Five Generations of a Mexican American Family in Los Angeles

Five Generations of a Mexican American Family in Los Angeles

Christina Chávez

ROWMAN & LITTLEFIELD PUBLISHERS, INC.
Lanham • Boulder • New York • Toronto • Plymouth, UK

ROWMAN & LITTLEFIELD PUBLISHERS, INC.

Published in the United States of America
by Rowman & Littlefield Publishers, Inc.
A wholly owned subsidiary of The Rowman & Littlefield Publishing Group, Inc.
4501 Forbes Boulevard, Suite 200, Lanham, Maryland 20706
www.rowmanlittlefield.com

Estover Road
Plymouth PL6 7PY
United Kingdom

British Library Cataloguing in Publication Information Available

Library of Congress Cataloging-in-Publication Data
Chávez, Christina, 1967–
  Five generations of a Mexican American family in Los Angeles / Christina
Chávez.
    p. cm.
  Includes bibliographical references and index.
  ISBN-13: 978-0-7425-3881-8 (cloth : alk. paper)
  ISBN-10: 0-7425-3881-8 (cloth : alk. paper)
  ISBN-13: 978-0-7425-3882-5 (pbk. : alk. paper)
  ISBN-10: 0-7425-3882-6 (pbk. : alk. paper)
  1. Fuentes family. 2. California—Genealogy. 3. Mexican Americans—
Genealogy. I. Title.
CS71.F9492 2007
929'.20896872079494—dc22   2006033964

Printed in the United States of America

∞™ The paper used in this publication meets the minimum requirements of
American National Standard for Information Sciences—Permanence of Paper
for Printed Library Materials, ANSI/NISO Z39.48-1992.

Contents

Gonzalez (2001), U.S.-born Mexican Americans drop out of high school at nearly the same rate as Mexican immigrants, 55 percent and 52 percent, respectively, and more strikingly still, U.S.-born Chicanos (29 percent completion rate) are less likely than Mexican immigrants (34 percent completion rate) to receive a bachelor of arts or bachelor of science degree. Despite their citizenship and English language proficiency, the latter point suggests that later-generation Chicanos are as economically and scholastically vulnerable as Mexican immigrants.

Because Latinos are the fastest growing minority, I argue that research on later-generation Chicanos be recognized and undertaken and where possible, in relation to their immigrant counterparts. The increase in the Latino population almost ensures an increase in the formulation of later-generation families. Combined with the ineffectiveness of current social and educational policy and practice to drastically change the Latino situation, Latino student academic failure, dropout, and low college attendance and completion are likely to persist. Without new ways of study and conceptualization, each generation of Chicano students remains vulnerable to the social obstacles and challenges their parents and grandparents experienced.

Crucial to improving the Latino situation today, immigrant or later generation, is altering the ways in which they are understood. First and foremost, the differences and commonalities between these groups, culturally, politically, socioeconomically, and socially should be studied. As academics, we tend to rely on preestablished theories and conceptualizations to understand phenomena. However, past theories and models of the immigrant/ethnic experience in America constrain the ways in which we see the later-generation Mexican American experience today.

For example, the assimilation/acculturation model, which continues to be a major framework to describe immigrant experience in the United States, claims that immigrants acquire mainstream manners and perspectives to belong to and participate successfully in U.S. society. If they do not, immigrants will continue to live unstably, marginalized, and disenfranchised from the American dream. In the end, an immigrant/ethnic minority's success is dependent on immigrants conceding to mainstream values and attitudes, despite any desire they may feel to retain their heritage culture.

Models and theories of assimilation/acculturation tend to be unilinear and monolithic.[2] One example is John Ogbu's notion of voluntary/involuntary minorities (1974, 1978, 1987). Revisited by Ogbu and Simmons (1998), the notion of voluntary and involuntary immigrants claims that immigrants' status creates the social stance by which they become minorities in society. Specifically, voluntary minorities begin as voluntary immigrants who enter the host society of their own volition in the pursuit of a better life; they establish a favorable stance to the host society because circumstances there are often better than their dire situations at home. Future generations are considered voluntary minorities as long as they retain their favorable reference. On the other hand, involuntary immigrants/minorities are co-opted into the host country via colonization, conquest, or slavery and therefore create oppositional spaces in society for themselves and their descendants. In this light, U.S.-born racial minorities—Chicanos, African Americans, and Native Americans—are viewed as continually opposed to the dominant group, with little to no hope of attaining full American status.

In line with the criticism of these academic models and theories, Chicano/Latino scholars have called for new approaches to studying the Latino experience (Acuña 2000; Blea 1997; R. Gutierrez 2000; Menchaca 2000; Mirandé 1985; Pizarro 2004; Trueba 1999). In addition to emic descriptive studies, R. Guiterrez (2000) claims that the "intersectionality" approach proposed and practiced by scholars, such as Anzaldua (1987), N. Foley (1997), and R. Garcia (1991), is more suited to the task of describing the dynamism of Chicano experience. Here, Chicano/Chicana scholars have viewed how the *intersection* of various factors (i.e., historical change, race, class, and gender) affected the lives of those studied. For R. Gutierrez (2000), this representation of Mexican American lives resembles the dynamic nature of ethnic identities and the worlds in which they are created.

Overall, the greatest shortcoming of assimilation/acculturation models is their inability to account for the complexity of immigrants' or ethnic peoples' experience and population but also to account for those experiences from the immigrant/ethnic perspective. In other words, if given the chance to speak for themselves, how might immigrant/ethnic individuals tell their stories? *Five Generations of a Mexican-American Family in Los Angeles* is the Fuentes family's telling of their own story that spans nearly a century, as five generations reveal the saliency of how the intersection of race, class, and ethnicity shaped their lives.

While the presence of race, class, and ethnicity is evident in the Fuentes account, the definitions of these terms are not obvious. In recent years, *race* has been the prevailing concept by which minority groups are studied. Social research fronts the importance of race, which is largely defined as the social construction of difference by phenotype, resulting in differential treatment of subordinate groups from the dominant groups (Darder and Torres 1999; Healy 2001; Sanjek 1994). Overall, race is seen as the *all powerful* reason for why racial minorities are the way they are. Darder and Torres criticize this approach claiming that "the significance and meaning [of race] are still attributed to the phenotypical features, rather than to the historically reproduced complex processes of racialization."[3] Instead,

Anderson states that race needs to be viewed and operationalized in the complex environment in which it exists, finding "a new way of thinking inclusively—recognizing the continuing significance of race and ethnicity . . . and recognizing the multiplicity of experiences of us all while placing this in context of an analysis of privilege and power.[4]

Therefore, race, in addition to the phenotypical difference of groups, also includes the institutional and social treatment (formal and informal policies, laws, practice, and ideology), intended to exclude subordinate groups because of their race, which has disadvantaged them from the dominant group.

Given academics' and society's preoccupation with race, many other concepts are misconstrued as race. *Ethnicity*, the cultural practices, behaviors, values, attitudes, and such of an ethnic group as manifestations of identity, and *class*, the material and social resources available as a result of one's social status, are frequently embedded in discussions about race. In this book, the difference between these terms must remain clear to truly understand how they have affected the Fuentes family.

Ethnicity has at times been interchangeable with race. This is a tragic error in that it often leads to the conclusion that ethnic minorities are genetically or culturally predisposed to their failure or struggle. For example, the link between ethnicity and race has been used for rationalizing the plight and condition of racial and ethnic minorities as viewed in the deficit and difference models. Because one's phenotypical appearance is the visual marker for one's ethnicity, this may be why most people are likely to confuse the two terms. However, in this book, ethnicity refers to the shared culture and ancestry of the Fuentes family, which originated with the first generation from Mexico and has transformed and transfigures throughout members lives in a U.S. context.[5]

Lastly, the Fuentes family does not exist outside U.S. social structures. Because of their race, ethnicity, and immigration, they have also been positioned in the American class system. Unfortunately, Americans are notorious for denying the effect of class on their lives, often believing everyone is middle class or at least has the opportunity to be middle class. Nevertheless, we must recognize that social structures, often established on racial and ethnic categories, have limited the economic mobility of certain groups, such as Latinos.

Class, or socioeconomic status, is perhaps the most elusive term of the three in that in the United States, it is often taboo to acknowledge that a class system exists, let alone discuss how that class system inhibits or advantages individuals' chances for success. However, sociologists have outlined how our society functions on a class system, noting that the majority of Americans tend to experience incremental amounts of social mobility from generation to generation (Kerbo 1983; Rossides

1997), and racial minorities' mobility is further dampened by their racial classification (Fiener 1994). Therefore, in this book, class encompasses the economic, material, social, and educational resources of the Fuentes family and is considered to have a significant effect on the lives they have lived.

These concepts should not be understood as separate but rather as intertwined and intersecting. One's race affects one's ethnic experience and class position; one's ethnicity affects one's class position and racial experience; one's class affects one's racial and ethnic experience. This is the messiness and complexity of human living. *Five Generations of a Mexican American Family in Los Angeles* seeks to disentangle these phenomena, even if momentarily, to experience and view the lives of this twentieth century American family.

NOTES

1. Many of the official Census statistics on Mexican Americans do not disaggregate for generation but rather disaggregate for foreign- and native-born Mexican Americans. Thus, few specific statistics exist for later-generation Chicanos, which almost exclusively refers to third generation.

2. While recent work on immigration has contended with influxes of Latino and Southeast Asian populations and the various group differences and uniquenesses (Booth, Crouter, and Landale 1997; Portes and Rumbaut 1996, 2001; M. Suárez-Orozco, C. Suárez-Orozco, and Baolin Qin 2005), assimilation theory has been based largely on accounts of southern European assimilation (Erdsman 1998; Handlin 1979; Novak 1971; Shrag 1971) to U.S. society during the 1940s and 1950s, which does not address the issue of race with which immigrants of color have had to contend (Steinberg 1989).

3. Antonio Darder and Rodolfo D. Torres, "Shattering the 'Race Lens': Toward a Critical Theory of Racism," in *Critical Ethnicity: Countering the Waves of Identity Politics*, ed. Robert H. Tai and Mary L. Kenyatta (Lanham, Md.: Rowman & Littlefield, 1999), 181.

4. Margaret L. Anderson, "The Fiction of 'Diversity without Oppressions': Race, Ethnicity, Identity and Power," in *Critical Ethnicity*, ed. Tai and Kenyatta, 17.

5. I acknowledge that the word and concept of *culture* is currently under debate (Boggs 2004; Kuper 1999; Ortner 1999; Smelser 1992). Some believe that culture is a single concept that has been either used for hegemonic purposes or has been poorly designed by scientific measures and should be eliminated from the field of social science altogether. Others believe that culture has effectively worked as a theory, which advocates for the reconfiguring of the human order as group oriented and liberal (Boggs 2004). My understanding of the term *culture* includes the classical definition in its simplest terms: the systemic order of a human group through symbols that members use to make meaning of their environment (Geertz 1973). Culture is learned and not genetic; it changes based on the advancements

of human society; "[It] is essentially a matter of ideas and values, a collective cast of mind" (Kuper 1999, p. 227).

My analysis of culture incorporates Rosaldo's (1993, p. 93) processual analysis that "resists frameworks that claim monopoly on truth. It emphasizes that culture requires study from a number of perspectives, and that these perspectives cannot necessarily be added together into a unified summation." In other words, I seek to describe the Fuentes family way of life, specifically as it relates to its Mexican cultural heritage and the family's everyday social adjustment to U.S. society, initially as immigrants, then as members of a racial minority. I accept that their expression of their experience may or may not include academic definitions or interpretations. I recognize that cultural manifestations can be shaped by individual differences or by historical, generational, regional, class, or gender experiences of the group, and any description of culture is but a point in an unfolding human experience in the social world.

Acknowledgments

In the tradition of the Fuentes family, we learn early on that we do not ever make it on our own. For this reason, I would like to thank several people for their participation in this project. Of course, this project could never have been completed had it not been for the willingness and graciousness of the participating Fuentes members. These members rose to the occasion by giving their stories, time, and energy for the sake of the family, to help the world learn of this untold Mexican American story that is quintessentially Fuentes. I have come to highly respect each one for their uniqueness, strength, intelligence, and perseverance. I am truly and eternally grateful to each for allowing his or her individual story to become part of the academic discussion. I hope that I have done them justice and done them proud.

I would also like to respectfully thank my mentor, Dr. Guadalupe Valdés, for encouraging, inspiring, and coaxing me to undertake and complete the study. She has definitely fulfilled her role as my "Mexican mother" throughout and because of her I have developed as a scholar. *Muchísimas gracias.*

Lastly, I would like to thank friends, family, and colleagues who encouraged me to publish this book and supported me through my doubts and dilemmas. Thanks for your energy, meals, and good wishes; all have nurtured my mind, body, and spirit through this long and strenuous yet extremely worthwhile intellectual journey.

Introduction

THE RESEARCHER: MY STORY AS A FUENTES

This story of the Fuentes family cannot begin without describing how I am situated within it. As anthropologists have noted (Clifford and Marcus 1986; Jackson 1990; Kuper 1999), the researcher no longer sits unattended outside the realm he or she observes and records but instead is incorporated into the scene. His or her personal characteristics and experiences, present or absent, as well as his or her ability to interact or not, influence the size, shape, and color of the completed written product. In this book, two outstanding characteristics foreshadow how the Fuentes's story will be told. One is my shared position with participants in terms of ethnicity, class status, and locale. The other is that I am a member of the family, an insider to the nth degree.[1] I have been privy to and have practiced their ways for much of my life; I possess a deep understanding of how they are and who they can be.

As a member of the Fuentes family, my personal story, as well as the larger one to be told in this book, brings to bear the many ways Mexican Americans have struggled to survive and succeed amid the narrow U.S. definition of success as upwardly mobile and highly educated.

Thus I begin my story at a time in my life when I had seemingly "made it." I was a freshman at a University of California, Santa Barbara (UCSB) campus, one hour and twenty minutes from the San Fernando Valley. When I bumped into Delia Esparza on the streets of Isla Vista, she introduced me to her family. "Come here. I want you to meet my star student," she said to her husband and daughter. I was as surprised as they were to

1

hear I was her star student. Up to that point at UCSB, I had felt like a for-eigner, always trying to figure out what people were saying and doing and why.

Delia was like no one I had ever met. She was dark like me and even grew up in the same small border town where I spent my childhood. While she was immediately familiar, Delia was also different. She was a doctoral student who spent her life reading and writing within the domain of social science. Previous to her, I only had experience with working people within the confines of my family: carpenters, masons, landscapers, gardeners, building contractors, factory workers, cafeteria workers, waitresses, receptionists, and painters. Thus the idea of being a star student was both curious and frightening to me. My only reference to college was my family's verbal edict that education would get me a better life—more money, more security. According to them, I would not have to scratch out a living but could make my way, having more power and control over my social and economic situation.

Long before college and my stardom, I had always been a star student in one way or another. Many factors went into my success as a young student, family encouragement, mentorship by teachers, and placement in a college preparatory track. Like other Latino students, some of these factors were easier to come by than others.

First, my mother's upbringing to be well mannered in the presence of adults and to live a good honest life kept me in the good graces of all my teachers. In the early years, I never spoke out of turn, I completed my assignments efficiently, and I kept to myself. As a result, teachers used me as the behavioral example for other students—behavior that was fostered at home. My brother, sister, and I did not learn specifically how to behave at school but how to behave period. School was just another public space where I was to represent my parents and family honorably.

The value of schooling was also present in my home. Mostly, my parents openly encouraged school by giving lectures about how an education can get one a better job and by insisting on perfect attendance. For a short period, my father, a Mexican immigrant with a junior-high education who excelled in math, helped my older siblings with their schoolwork. Mom would ask if my siblings and I did our homework or she would direct us to do homework when we arrived home.

To support our family, both my parents worked eight- to ten-hour jobs in the service industry. Dad was a jack-of-all-trades: a painter, laborer, sheet metal worker, and eventually a real estate agent. Mom, a third-generation Mexican American with an eleventh grade education, raised three children, and once they were school-aged, worked part-time as an assembler in a factory and eventually as a janitor for the public schools. If there was time left over from their day, my parents spent it with us, doing family things, out-ings together to the park, visiting friends, or going shopping across the border. They were focused on survival—feeding, clothing, and sheltering their children and every once in a while, giving them a little happiness. As is the case with many working class families (Rubin 1994) the large amount of responsibilities and little disposable time, income, and energy often factor vigorous parental involvement out of the survival equation. In those days, what I remember most was that they were always working.

Although my parents may not have been of a traditional[2] mind toward schooling or had the time to participate in the way scholars recommend, on further examination, they supported education in subtle yet important ways. My mother always bought us pens, pencils, paper, crayons, records, books, and occasionally took us to the library. Even though my mother or father did not read to us, my older sister fulfilled that role from time to time. My innate creativity and curiosity led me to hatch new ideas for inventions and art projects, and my mother made sure I had the supplies to innovate. While my parents often just made enough to sustain a family of five, I always knew that they did what they could when it came to school.

In kindergarten in a Texas public school, Mrs. Schiender introduced me to the world of school, teaching me to read and write and to love academic learning. For example, weekly spelling tests provided a challenge. Mrs. Schiender routinely encouraged me to aim for achieving a perfect score. "You're a smart child. You should be getting all the words right. Work hard to get them all correct next week." I nodded. I knew what hard work was; I witnessed it every day. My parents' hard work provided food, clothing, and housing for our entire family. I set my mind to it, spelling words while I walked to and from school or enlisting my sister to repeatedly quiz me. After that week's spelling test, Mrs. Schiender called me to her desk. "Christina," she said, "I knew you could do it. You are a very smart girl. I think you should think about going to college some day. I think you would do well there." I beamed, grinning from ear to ear, then thought and asked her, "What's college?" "It's a school like this one, where you do the same things, reading and writing. But it's much bigger." "Oh," I said. From that day forward, even with the vague notion of what it entailed, going to college became my life's dream.

With college education as a goal and the structural and behavioral requirements in my home, I excelled at school. I was an A student for all my years in Texas, almost always making the honor roll. In Los Alamitos (Texas) schools, if one excelled, one was recognized for it. Teachers held high standards and expected students to meet them, and most students responded with eagerness. At home, I became branded the "brain" in the family. When in the presence of company, my mother instructed me to espouse my desire to attend college or she proudly talked about my perfect grades. Under these circumstances my academic achievement emerged.

Unfortunately, matters changed, and life became more difficult when my parents separated.

After my parents' separation, my mother, siblings, and I moved back to Los Angeles to be around my mother's family—the Fuentes family. We had been away for seven years, and my siblings and I neither remembered the place nor the people. Nevertheless, knowing we were among family made the adjustment easier. With a single mom with little less than a high school education and work experience in janitorial services, our family had to adjust to a different standard of living. My mother applied for welfare, and our relatives helped her get a two bedroom apartment and a used car. We were three teenagers and one adult in a second story apartment in a lower working-class neighborhood flooded with newly arrived Latino immigrants. Though we had previously lived among Mexicans (or Mexican immigrants) in Texas, the social space between the *Mexicanos* in our neighborhood and my family was qualitatively different. The social landscape had changed so drastically from Los Alamitos, which made school challenging for different reasons.

My experience in school in L.A. illuminated my lack of understanding about the social environment outside the school campus. Suddenly, there were lines and territories I was not familiar with, and I had no idea where I belonged in reference to them. In L.A., my ethnic affiliation defined everything down to how I was treated on the street, in stores, and at school. My first social trauma arose out of the local and historical separation between white and brown people. On school campuses and in my neighborhood, *cholos/cholas* (male/female Mexican American gangs or social cliques) were a legitimate ethnic affiliate for some Mexican and Mexican American youth. I did not know this in sixth grade and I was approached by cholas who harassed me for "hanging out with the wrong people"—white people—whom I befriended because they happened to be the majority of students in my class. Ethnic affiliation aside, I could not befriend these girls had I wanted, because I had learned they routinely invited trouble. At this point in my life, my mother, who was working so hard to survive, wanted only one thing from my sister, brother, and me— *to stay out of trouble.* I could not disappoint her by getting involved with these girls. As a Fuentes member, my first affiliation and loyalty was to family.

In Texas, the ethnic/racial issue was moot. Most everyone was of some Mexican origin, speaking both Spanish and English. The Anglos themselves often spoke both languages. Of course, there were different social classes, but people were generally of a like mind when it came to raising good families and doing well in school. What I found in L.A. was brutal, harsh, and cruel; groups of people fighting for a rung on the socioeconomic ladder. There was a war going on between the newly arrived "boat" people who received low interest home and small business loans and the well-established minority groups who had little to show for their families' toil over generations. I soon realized that I, too, was fighting for recognition and a slice of the American dream.

Unfortunately, this task would not be easily achieved for two reasons. First, my home life was complicated by having only one parent and one income. Mom had to go back to school to be trained as a data processor, and she cleaned houses on the side for extra money. Once again, she was always out of the house. I was left to figure out problems with school and schoolwork on my own.

Second, school had become unchallenging. One day in the eighth grade, I took inventory of my life by paying attention to the events and people around me. In most of my classes, my fellow classmates were immigrants, discipline problems, and the academically distressed. The classes themselves consisted of outdated textbooks presenting rote lessons in a color-by-numbers fashion. Teachers did not teach but directed students' attention to the assignment for the day, insisting students work individually and silently. With the slightest noise, teachers lectured us on responsibility, hard work, and discipline. These classroom routines were a veiled attempt at disguising the fact that much of what happened in class was void of stimulation. Regardless of my desire to excel, I had been assigned to a chain gang, whose punishment was six periods of tedious intellectually deprived labor under the supervision of a moral overseer—an educational experience had by many students in the lower tracks of secondary school.

Interestingly, however, most of my friends were not in any of my classes. I had miraculously managed to befriend (or they befriended me) middle-class white, Jewish, or Asian girls from the accelerated track, with whom I hung out during the morning recess and lunch. When they talked about their school assignments, I became envious of their fortune to be intellectually stimulated. They read Shakespeare, wrote reports in story format, and worked in groups on their science projects. I thought nothing of the difference between their and my school experience, believing that the counselors knew what they were doing, and I was where I needed to be.

Then one lunch period one of the girls mentioned that she was going to get help preparing for college in one of her classes. I asked her to fill me in, and as I listened, I reflected on the classes I was taking: Sewing, Woodshop, Social Studies, Pre-Algebra, and Health. Nothing special. I quickly realized I would not be receiving any such instruction to help me get into college. With my mother's inability to participate in my schooling because of her work schedule and the fact that I had no allies in teachers or counselors, I realized I had no recourse. My college ambitions began to fade.

Once in high school, I knew I had to change my lot in academic life if I was going to make it to a university. Prior to my sophomore year, I received my school schedule in the mail only to discover I had been put in the same pathetic classes I had been in junior high. I was supposed to see my counselor about getting into the marching band, so I thought I would take that opportunity to get placed into the college-prep track.

My counselor, a middle-aged white woman, whose advice my sister and brother never found useful, seemed friendly enough when I asked to be put into marching band. When I said, "I want to change some of my other classes. I want to go to college and I need other classes so I can do that." "Well, what do you want to change?" she asked with a weak smile. I told her I wanted to change almost all the classes on my schedule. Her face turned sour, and she said, "Christina, I don't think making all those changes is a good idea. All those people in those classes have had the same classes in junior high. You don't have the background. You have such good grades. I'd hate to see you ruin your record by going into these classes without the right preparation."

I was stunned by the fact that this woman, assigned to me as a guide, as a helper, was resistant to my desire to better myself. My heart felt heavy as I thought about having to endure three more years of the same boring material I had tolerated for the last three. *What could I do*? My mother could not come and speak on my behalf, because she was working three jobs at the time. Desperate, I blurted out, "Well, my mother said if I had any trouble getting these classes that I'm supposed to make an appointment for her to come in and talk with you." Shock and silence. "Oh, you mean your mother knows about this? Well then, if she wants this, I think it will be okay," she said as she crossed out classes and penned in my college-prep courses.

In the college-prep track, I did well. My desire to learn returned. I was again stimulated, writing satire, learning about women's issues in American literature, and discussing politics. I also found myself happily challenged by my position as trumpet section leader in the marching band, an instrument I started to learn in Texas. It was clear to me, as well as others in my family, that school had become the center of my life.

But often, my role as college-bound student and leader conflicted with the one I had to play at home, as is the case with many working-class Mexican American children. The ability to maintain the same consistent and supportive structure for my studies dwindled as my mother single-handedly provided for three teenagers. Additionally, my older sister had just had a baby and my younger brother was having problems in school. Though I worked to pay for my car and insurance, I was now responsible for buying myself the necessities my mother could no longer afford. My senior year was especially difficult. I often had to balance my school commitments with babysitting my niece while my sister attended school or went to work. Everything in my life suffered: grades, friendships, and my family duties. During this time, I had entirely forgotten about my goal of going to college. If it were not for a teacher who had taken special interest in me, I am almost certain my aspirations would never have been realized.

Her name was Kaye Barnes, and she was the wife of my junior high band director, the school's college advisor, and my biology teacher. She called me into her office one day and asked me if I was thinking about going to college. I told her yes, but at the moment it was not a good time: "My family needs me." She assured me that my family would always need me, but the time to go to college was now. Immediately, she scheduled me to attend an application workshop the following week with a University of California recruiter. Although deadlines for admissions had already passed, the recruiter claimed his position as a minority student advocate allowed him to help me apply late. As a direct consequence of affirmative action legislation, the workshop provided me with invaluable assistance I would not have otherwise had as a first-generation college student.

After mailing the thick application envelope, I returned to my hectic life only to completely forget about the probability of going to college. It was not until spring semester that I recollected I had even applied. After returning from band practice one afternoon, my mother handed me a letter from UCSB and in the corner was printed Office of Admissions. I opened the letter and read that I had been accepted. I could not believe it. I was going to college. That joyous moment and the subsequent ones where I informed my relatives heavily masked the fact that I had no idea what I was getting myself into.

To end here, most would agree that my life plays like a success story— underprivileged individual fights the forces and circumstances of her disadvantaged life to rise to excellence. However, this narrow and simplistic definition of success, as upwardly mobile, overlooks other important factors in my life that contributed to my success. Furthermore, it neglects what is most disturbing about the social system in which this story is embedded. That is, despite my eagerness and desire to academically achieve, my race, ethnicity, and class mediated the type of treatment I received in schools; I experienced school much in the way that the majority of Latino and working-class students do.

MY STORY AS A REFLECTION OF THE FUENTES'S STORY

My story, as well as that of the Fuentes family, has to be understood in the historical and social context of all other Latinos. Specifically, Mexican

Americans and other Latinos are known for how they remain outside the mainstream. Aside from cultural/ethnic differences, indicators of their difference lie in their high rates of drop out and poverty and low levels of academic achievement (Chapa and de la Rosa 2004; Marotta and Garcia 2003).

The causes of Latino students' academic situation are many and are commonly attributed to factors outside of schools. For instance, some scholarship identifies community and social groups as crucial factors, while others target language and cultural differences. Ogbu and Simmons (1998) claim that Mexican Americans, as a caste minority, have a history of colonialization, which causes them to generate an oppositional attitude toward schools and school success (Ogbu 1987). Others claim that social groups promote underachievement as a symbol of group affiliation/ identification (Flores-Gonzalez 2002; Gibson, Gándara, and Koyama 2004; Matute-Bianchi 1991). Language, the need to acquire English and American culture, and a devaluation of formal education have been major reasons that some studies claim Latinos do not do well academically (Carter 1970; Valencia 2002).

However, unlike more successful immigrant populations, Latinos are continually perceived through their immigrant roots and perceived in a perpetual state of assimilation or acculturation. In other words, it is the influence of the Mexican culture, its lack of value for formal schooling, and its strong value of family and work, which distracts Latino students' attention away from their academic endeavors (E. Garcia 2001).

Rarely if ever are later-generation Chicanos, those born and raised in the United States of third generation or more, considered. Later-generation Chicanos have been characterized as different from Mexican immigrants and their children. They have different attitudes, values, and preferences; they primarily speak English, celebrate U.S. holidays, and are oriented toward an American identity (Keefe and Padilla 1990; Menchaca 1995; Ochoa 2004; An. Valenzuela 1999; Wells 1981).

Unfortunately, the research on Latinos does not go much further than this type of description, creating a gap in understanding how Mexican immigrants and later-generation Chicanos differ from each other. It has failed to critically and operationally investigate the following questions: How are these two groups the same? How are they different? What, if any, of the Mexican culture persists in later-generation Chicanos? What factors are attributed to the similar social treatment that both groups receive as members of a racialized group? Why does the social and cultural capital of U.S.-born Chicanos not translate into greater representation in the middle class or in higher education?

To this end, the Fuentes's story, a five-generation account of a single Mexican American family in L.A., can contribute much to understanding the way the immigration/acculturation experience affects a Chicano family over time and what influence it might have on the family's consistent educational attainment. More succinctly, what aspects of the Fuentes's experience across generations (at home, at work, and in school) can help us understand their school experience? My own story, told earlier, reflects some of the telling elements of Fuentes family life, elements that suggest a dynamic interaction and intersection between race, ethnicity, and class.

THE FUENTES FAMILY AND ME:
A PRELUDE TO AN AMERICAN STORY

The Fuentes family story starts with the immigration of Mario and Manuela Fuentes through the land port of El Paso, Texas. They married and migrated west to California, settling in the heart of the San Fernando Valley. The Fuentes family, initially as migrant workers, then as factory workers and tradesmen, then as lower white-collar workers, cultivated their lives and identity through the valley's transformation from an agricultural area to a large-scale suburb. Like other parts of L.A. throughout the twentieth century (Monroy 1999; Ochoa 2004; Sanchez 1993), Mexicans were laborers and service workers segregated into their own ethnic enclaves, fragmented from the white working- and middle-class neighborhoods that surrounded them. The Fuentes family was among the first after World War II to move into white working-class neighborhoods, as they gained more stable employment or as a result of the privileges Fuentes men gained from participating in the armed forces. Their success as a later-generation Chicano family lies in their desire for and attainment of a higher and stable standard of living across five generations. From this toil and tradition, I was born, and it has been the fodder for my success and the success of all Fuentes.

The first factor in my success is the importance of family. Research claims that one of the stalwart and consistent elements of Latino culture is familism (the strong emotional and social bonds between family members, immediate and extended), which is generally seen as positive (Buriel and De Ment 1997; Gaitan 2004; Griswold del Castillo 1984; Keefe 1980; F. Martinez 1993; Rueschenberg and Buriel 1989). Regardless of generation, the importance of family as an informational, social, and financial resource persists. However, the literature on education suggests that the Mexican American family is one of the chief causes of Chicano student academic failure. Despite the overwhelming evidence that families are poor or working class, it is held that the Mexican American family diverts students' endeavors away from school and toward the labor market to supplement family income. Subsequently, it is assumed that the value of formal education that is present in white middle-class families does not exist in Mexican American families, neglecting to account or recognize the additional resources and access that middle-class status affords (Brantlinger 2003; Lareau 2003).

How is it that Chicano families play such a contradictory role in Chicano student academic performance? Given that many of those who study Chicano students do not share their social, economic, cultural, or racialized experience, the question or approach to the problem of Latino student underachievement is invariably couched in these terms: How can we get *their* families to be more like *ours*? Rarely has the question been asked from a positive interpretation of the Chicano family: In what way does or can the Chicano family aid Chicano student success?

The Fuentes's case, as seen in my individual story, depicts the many ways that familism promotes or encourages schooling. For example, my family instilled in me the value of schooling, if for nothing else, to obtain a higher standard of living. My family also reinforced my "school kid" identity (Flores-Gonzalez 2002). More importantly, despite the conflicts I sometimes felt between my family and school, the presence of family ties and relationships provided a safe and secure haven to retreat during difficult times. This latter point suggests that Fuentes members understand that the well-being of Latino students (as I am sure is the case for all students) cannot be confined to their school lives and identity.

The Fuentes family story offers an account of Mexican American life that has often been omitted from the description of the Chicano student experience. My family's core values of being a respectable and respectful person (*bien educado*), the value of hard work, and the importance of school gave me the discipline and drive to succeed academically, as many Latino students will attest. Likewise, these values and others (the value of family, the value of saving and investment) play a crucial role in the lives of Fuentes members in and out of school and has established a social safety net for members, who live a precarious and unpredictable life as working-class individuals (Rubin 1987).

Furthermore, when discussing Latino school performance, the literature tends to focus on two spheres primarily—family/community and school. However, Sanchez (1993) points out that a third sphere—the world of work—is often excluded from research on Mexican American experience despite the major role it plays in Mexican American life. As has been documented, Mexican Americans in the early and mid-twentieth century had little to no hope of higher education and were often encouraged and directed to the labor market. Schools played a primary role in this unofficial social policy by segregating students and providing them with largely vocational training. These are the tangible experiences of at least the first three Fuentes generations. Seldom recounted in the literature of Chicano students are the consequences of such measures on the lives of these young people. The reality for these Fuentes generations was the limited work opportunities they had, having been schooled in a general or vocational specialization coupled with the fact that their race limited which occupations were open to them.

In addition, my story told of the prominent role that the world of work played in my life, as it has for the rest of the Fuentes family. My parents' working-class jobs provided scarce resources (money, time) for my siblings and me; their own school experience denied them the possession of the educational capital necessary for higher education. As a teenager, I worked to buy the things I needed that my mother could not afford as well as to provide transportation to and from work. Like many of the other Fuentes members, the world of work was a place where I, from an early age, exercised my independence, but it was also a direct means to subsistence and modest luxury.

While I may have made it in school, the majority of the Fuentes family members did not. Like other Latino students (myself including), they were prone to the influence of gangs, the relegation to general/vocational/remedial tracks, the negligence of teachers and other school personnel, gatekeeping by counselors, administrators, and teachers, and the challenge of contending with a "boring" curriculum (Carter and Segura 1979; J. Moreno 1999; San Miguel and Valencia 1998). Like the vast majority of Latino students (and unlike me) most Fuentes members had no mentors, did not participate in school activities, and did not have access to friends who were high achievers (Stanton-Salazar 2001).

Though a few dropped out, most stayed and completed their high school education, and all the while the reason for staying was the insistence and encouragement of family to get an education.

What then is the moral of the Fuentes's family story about to be told? The Fuentes's story implicates, not indicts, at least three factors, race, ethnicity, and class, as manifested in the home, in the workplace, and at school as salient in the family situation over five generations. Equally important has been the interaction and intersection of these factors within these social spheres. For example, the Fuentes family's encouragement of schooling increased the family's graduation rate; Fuentes members' consistent placement in general and remedial tracks made available working-class occupations after high school; the family's value of hard work ensured members' success on the job and resulted in an increase in standard of living.

More importantly, the Fuentes's story encourages academics to set aside the traditional ways we have come to understand and listen to Latino individuals/families' accounts of the world, versions that have been preestablished and presorted through academic frameworks and conceptualizations. The Fuentes's story says to us, as is echoed in Darder and Torres (1999), that race, ethnicity, and class interact dynamically to generate relatively identical experiences at home, at work, and in school over five generations, suggesting the consistency and constancy of social structures in these three realms. Specifically, it notes that moderate changes in any one area may not be enough to hurl minority working-class members of society into the upper echelons of society. Rather attention to all three, recognizing how all three may influence Latino youth's success or failure, and then incorporating all three in a comprehensive plan makes available the broader opportunities other youth experience.

The second moral of the Fuentes's story emerges when we listen to the Fuentes family account, imagining ourselves in their place instead of how they should be in white, middle-class Americans'. Particularly, one learns that the Fuentes family's American experience has granted them a different definition of success. I have managed to become successful in the mainstream definition: highly and formally educated, upwardly mobile, and a newly born member of the middle class as a university professor.

The Fuentes family, on the other hand, might be viewed as unsuccessful by mainstream standards because of their low rate of college graduation and prominence in working-class and lower white-collar occupations. However, in Fuentes members' eyes, the family is successful. Despite the historical discrimination and social injustices against Mexican Americans, the Fuentes family has over the course of five generations focused on raising good children, increased its socioeconomic standing, increased its rate of education, and maintained a cohesive family network, one which is still vital in assisting its members in times of need and hardship as well as in times of joy and celebration. Their success lies in their ability to be honest, hardworking, well-meaning human beings. The problem lies in that the narrow mainstream definition excludes and denies my family their right to be seen as successful, despite their respectable and productive contributions as full-fledged Americans for nearly a century.

ORGANIZATION OF THE BOOK

This book is organized into eight chapters. Chapter 1 provides a demographic overview of the family in relation to their immigration, family interaction, and social status (wealth, occupation, and education) as well as synopsis of the participating Fuentes members. In chapters 2 and 3, I present the Fuentes's family value system as experienced from the first-generation to later-generation families, connecting the family's social status to their sociocultural context. Chapter 4 depicts Fuentes members' experience in the labor market and the workplace, linking it to Fuentes's home and school experience. Chapters 5 and 6 describe how Fuentes members experienced school and how school activities were addressed in the home, particularly language and literacy. Chapter 7 presents the role that parent involvement had in Fuentes's homes, through both parents' and children's perspectives. And chapter 8 highlights the invaluable lessons the Fuentes family account illuminates about the Latino families in American society. It discusses the need for designers and implementers of school policy and practice to reevaluate their understanding and perception of Latino families by acknowledging the vital role they play in Latino students' well-being and discusses specific strategies to address the relationship between Latino families and schools.

NOTES

1. It has not been until recently that insider scholarship (Baca Zinn 2001; Kikumura 1998) has been recognized as worthy and valid. The controversy has been over accepting and recognizing insider research, where the researcher possesses shared understanding and views with participants believed to compromise his or her objectivity as opposed to the strict belief that an outsider researcher was the optimal position, given its objective perspective. Now, anthropologists believe that all researchers, regardless of outsider or insider status, possess limitations, requiring them to incorporate reflexive research methods, where they acknowledge the ways in which their identities, attitudes, and behaviors influence participants and the final research product (Jacobs-Huey 2002).

My Fuentes family membership and identity as a scholar gave me immediate access to the family and legitimacy with many family members. However, like other insider researchers have noted (Baca Zinn 2001; Jones 1970; Kondo 1986; Narayan 1993; Stephenson and Greer 1981; Zavella 1996), I was sometimes constrained by the social roles (women, daughter, or cousin) and identities (student and teacher) that participants perceived of me. I also felt the ease at being an insider researcher in that I understand the cognitive, emotional, and psychological precepts of participants and their everyday lives and possess a profound knowledge of the history of the field and daily life. As Aguilar (1981) proposes, I had access to more in-group activities, was less likely to "alter social settings," and was more likely to stimulate natural interaction and behavior. I also incorporated strategies to contend with issues insider researchers have confronted, such as living at a distance from central activity and reflexively thinking about the research process and product (Kondo 1986; Narayan 1993).

From the summer of 1998 to the summer of 1999, I interviewed thirty-three members of the Fuentes family, who ranged in age from seven to ninety-one. I met some participating members at large and small family gatherings, introduced the topic, and made my intentions to interview known. Others, I contacted through relatives or over the telephone. These methods resulted in the primary data: sixty-six oral history interviews with thirty-three members. In accordance with the intent of oral history, to study "the recent past by means of life stories or personal recollections, where informants speak about their own experiences" (Henige 1982,

p. 7), interviews were designed to reveal Fuentes members' lived experiences and current situations; these experiences covered childhood to adolescence to parenthood to retirement. Even though the process of interviewing was not a practice in our family dynamic, the interviews themselves were much like conversations I might have had with members at gatherings. The atmosphere was relaxed as interviewees freely moved from topic to topic, and the flow and activity of household happenings frequently weaved into the event. My relatives found the event a refreshing experience as they had been given the opportunity to recall a life lived, often uncovering special moments and experiences they had not thought about in years.

As a secondary source of data, I attended and observed six family events from summer 1998 to spring 1999: four large events and two small (where only my grandmother's family attended). Large family events were an annual Easter gathering, a family camping trip, an anniversary celebration, and a funeral; small family events were Christmas and Thanksgiving celebrations. I was invited to all events and attended each event for a duration of anywhere from two to five hours.

My experience as a researcher resembled that of other insider investigators, in that the project enriched the lives of participants as well as that of the researcher (Echevarria-Howe 1995; Kikumura 1998). Most importantly, I gained a profound respect for the lived experiences of my loved ones. I was able to see how the family social web extended to the lives of later generations and how the original lives of Manuela and Mario Fuentes were the foundation for the lives of Fuentes today.

2. *Traditional* is a term that has changed as new attitudes about and expectations of education have changed (Cutler 2000). What was meant as traditional before the twentieth century, that families "maintain primary responsibility for the moral education of children and . . . influence over their cognitive development" (16), is no longer the case for the beginning of the twenty-first century, where parents are asked to "give their time, assist with student learning, and join in school planning and decision-making" (201). The debate over parents' role in schooling has been and remains politically charged as to what the responsibilities are of the home and school, as schools have assumed much of the power to determine what is acceptable parent/family involvement.

1

The Fuentes Family
An Overview across Generations

Contrary to the images of Latinos as newly arrived immigrants, the Fuentes family has had a long presence in California, in Los Angeles in particular. The Fuentes family story in America begins with the immigration of Mario and Manuela Fuentes, my great-grandparents, and extends to the lives of roughly one hundred living descendants.

GENERATIONS OF THE FUENTES FAMILY

The Fuentes's Immigrant Beginnings

Mario and Manuela Fuentes immigrated to the United States separately. Arriving some time between 1910 and 1920, they came with the second wave of Mexican immigrants, who comprised mostly, "the working class, including, nuclear and extended families, women alone with children, single men and single women," trying to escape the heightened political and social turmoil of the Mexican Revolution (Camarillo 1990, p. 34). Both came from Acámbaro in the state of Guanajuato, Mexico, and entered the United States through one of the major land ports at turn-of-the-century El Paso, Texas.

Mario, a dark-skinned, thin, wiry Mexican, was known as a quiet and introverted man. For several years he worked sun up to sun down to feed his family of twelve, earning himself a reputation as a hardworking family man. He spoke little, even to his own children, but his voracious appetite and penchant for cutting his own hair became fond family memories. I remember him as an ancient Indian-looking man, who mumbled when he spoke and spent hours sitting quietly as the hustle and bustle of Fuentes family activity swirled around him. I learned from watching others that he was a man who commanded respect and admiration from his children, grandchildren, and great-grandchildren. This is how I treated him even for the short time I knew him, only fully understanding the justification for this when I completed this study.

From the few conversations Mario had with them, the Fuentes children learned that he had married once before marrying Manuela and that he was widowed after the birth of his first son. He lived a transient life, migrating to other parts of the country seeking work in the coal mines, on the railroad, and in the fields. He met Manuela during a period that he worked near the Texas-Mexico border in the early 1920s.

Manuela's life and experiences were more known than Mario's. Fuentes family members view her as the glue that held the family together, many mentioning that her passing in the 1980s changed the nature of how the Fuentes family gathers and relates. Manuela, a dark-skinned petite woman, was kind, generous, hospitable, affectionate, and nurturing, always having advice for those in trouble and food for those who stopped by. This is how I remember her, smiling, with a sparkle in her eye as she herded us to the kitchen to eat freshly made flour tortillas and *frijoles* (beans). Manuela was a good mother and a good wife and a fascinating and complex human being.

Manuela's story begins in the late 1800s when she, her sisters, and mother lived in Guanajuato, and they frequently had to hide from renegade bandits because they were without a male in the house. After her mother died in the great influenza epidemic, Manuela and her two sisters went to live just outside of Mexico City with her maternal grandparents. Manuela's passion to study conflicted with her grandfather's belief that school was unnecessary for young girls, because they only became wives and mothers. Despite being identified by convent nuns as an exceptional student, Manuela only attended school until the third or fourth grade, where she learned to read and write. In her teens, she rebelled against her grandparents' strict upbringing and decided to head for the border to live with her father, the man her mother had married and who had abandoned her family.

As a *contratista* (labor contractor), Manuela's father helped her cross the border while masses of other Mexican citizens were turned away either because they did not have the head tax or could not pass the literacy test as dictated in the Immigration Act of 1917 (A. Garcia 2001; M. Garcia 1983). In El Paso, Manuela lived with her father and stepmother and came in contact with many people through her father's work, one of who was Mario. On meeting each other, Mario and Manuela realized they both were from the same town in Mexico and shared a sense of the past and the familiar. Feeling like she wanted to escape her father's crowded household, Manuela, at sixteen, eventually married Mario, who was eighteen.

Now married and living with two children in El Paso, Mario worked as a barber in his own shop, which afforded his family a small apartment in the city. At home, Manuela raised her stepson, Pedro, and first child, Saul, as a "city woman," accustomed to modest luxuries and moderate amounts of household chores. To Manuela's surprise in 1921, Mario returned home and announced that they would be going to California, telling her that he had sold his shop and would leave immediately to find work and a house before she and their sons arrived. Like other Mexican families of the time, the possibility of work in the West is likely what pulled the Fuentes family from their border town existence to the rural and agricultural life in the San Fernando Valley (M. Gonzalez 1999).

Some months later, Mario sent for Manuela and their sons, who arrived to find Mario employed as caretaker for a local grower who gave Mario a canvas tent to live in on the property. The orchard he worked was located in the San Fernando Valley in a town called Zelzah (then one of the major agricultural areas for Los Angeles County). This was the original site and surroundings for the Fuentes family.

My great-grandparents' lives in California began like other Mexican families in the greater southwest at the time (M. Gonzalez 1999; O. Martinez 2001; Monroy 1999). The first Fuentes home was a canvas tent furnished with a tabletop wood-burning stove atop a small table, a few chairs, and a bed on a floor of compacted dirt. The next three Fuentes children, Katarina, Michael, and Yvette, were born in this tent. Soon after Yvette's birth in 1928, the Fuentes family "inherited" a small four-room house—two bedrooms, a living room, and kitchen—left by Manuela's sister, Amanda, who had moved to a neighboring town where her husband was offered work. They paid six dollars a month to rent the house, where they remained through World War II. As the years went by, the family grew and Mario, Manuela, and their children experienced a life based on the tentative nature of immigrants during one of the toughest economic times in American history—the Great Depression.

While living in the four-room house, the Fuentes family had ten children by 1939. The size of the Fuentes family made feeding and housing its members difficult, especially because they had to endure the poverty of immigrant life and the Great Depression. For example, Fuentes children recalled having only one pair of shoes each, and new shoes came only when there was money. Manuela made and altered the older siblings' clothes to be handed down to the younger ones. Seldom were items purchased from stores, and Fuentes children claimed there was no money for personal pleasures like toys and candy. Nevertheless, all second-generation Fuentes members said they grew up happy even though they had little material wealth or possessions.

The Fuentes family's standard of living was like those of other accounts during the Great Depression (Edsforth 2000; Terkel 1970). Michael, the third child, likened the family's experience to those families depicted in the film *The Grapes of Wrath*, because everyone in the family worked for their survival, and shelter and other household needs were sometimes fashioned from discarded material. After recalling his family's situation in comparison to those who migrated from the Dustbowl, Michael realized that his parents had strategies and resources for meeting the family's needs that were a result of their preestablishment in the Valley. The family raised livestock for food and extra income, selling it to a local slaughterhouse; they also tended a garden that provided the family with fresh fruit and vegetables, making rice, beans, tortillas, meat, vegetables, and fresh milk from cows and goats part of their staple diet. Both these strategies are characteristic of other Mexican immigrants in the Los Angeles area of the time (Monroy 1999; Sanchez 1993).

After a long day, the Fuentes family spent the evenings at home. Using kerosene lamps to light the house for a few extra hours, they sat around talking. When the family was able to afford small luxuries, like a radio, they spent evenings listening to programming. Mario and Manuela listened to the few Spanish language programs, and their children to English language programs like the *Green Hornet* and *Amos and Andy*. The family owned few possessions other than the radio and Manuela's sewing machine, which was used to make clothing. Mario purchased his first used car in the late thirties, a 1929 Chevy two-door sedan, and in 1942 or 1943, he purchased a used Model T. Fuentes children remember that each of the new acquisitions was a landmark event in the home.

Through the years, the Fuentes moved a few times, more than likely in hopes of improving their standard of living. Around 1941, the Fuentes rented a larger house a few miles from their initial home. During the war, the grower who owned the house wanted to demolish it to build stables on the property. Instead he decided to offer the house to the Fuentes for $1,000, which had been owned by an interned Japanese American family. Manuela's insistence on homeownership and the pooling of family wages allowed the Fuentes to purchase the house in addition to a few parcels of land, and they moved the house to *El Barrio de Los Compadres* (The Neighborhood of Friends), a Mexican barrio that had emerged in Zelzah.

Around 1942, about the time my great-grandparents bought their first home, the older cohort were beginning lives as adults. Sons enlisted or were drafted into war; and daughters found spouses and married. As a consequence of the postwar economic boom experienced in the nation,

Mario was able to change professions from stoop labor to construction. He joined the local chapter of the laborers' union. The family picked northern crops more infrequently until they stopped altogether in the 1950s, once Mario had stable work in construction. In addition to the purchase of the house and property, the family's increased income and stability brought the acquisition of other conveniences, such as an electric iron and motorized Maytag washing machine. Older Fuentes children recalled a hard life of work, while the younger ones remembered having the personal and monetary freedom for occasional luxuries, such as movies, records, and clothing.

In sum, my Fuentes great-grandparents and their children experienced extreme poverty because of a large family size as well as the economic effects of the Great Depression. Despite this predicament, their priorities for food and shelter (and the strategies they used to acquire them) put the family in a better position to endure these harsh conditions. Once the nation rebounded from its economic troubles, the Fuentes family elevated their economic standing through plentiful employment and pooling wages. They had fulfilled Manuela's dream of becoming homeowners and together worked to raise their standard of living, an invaluable legacy for future generations.

The Second Generation: Raising Mexican American Children

The second-generation Fuentes includes my grandmother and her brothers and sisters. Prior to the study, I had revered and respected them for being hard working and for creating a strong sense of family that established and nurtured my connection to other Fuentes members. However, I and other members learned that they wrestled with balancing their parents' Mexican traditions and their lived experience as Mexican Americans (Monroy 1999). Sons were soldiers and dressed in zoot suits, while daughters married young and worked to support their families.

In the forties and fifties, the second-generation Fuentes married and started families at a relatively young age. With the exception of one son who remains a bachelor today, all the Fuentes children married and moved from their parents' home between the ages of fifteen and twenty-five. Fuentes sons often left home to enter the military. In three out of five cases, Fuentes males were drafted or enlisted in the armed forces and then lived with their parents on returning home. They found spouses and married, moved to small apartments in other Valley cities with barrios, like San Fernando and Van Nuys, while they saved enough to buy their own homes. On the other hand, daughters quit school to work to support the family or to marry. After they married, they lived with their parents or other relatives for short periods of time to save money to purchase homes.

They tended to stay home to raise children but experienced periods of working to supplement husbands' incomes.

Both sons and daughters of the second-generation Fuentes family found spouses through community-sponsored events and personal networks, which were often outside the scope of their parents' circle of friends. Likewise, their homes were unlike the ones that their parents first owned. In general, the homes had two or three bedrooms, a living room, a kitchen, a dining room, and a backyard. Husbands of older Fuentes families built family homes, often using blueprints and building material from their jobs, while the younger members bought prefabricated homes, which became readily available after rapid and expansive urban development in the Valley after World War II.

The neighborhoods where second-generation Fuentes lived before owning their homes were also different from those of their parents. Once they decided to permanently settle, they moved, like other Mexican Americans after the war, "across the tracks, and into Anglo neighborhoods; or into neighborhoods now being evacuated by Anglo Americans moving to the suburbs."[1] Most bought or built homes outside barrio communities and in largely white working-class neighborhoods. Similar to Chicanos in other parts of Los Angeles County (McNamara 1957; Ochoa 2004; Peñalosa 1963), older Fuentes members experienced considerable discrimination outright purchasing land or houses and employed covert strategies, such as buying from a third-party realtor. Younger Fuentes members described no discrimination when they bought homes, more than likely because a single Mexican American family moving into a neighborhood posed no threat in the new urban setting.

Second-generation Fuentes families owned more modern conveniences than their parents. Over time, members filled their newly acquired homes with secondhand furniture: TVs, washing machines, stereos, refrigerators, and stoves. In addition, both husbands and wives eventually had a secondhand car. Husbands worked as landscapers, laborers, carpenters, and masons, and wives worked in factories.[2] On average, these families had four children, as few as two and as many as seven.

Growing up in the fifties and sixties, second-generation Fuentes children (third generation) recalled childhoods with more material luxuries than their parents. Excluding the early period of older second-generation Fuentes members who struggled with stable employment, third-generation children always had food and clothing and occasionally received store-bought toys: roller skates, dolls, and bikes. In these families, TV took the place of the radio, as children watched shows like *Howdy Dowdy*, *Rin Tin Tin*, and *Lassie*. While their mothers made Mexican food (tacos, enchiladas, and beans), third-generation children also ate American cuisine: hamburgers, hotdogs, pizza, roast beef, and mashed potatoes. Unlike their parents, children played, often at the encouragement of their parents; they rode bikes, played hide-and-seek and tetherball, and visited the homes of their neighborhood friends.

Just as in their parents' generation, third-generation members joined the workforce in adolescence. All but one member had jobs (part-time or temporary) that they used to supplement what their parents' income could not afford. They purchased the latest fashions and music as well as paid for excursions to movies and amusement parks. In later adolescence, more for the older cohort, money earned from employment was used to purchase used cars. Unbeknownst to them, entering the workforce became the next step in their passage into adulthood, marriage, and raising families.

Third-Generation Fuentes Families: Carrying over the Family Tradition

Third-generation members were cousins to my mother and her siblings. They grew up with more affluence and stability than their parents but always maintained a deep respect and admiration for their elders. Their world was Bobbie socks, cruising, car clubs, and Motown. They struggled with divorce and layoffs but did not lose sight of their dedication to their families, working hard for their children to have better futures.

Similar to their parents' lives, third-generation Fuentes adolescence influenced their adulthood. During their teenage years, these members lived with their parents and attended high school. Nine of the eleven graduated from public high school, and no one attended private school. The jobs they held during their adolescence were in the labor, manufacturing, and retail/service sectors, and they usually stayed in these jobs until they married and had families.

In choosing spouses during the late fifties through the early seventies, the older third-generation Fuentes members mostly married Chicanos from the personal networks they established in junior high and high school. Potential spouses resulted from attending casual parties or introductions by friends. In the few cases of exogamy, members met their spouses as a result of work relationships. They married roughly at the same age as their parents—between the ages of eighteen and twenty-five—and had children within a year or two. The average number of children was three, with as few as one child and as many as five.

One distinct characteristic of third-generation Fuentes families is the increased divorce rate, which has been an indicator of assimilation/acculturation (Grebler, Moore, and Guzman 1970; Rosenfield 2002). In the second generation, only one of seven members had been divorced compared to five of eleven in the third generation. Once earning a living and married, many third-generation members experienced a similar residential pattern to the younger second generation. Specifically, members moved to apartments in low-rent cities, some of which were barrio communities, prior to moving into their own homes. Eight of eleven cases in this generation resided in homes owned by their parents or in-laws for a short period (only three cases existed in the previous generation). Here, children were expected to pay rent but usually considerably lower than the market value so that couples could save money for a down payment on a house. These homes, unlike apartments, were in white working-class neighborhoods. In time, however, a few third-generation families upgraded their residences—moving to more affluent middle-class neighborhoods outside the Valley.

Third-generation parents provided slightly more materially for their children than the previous generation. Houses were approximately the same in size as that of second-generation families, and families purchased used cars through dealerships, occasionally buying a new car. Fourth-generation children recollected having store-bought toys and playthings, like bikes and skateboards. Food was plentiful and a few families could occasionally afford small vacations with their children.

Beyond necessities (home, food, and clothing) fourth-generation children remembered wanting. Growing up in the eighties when consumption of name brand products was en vogue, third-generation parents could not buy their children the culturally relevant attire or artifacts identified with popular social groups. Parents could also not afford cars for their children when they came of driving age, another cultural symbol for adolescents at the time. Instead, fourth-generation Fuentes members used the family car or recalled having to work while going to school to pay for half the cost of a used car, including insurance and maintenance. Any of the luxury items they wanted, clothing or excursions, had to come from their own earnings. In conclusion, with help from family, third-generation Fuentes families provided a slightly higher socioeconomic living situation for their children.

Fourth-Generation Families Making Fifth-Generation Fuentes'

My generation of Fuentes members grew up with Yuppies, the brat pack, and name brands.[3] As adolescents we struggled with fitting into a social landscape that forced us to choose between extremes, Mexican (immigrant) or American (white). We played with Rubik's cube, watched MTV, and went to the mall. Nevertheless, the constant was our bond to family, established through the time we spent with them on weekends, at celebrations, and on holidays.

Fourth-generation Fuentes' began to work in their adolescence. In most cases, they worked to purchase the personal items their parents could not afford. Often while going to school, they worked mainly in food service and retail. A few members dropped out, but most finished high school either with a diploma from public high schools or general education diploma (GED). After graduation most went directly into the workforce, moving from job to job in search of a career, sometimes attending vocational school or community college simultaneously.

These Fuentes' also met their spouses in similar ways to their parents through personal networks outside of family, at school or work. Of the seven members who participated only four were married at the time of the study (currently six are married), marrying between the ages of twenty-three and thirty-two, a markedly older age compared to previous generations. Although never married, one male had three children with a long-term partner whom he met through friends in high school. Different from the third generation, three of the four marriages (all of the female Fuentes in this generation) were to members of different ethnic groups, a biracial African American, a Filipino American, and a Native American, and are all college graduates. To date, there are no cases of divorce in the fourth generation, and marriages range in length from six months to fifteen years.

My siblings and Fuentes cousins have tended to stay in and around the Valley area, and all but one live in Los Angeles. After graduation most remained in their parents home or experienced times on their own followed by a return to their parents' or relative's home (both alone and with children). Currently, six of the married couples own their own homes, two homes in mixed ethnic working-class to lower-middle-class communities and the other in a townhouse complex in a suburb outside the Valley. At the time of the study, one male member (Francis) and his two sons resided with his mother in a mixed ethnic working-class community in transition of incorporating Latino immigrants, but they now live in an apartment in a lower-middle-class community.

Fourth-generation homes resemble their parents' homes in that they provide basic necessities and a little extra. Homes had ample food supplies along with some new or secondhand furnishings. These Fuentes families had an average of two cars and provided fashionable clothing (often discounted) for their children. In addition, at the urging of their parents, fifth-generation children participated in extracurricular activities, like Little League, track, and music lessons. Homes averaged two televisions, a VCR/DVD, and other modern appliances. Only two of the families had personal home computers at the time of the study, while currently all families have one. Children also possessed store-bought playthings like bikes, skateboards, stereos, and videogame consoles.

The aforementioned families and homes are the living context for my nieces and nephews and my second cousins. At the time of the study, fifth-generation children were all enrolled in school, five in elementary and one in middle school. Currently, they are all teenagers attending high school. All but one (who attended a private parochial school) attended a public school and had participated in some type of extracurricular activity at various times. Many aspired to professions that require a college education (i.e., veterinarian, scientist, doctor, and inventor). These children expressed a fondness for spending time at large functions with their extended family. In fact, before two moved to the Midwest in their toddler and preschool years, all six were a close-knit group, attending one another's birthday parties and going on excursions together.

FAMILY TIME: FUENTES FAMILY INTER- AND INTRAGENERATIONAL ACTIVITY

Since its inception, the Fuentes family has established a tradition of intergenerational gatherings. These happen at two levels, as whole family and single-branch events. Since the first generation, Manuela and Mario's house in the barrio became the site for both spontaneous and planned family celebrations.

When the younger second generation had families, Manuela and Mario moved to the northwest side of the Valley to a small house that could not accommodate large gatherings, making them more infrequent. Nevertheless, many recollected how there was a steady stream of visitors at the house whenever they visited. Even fourth-generation members, like Lydia Lopez, had vivid memories of visits to their great-grandmother's house:

> First, we would not go through the front door. We would go through the garage, through the laundry room, through the kitchen. There were cookies or tortillas [Grandma] just made. . . . Sometimes more than just my parents were there. . . . You never knew who was there. The people would always be dropping in.

Larger family events at Christmas and other holidays were easier to have when the family was only three generations large. As the family grew and once Mario and Manuela passed away, large intergenerational contact occurred less frequently and then only on certain holidays. Two third-generation females assumed the responsibility for certain celebrations, annually hosting Fourth of July, Christmas, and Easter parties in their homes. In addition, family reunions began at the end of the 1970s and occurred every two years for about ten years; recently, this tradition has dissipated given the retirement of second-generation Fuentes members. Other large family events that gather Fuentes from all generations are birthdays, funerals, anniversaries, and wedding celebrations.

In addition to holiday celebrations, intergenerational contact exists at a smaller level but more frequently. During Christmas, for example, second-generation families, comprised of three-generation families (grandparents, parents, and children) have separate gatherings in the grandparents' homes (usually). These types of gatherings also happen spontaneously on weekends, and grandparents and parents talk several times during the week.

At large family events, clear divisions exist between social spheres: Men play horseshoes, watch sports, or gamble; women sit and talk; and children play freely, usually outside away from adult activity. In general, however, men and women share space drinking and talking or playing card games. Often second-generation Fuentes family members tend to sit together and talk among themselves for most of the event, as other members periodically walk by to chat. Overall, the atmosphere is enjoyable: Children running and playing; adults talking and laughing; music playing loudly in the background, an abundance of food and drink spread out on a large table while conversations happen in and across the room or house. This type of inter- and intragenerational contact is one of the mainstays of Mexican culture in later-generation families (Keefe 1980; Keefe and Padilla 1990; F. Martinez 1993). Given this type of family interaction, it can be said that the Fuentes family maintains a connection between members even in the face of its unmanageable size. Family remains an important part of Fuentes life.

THE FUENTES FAMILY AS
WORKING-CLASS AMERICANS

In the United States, it is often taboo to acknowledge that a class system exists, let alone discuss how that class system inhibits or advances individuals' success. Despite our reliance on Horatio Algers stories as American exemplars, the majority of Americans tend to experience incremental amounts of vertical social class mobility from generation to generation (Kerbo 1983; Ransford 1980), and racial minorities' mobility is further affected by their categorization (Rossides 1997). Like other American families, the Fuentes family has been defined by its racial and class designation. Specifically, they have risen from lower class in their immigrant roots and plateaued at working class, like the majority of Mexican Americans (Ortiz 1996; Ramirez and de la Cruz 2002). Yet, most Americans would place the burden of blame on the family itself, claiming it was not ambitious or industrious enough to make it. However, sociological research (as noted in the Preface) begs to differ.

Sociologists have various classifications of American social class system yet use relatively similar characteristics or indicators to measure class.[4] One general scheme is five classes: upper class, corporate class, middle class, working class, and lower class. The important distinction, here, is between middle and working class.[5] While both describe full-time skilled employees who own their own homes, middle-class Americans tend to have more social resources in which to achieve social mobility. For example, middle-class people have at least a college education, work in managerial positions, and have access to other financial and social resources that improve their standing (i.e., health insurance, credit, and banking institutions). Working-class individuals, on the other hand, have high school education, work in wage labor occupations, and have limited access to other financial and social institutions.[6] While the Fuentes family may be said to border on the middle class based on their income, their education, occupation, and wealth demonstrate their constant and consistent place in the working class.

Like sociologists, I used occupation, educational attainment, and wealth as indicators of social class (Gilbert 2003; Jeffries 1980; Rossides 1990). Table 1.1 displays these factors for the Fuentes family participants.

Regarding occupation, table 1.1 displays the distribution of Fuentes family members by generation and occupation type. We have learned that Mario, the first-generation worker, was an unskilled laborer all of his life. From this table, we can see that Fuentes descendants three generations later have moved through semiskilled and skilled jobs but not much further. Despite that some jobs are white collar in nature (office staff), the Fuentes family still largely possesses jobs that require only some specialized vocational schooling and certification and pay hourly wages. Excluding me, the only participant who has a middle-class job (business owner) also possesses a master's in business administration (MBA).

What cannot be seen on this chart is that all Fuentes members experienced passage from unskilled to semiskilled to skilled jobs. That is, most began their employment in adolescence with unskilled work (laborer, fast food server, babysitter, or factory worker) and moved to semiskilled and skilled jobs through the course of their lives. One difference between generations is that third- and fourth-generation Fuentes members experienced accelerated job mobility compared to the second generation, likely because of the opening of the job market to Mexican Americans in the middle of the twentieth century (O. Martinez 2001). Despite this change, occupationally, few Fuentes have moved from their working-class roots.

Educational attainment or level has been another indicator of individuals' socioeconomic position. First, table 1.1 indicates that the greatest

Table 1.1. Occupations, level of education, and personal wealth by generation

Factors	Second generation	Third generation	Fourth generation
Occupation[a]	Unskilled, semiskilled, and skilled (7) (laborer, factory workers, housewife, retail assistant, blue print schematic reader, electric generator mechanic)	Semiskilled and skilled (10) (masonry contractor, cafeteria manager, legal assistant, medical assistant, administrative assistant, payroll officer) Middle class (1) (business owner)	Skilled and lower white collar (7) (medical assistant, party planner, escrow officer, hospital clerk)
Education	Ninth to eleventh grade; high school graduate (3)	Eleventh grade (3); High school graduate (8); Associate degree (1); Bachelor degree and master of business administration degree (1)	Eleventh grade (1), High school graduate (7); some community college courses (6)
Wealth	Homes (7), cars (7), real estate (rental properties) (6)	Homes (9), cars (11), some real estate (2), some stocks (2)	Homes (6), cars (7), some stocks (5)

Note: Number in parentheses indicates number of members.

[a]Occupations requiring no skill or training are unskilled jobs; those requiring some skill or training are semi-skilled; and those requiring long apprenticeships or certified training are skilled occupations. The chart measures the types of jobs Fuentes members held as heads of households throughout a lifetime.

trend in educational attainment for the Fuentes family has been the dramatic and consistent rate of high school completion with each subsequent generation. Where three second-generation members graduated from high school, more Fuentes' completed high school by the third and fourth generations, eight and seven, respectively.[7] Second, more Fuentes members in third and fourth generations have college attendance or earned a degree (one each of a bachelor of arts [BA], associate of arts [AA], and MBA in the third generation) and six in the fourth generation who completed college courses. I am the only member with a BA, master of arts (MA), and doctor of philosophy (Ph.D.). All this to say, the Fuentes family has experienced educational mobility aligned with working-class Americans—high school completion and some community college. These trends resemble those of other Mexican Americans (A. Gonzalez 2001; Groger and Trejo 2002), who graduated high school and attended some college but did not complete a four-year degree.

The final indicator of class is wealth.[8] Zweig (2000) measures wealth based on moneymaking assets (ones used to produce more capital) and personal use assets (ones used daily which depreciate over time). He claims that the bottom 90 percent owns roughly between 9 percent and 18 percent of the moneymaking assets, like stocks, bonds, real estate, and businesses and between 56 percent and 75 percent of the assets for personal use (autos, homes, and life insurance). In this light, working-class individuals possess predominantly personal use assets and little or no moneymaking assets.

Table 1.1 shows the type of assets Fuentes owned at the time of the study. Generally speaking, Fuentes' in all generations own personal use assets—homes, cars—and each generation own some moneymaking assets (real estate, savings bonds, or stocks). Now most own homes (twenty-two of twenty-six), and all own autos, averaging two cars per family. In the fourth generation, only two owned homes at the time of the study, and four purchased theirs between the completion of data collection and publication of the book. With regard to real estate, it is apparent that the second generation owns more than the latter two generations. This is for two reasons. First, second-generation members have had a lifetime of employment and have had the opportunity to redirect their money toward investments, while third- and fourth-generation families are still raising children and working. More importantly, this generation purchased rental properties when housing was cheaper in the Valley and before the passage of Proposition 13, which fixed property taxes. Later generations have not had, and do not have, access to these opportunities, making investment more challenging.

With regard to stocks, those Fuentes members who own stocks did not purchase them individually. In fact, third- and fourth-generation stockholders were part of a Fuentes family investment group that bought and traded stocks until 2002 (Fieldnotes, July 22, 1998), suggesting that members may not have been able to partake in the stock market had it not been for the pooling of funds.[9] The ownership of assets, regardless of type, clearly shows that the Fuentes family is oriented toward the future and working toward upward social mobility. While across generations there has been a rise in the standard of living, one must keep in mind the increase in cost of living and periods of inflation that have a profound effect on the working class.[10]

The remainder of this book delves into the lived experiences of Fuentes members at home, in the labor market, and in schools to understand why they have not had the dramatic mobility often promised to immigrants and citizens alike. I contend that the lives and livelihoods of the Fuentes family are more complex than studies of American ethnic groups have described and present the Fuentes view of themselves as survivors of a rough American voyage.

GETTING TO KNOW THE FUENTES: SKETCHES OF PARTICIPANTS

Given the number of Fuentes members that are part of this study, I will present a partial family tree in figure 1.1 and brief personal sketches for each member to help the reader follow the generational accounts.[11] Personal sketches incorporate information about members in the six years since the study. All second-generation members are Manuela and Mario's children, and members in bold are no longer living.

First Generation

Amanda Fuentes—At the age of 91, Amanda was a small dark-skinned Indian-looking woman, living with her son and only child. In the pattern of most immigrants, she had followed her sister to the San Fernando Valley, living with her for several years, and later marrying Mario's nephew. In her interviews, she demonstrated her incredible clear mindedness, recalling lucid and vivid details of her family's life in Mexico and immigrant life in the United States. Amanda passed away in the spring of 1999 at the age of ninety-two, and the family gathered at her funeral to celebrate her spirit, sense of humor, and zest for life.

Second Generation

Katarina Quiñones—Katarina lives with her daughter and grandchildren in her family home. A small, gray-haired, eighty-year-old woman with a dark complexion, Katarina has been widowed twice and spent most of her life as a housewife and mother to two sons and a daughter. As the oldest, she quit school in the eleventh grade to help the family. In her later life, Katarina, quiet but highly respected, worked as a hostess at a restaurant to stay active, a characteristic Fuentes trait.

    Michael Fuentes—Like his older sister, Michael's academic life ended in eleventh grade when he enlisted in the U.S. Navy in World War II. He is a proud veteran, attending his Navy reunion every year, and an avid deep-sea fisherman, who organizes a yearly summer family trip. Standing at just under six feet tall with dark skin, dark eyes, and a full head of salt-and-pepper hair, Michael has been a bachelor all his life, devoting his

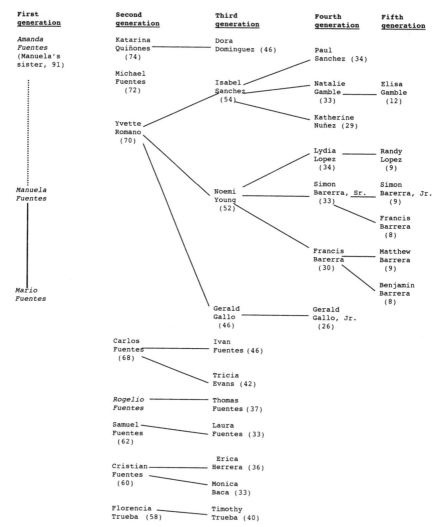

First generation

Amanda
Fuentes
(Manuela's
sister, 91)

Manuela
Fuentes

Mario
Fuentes

Second generation

Katarina
Quiñones
(74)

Michael
Fuentes
(72)

Yvette
Romano
(70)

Carlos
Fuentes
(68)

Rogelio
Fuentes

Samuel
Fuentes
(62)

Cristian
Fuentes
(60)

Florencia
Trueba (58)

Third generation

Dora
Dominguez (46)

Isabel
Sanchez
(54)

Noemi
Young
(52)

Gerald
Gallo
(46)

Ivan
Fuentes (46)

Tricia
Evans (42)

Thomas
Fuentes (37)

Laura
Fuentes (33)

Erica
Herrera (36)

Monica
Baca (33)

Timothy
Trueba (40)

Fourth generation

Paul
Sanchez (34)

Natalie
Gamble
(33)

Katherine
Nuñez (29)

Lydia
Lopez
(34)

Simon
Barerra, Sr.
(33)

Francis
Barerra
(30)

Gerald
Gallo, Jr.
(26)

Fifth generation

Elisa
Gamble
(12)

Randy
Lopez
(9)

Simon
Barerra, Jr.
(9)

Francis
Barrera
(8)

Matthew
Barrera
(9)

Benjamin
Barrera
(8)

Figure 1.1. Fuentes family tree of participants[a]

[a]Cohorts. Ages of Fuentes at the time of the study are presented in parentheses. First, the six-year separation between Carlos Fuentes and Samuel Fuentes indicates a separation in cohort experience. Reference to the older cohort in this generation is from Katarina to Carlos, while the younger cohort extends from Samuel to Florencia. For third- and fourth-generation Fuentes, the tree also indicates overlap in age groups of participants, which implies an onset into marriage and family. For this reason, the older third-generation cohort consists of members between 54 and 40, while the younger cohort is between 33 and 37.

energies to work and investing his money. Even at seventy-eight, he is known as the jokester of the family and respected as the eldest living male who cared for his parents for a period of his life.

Yvette Romano—Yvette, a small seventy-six-year-old fair-skinned woman with dark black hair who exudes grace and style, is my grandmother. After leaving the eleventh grade to marry a boy from the barrio, she lived as a housewife and mother of four. When money was tight Yvette worked as a migrant or factory worker. She eventually divorced her husband and supported her youngest son as a blueprint schematics reader for Hughes Aircraft. Later in her life, she remarried, traveled to foreign countries like Morocco and China, and retired at the age of sixty-two. Currently, she volunteers as an interpreter at a social service agency and works part-time in a retail store to remain active.

Carlos Fuentes—At the age of seventy-four, Carlos has retired as a building contractor and is a father of two sons and two daughters. Carlos is a small, dark, wiry man who fashioned a ponytail for much of his adult life, recently cutting it off after the passing of his wife of over fifty years. Carlos's reputation in the family is as a hard worker and family man and is shown in the amount of respect and devotion he receives from his children and grandchildren.

Samuel Fuentes—A father of three daughters and a retired electric turbine mechanic, Samuel Fuentes is an intelligent and religious man. In retirement he maintains his rental homes, in which two of his daughters live. Having served in the Army Reserves as a strategy against unemployment, Samuel initially trained as TV repairman and worked as a warehouseman after graduating from high school. He, a short, strong, dark-skinned man, spends much of his time counseling and enjoying his nine grandchildren who visit frequently.

Cristian Fuentes—Cristian is well-known for his trademark handlebar mustache and red company landscaping truck, a company he has worked with for over thirty years. Living in the heart of the Valley, Cristian and his wife bought and moved into a house down the street from the first house they purchased, where one of his daughters lived until recently. He was a paratrooper during the Korean War; he enlisted after finding no employment after high school graduation.

Florencia Trueba—As the youngest member of the family, Florencia cared for my great-grandparents in their old age, currently living in the house they last owned. She married at fifteen and became a mother of three. Now, a caramel-colored woman who wears glasses and has long highlighted hair, Florencia works as a retail assistant. She is a serious, soft-spoken woman, and devout Christian who attends a Bible study group regularly.

Third Generation

Dora Dominguez—Katarina had Dora, her only daughter and baby of the family, ten years after her two sons. Dora has been a single mother for much of her life, raising two boys and a girl, in her mother's home. Her training as a cosmetologist shows in her highlighted hair and makeup, doing nails for family and friends. Dora's fond memories of Manuela have prompted her to assume responsibility in gathering the family on some holidays. A fifty-four-year-old, heavyset light-skinned woman, Dora is currently focused on getting her daughter into college.

Isabel Sanchez—The oldest of Yvette's children, Isabel, graduated at eighteen, married, and had three children. She is a cocoa-colored, sixty-two-year-old woman who wears light-sensitive glasses, and works as a cafeteria worker at the local high school. Isabel coordinates the annual Fuentes family Easter party at her home, where there are horseshoe tournaments, an egg hunt, and raffles.

Noemi Young—Yvette's second child, Noemi is fairer skinned than any of her siblings. She married a young Mexican immigrant at the age of eighteen and had three children. She and her family lived in Arizona until she and her husband separated, when she subsequently moved back to the Valley. With an eleventh grade education and few job skills, Noemi raised her three children working in food service. Now, sixty years old, a manager of a public elementary school cafeteria, she has remarried and takes tremendous pride in her great-granddaughter, the first sixth-generation Fuentes member.

Gerald Gallo, Sr.—Gerald is Yvette's youngest child, who frequently jokes about his "Indian" hair and has been married for thirty-six years. Self-employed as a masonry contractor, Gerald's dark tan testifies to many years of working outdoors. He is known as a fun-loving guy and enjoys camping in his RV when he can. Nevertheless, Gerald takes extreme pride in his craft and works long, hard days. At the age of fifty-four, Gerald adores his two granddaughters.

Ivan Fuentes—Ivan, Carlos's second child and second son, followed in his father's footsteps and became a self-employed building contractor. Like Gerald, Ivan takes extreme pride in his work and is the only one in his family with an associate degree. His signature long mustache and dark tan complement his Levi jeans, white T-shirt, and work boots. A relatively quiet man at family functions, Ivan is fifty-four, the father of four, three girls and a boy, and a veteran of the Vietnam War.

Tricia Evans—Tricia is a petite fine-featured, light-skinned, dark-haired woman, a look she inherited from her mother's Spanish background. Like her brother, Ivan, she has four children, three from her first marriage and one from her second. A quick-minded person, a skill she attributes to hanging out with her father at work sites, Tricia has worked as a grocery cashier and bookkeeper but now stays home due to a condition as a result of an automobile accident. At forty-eight, Tricia is a dedicated mother who takes tremendous pride in her children.

Thomas Fuentes—The second oldest child and first son to Rogelio, Thomas, a forty-five-year-old with a dark complexion, is a highly educated man with a bachelor degree and MBA. His passion also lies in his love for surfing and his two children. Recently divorced (something that happened after the study), Thomas juggles the responsibilities of owning his own business and being a father.

Laura Fuentes—Laura, a tall, heavyset, dark forty-one-year-old mother of four, is Samuel's middle daughter. She has been married twice and trained as a medical assistant but has been considering a career as a legal assistant. As a single mother, her parents have been caregivers for her children, and her oldest son and father have developed a special relationship as a result. Laura is a warm-hearted and friendly person who smiles a lot and is set on giving her children the warm and close family life she had growing up.

Erica Herrera—Shy and quiet in her adolescence, Erica, a light brown-haired woman with a beautiful complexion, remains much the same in her adulthood. As Cristian's eldest daughter, this forty-two-year-old single mother, married young and divorced, afterward living with her parents until she could afford her own condo. Completing a degree at a local private business college, she has managed to work her way up in a wealthy school district as a payroll officer, a job that paid well enough to put her son through a private school education.

Monica Baca—As Erica's younger sister, Monica could not look or be more different. A sociable, dark, thin woman with long straight black hair, Monica and her family live a few houses down from her parents in their rental home. She dropped out in eleventh grade and began working at a bank, quickly moving up. At forty-one, Monica now works as a legal secretary for a law firm and is courting the idea of becoming a paralegal. Both her son and daughter attend the same private school as Erica's son.

Timothy Trueba—Timothy is a tall, tanned forty-eight-year-old who works as a postal carrier in a barrio community in the Valley. The large amount of time he spent with Mario and Manuela as a child have given him bilingual ability, which he enjoys exercising when he delivers the mail. Florencia's eldest child, Timothy is the father of five, two from his first marriage and three from his second. He infrequently attends large family gatherings in that his wife, a nurse, and he have a spilt schedule to care for their children.

Fourth Generation

Paul Sanchez—The oldest of Yvette's grandchildren, Paul, a thin, tanned, well-dressed young man, is known for his boyish looks and penchant for mischief. Prior to his engagement, he was believed to remain a lifetime bachelor like Michael Fuentes, often returning and sharing his tales of far off places like, Costa Rica, Cuba, Italy, and Egypt. Paul plays golf and tennis and rides his mountain bike. At the age of forty-two, he has owned his own business, as a result of taking many community college business courses and has worked nearly fifteen years with a party planning company.

Natalie Gamble—Natalie, a forty-one-year-old mother of four, frequently hosts spontaneous family gatherings at her home. Her house is filled with examples of her creative and artistic ability, from a tropical-themed bathroom to handmade salt and pepper shakers. Natalie, a tall, copper woman with auburn highlights, is licensed to do nails, often doing them for friends and family from home, and dreams someday of owning her own business. As a mother, she is firm, focusing on raising her children to be polite and well-mannered people.

Katherine Nuñez—Younger sister to Paul and Natalie, Katherine is thirty-seven years old, five feet, two inches tall, with long straight black hair. She is known for her sociability at family functions, frequently chatting with various members throughout events. She graduated high school, after which she held many jobs where she did well, then attended school to become a medical clerk. She claims she enjoys the job given the opportunity to work in various areas. Katherine met her husband, a registered nurse, on the job and now has one daughter.

Lydia Lopez—Lydia, an olive-skinned woman with brown hair and glasses, is the eldest of Noemi's children. Lydia met her husband on the job at the Internal Revenue Service, her first job at the age of eighteen. Her two daughters have only been to private Catholic schools, and the family lives in the heart of the Valley. Lydia's love for reading and thirst for knowledge has positioned her as somewhat of a family librarian, where she passes on books she has read to other members. She also has taken an active role in consistently interacting with second-generation members. When her eldest daughter had a baby, Lydia became a grandmother at the age of thirty-nine.

Simon Barrera, Sr.—Simon, Lydia's brother, is the only fourth-generation member to complete a tour of duty in the armed forces. His demeanor exemplifies his disciplined and regimented military training, and he runs his household in a like manner. Simon is a devoted father of four, three boys and one girl, and is married to a woman from Mexico City. Out of the service, he has had a number of jobs and currently works as a truck driver and runs a small home business. Feeling his opportunities were limited in Los Angeles, he is one of few Fuentes members who has moved away.

Francis Barrera—The youngest of the Barrera children, Francis, who stands about five-feet nine inches, has a medium brown complexion, sports short, wavy, black hair, a goatee, and wears dark sunglasses. Others are often astounded by his knowledge of U.S. and World history. He is the father of three, a girl and two boys. He never married the mother of his children, but at the age of about twenty-five, assumed sole custody of his sons. He lived many years with his mother, Noemi, who helped with child care and child raising. Francis worked his way up in a telemarketing firm, starting as a caller and moving up to a supervisor by the age of thirty.

Gerald Gallo, Jr.—Gerald, son to Gerald Gallo, Sr., is an only child in a dual-income family. For this reason, Gerald had many advantages that his Fuentes cousins did not. Nevertheless, he credits his cousins with giving him a family, the brothers and sisters, he never had. Standing taller than most Fuentes at five eleven with short, straight dark hair like his father, Gerald also sports tattoos aligned with his ethnic pride; one in particular spells out *Brown Pride* across the top of his back. Having married and had two daughters in the last few years, his current ambition is to start his own pool cleaning business.

Fifth Generation

Elisa Gamble—Elisa is the oldest of this cohort of the fifth generation. As a child, she was known for her high academic performance and extremely mature personality. Oldest sister to three younger children, Elisa proudly and willingly assumes her role as a big sister. At family functions, she can be seen changing children's clothing, comforting a crying baby, or reprimanding those who misbehave. Now twenty, she works at a personal gym as a receptionist and is graduating from high school.

Randy Lopez—Lydia's youngest daughter, Randy, is the exact likeness of her Navajo father. Randy is tall, dark, and small featured and loves to run cross-country, a sport her mother introduced her to with tales of her track competitions as a girl. As a child, Randy was a good student and quick learner. At the age of seventeen, she spends time with Elisa and Francis' daughter, Sonia, and attends a top-ranked all-girls Catholic school.

Simon Barrera, Jr.—Simon, Jr., or JR, is the eldest of Simon's children. From the beginning, JR has always been known as a talkative and inquisitive boy, often asking questions well beyond his years. During the study, I recall having a car ride discussion about cross-cultural issues after he had made a friend from Japan at school. This tall, dark-skinned boy has also been known for his love of TV and animation and dislike for household chores. Now seventeen, he talks about getting into a school to do computer graphics and design.

Francis Barrera—JR's younger brother, Francis, could not be more unlike JR. Francis enjoys a challenge and working to the completion of a task. He is short and light-skinned like his mother and is quiet and timid in new social situations. He is highly athletic, excelling at just about any sport he plays. At the age of sixteen, he has become an excellent electric guitarist.

Matthew Barrera—Anyone raised by Francis (male or female) is bound to be exposed and encouraged to play baseball. Matthew is no exception. A thick light-skinned boy, Matthew, at the age of five, took to baseball like second nature, more than likely because his father likes sports. He is a sweet boy but like his cousin, JR, does not like household chores. From an early age, Matthew has shown a strong ability to draw. At seventeen, he is close to six-feet and plays in a rock band for which he writes songs.

Benjamin Barrera—Like his older brother, Benjamin plays and loves baseball. Yet, Benjamin is softer than Matthew. A small, dark, and chubby-cheeked child, he frequently helped his father, grandmother (Noemi), and grandfather and especially liked to care for family pets. Benjamin is also a warm-hearted and sensitive human being who often empathized with others. Grown now to about six feet at the age of sixteen, he has retained some of his original character, even in the face of becoming a man.

NOTES

1. Clark S. Knowlton, "The Neglected Chapters in Mexican American History," in *Mexican-Americans Tomorrow: Education and Economic Perspectives*, ed. Gus Tyler (Albuquerque: University of New Mexico Press, 1975), 42.

2. The second-generation Fuentes women's careers predate the identification of the dual-income family (Waite and Nielsen 2001) and align themselves with Griswold del Castillo's (1984) thesis that working-class and poor Mexican and Mexican American women worked for needed income and family subsistence. The third generation of females appears to follow their mothers' example and the American trend for women to work, and fourth-generation women tend to work in that even American families can no longer survive on a single income.

3. Marrying outside the ethnic group, usually to Anglos, is noted as an effect of Americanization (Murguía 1982). While these marriages may be seen as acts of assimilation, the motivation for marriage was for love and for their strong potential as providers and family men. Over the years, their professional and personal qualities have become invaluable to the Fuentes family; they have been good men and involved and present husbands and fathers.

4. Unfortunately, while this analysis identifies the Fuentes as working class, caution must be taken with this seemingly facile classification. Specifically, the categories of jobs are merely descriptive of particular labor fields, but they disregard idiosyncrasies that blur categorization. For instance, a food service manager and a supervisor are in managerial positions. According to Perruci and Wysong (2003), managerial positions are labeled middle class, because they assume a disciplinarian role, organize other subordinates, and usually require a college education. Nevertheless, I decided to classify the aforementioned as skilled occupations, because they were obtained through experience, seniority, and some degree of training. Thus the strict use of occupation as a class identifier can prove problematic.

5. Middle-class Americans are small business owners, self-employed individuals, semiprofessionals (police officer, teacher, or nurses), and middle management, and working-class Americans have high skilled, semiskilled, and unskilled jobs, like factory workers, truck drivers, welders, and secretaries. Some jobs in both categories may have comparable incomes, such as teachers and plumbers, yet the nature of the work is qualitatively different. Middle-class jobs have more prestige, require less physical labor, and deal with abstract ideas; on the other hand, working-class jobs are repetitious, low prestige, and more physically demanding.

6. General scholarship on working class in the United States (Fussell 1983; Le Blanc 1999; Levitan 1971; Shostak 1969) does not incorporate the experiences of most minorities. Except where class and race have been studied in minority groups (Bettie 2003; Dohan 2003; N. Foley 1997; R. Garcia 1991; Griswold del Castillo 1984; Hart 1998), the analysis of Mexican American lifestyle and experience as working class is based on standard measures, which are extrapolated from white working-class accounts. The unique experiences and nuances of the Latino working class have yet to be thoroughly and comprehensively studied.

7. Research claims that there is a dramatic increase in attainment between first and second generations and minimal gain in third (A. Gonzalez 2001; Groger and Trejo 2002). Groger and Trejo claim "the huge educational gain between first- and second-generation Mexican Americans should produce a sizeable jump in schooling between second and third generations. . . . Yet, the improvement in the schooling we expect to find between the second and third generations is largely absent," (p. 17).

8. Given the sensitive nature of disclosing one's financial resources, the use of income was not chosen as a direct measure of class. Instead, material wealth, one's personal possessions and assets were used.

9. For clarity and efficiency, references to participant interviews and fieldnotes are not noted in the bibliography and are solely referenced in text by name of the participant or by date of the fieldnotes.

10. Despite America's economic prosperity in the mid-twentieth century, some scholars have claimed that certain groups, especially the working class, experienced negative effects of harsh economic forces in the latter part of the century (Bernhardt et al. 2001; Osterman 1999; Parker 1972; Zweig 2000). For example, Bernhardt et al. describes that period for the U.S. worker as follows: "Starting in the mid-1970s, real wages stopped growing and even declined for certain groups in the labor force, a marked reversal from the postwar economic boom. To make

matters worse, the degree of inequality in wages grew by roughly 30 percent. Either one of these trends alone is cause for concern, but in combination, they indicate a truly worrisome deterioration in workers' economic welfare" (p. 2). Surviving these conditions, let alone thriving in them, poses an extreme challenge to working-class families.

11. Pseudonyms have been used for all Fuentes members, including the family name. I also created names for some locales and altered details of personal information and events.

2

Home, Part I
The Original Fuentes Home

In this chapter, I focus on both continuity and change of the Fuentes family home life, starting with the immigrant and second-generation Fuentes', which leads to subsequent Fuentes generations in the following chapter. I examine the values system that Fuentes parents instilled in their children at home, describing and demonstrating the values Fuentes parents and children perceived important in raising children. In summary, I illustrate how elements of original Mexican values existed in the first Fuentes home and were passed on to later generations.

THE ORIGINAL FUENTES HOME:
FIRST-GENERATION PARENTS RAISING CHILDREN

Given Mario and Manuela Fuentes's national origin, it goes without saying that the second-generation Fuentes' were immersed in what can be described as the Mexican tradition of family.[1] The descriptions of the second-generation Fuentes' upbringing, as well as comments by Amanda, Manuela's sister, detailed the presence of Mexican cultural values. Further, Mario and Manuela provided a home and family life that exemplified and promoted a sexual division of labor, Spanish language use, and other religious/social traditions (e.g., *compadrazco* [godparentship]).

The socialization of Fuentes second-generation members resembled that of other Mexican American families. Griswold del Castillo (1984) claims that "the socialization of Mexican American children in the late nineteenth century and early twentieth century occurred through 'parental example and teachings'" or *consejos* (advice).[2] According to the interviews with second-generation members, this type of instruction existed in the Fuentes home.[3] Despite Manuela's demanding schedule and responsibilities, all second-generation members recalled advice their mother had given them, a good deal of which will be presented in the next section. Michael, the second eldest son, characterized her advice like this: "Oh, she gave us a lot of advice. Advice like going to school, keep clean. Stay away from the kid that got in trouble. Everything that had to do with life itself." More poignantly, Florencia, the youngest, articulated that her mother was indeed the example they were meant to follow: "I don't think she really taught us . . . she was an example of how we should treat each other. I would say that to me that would be the best thing that she could have done."

Regarding parent socialization styles, the first-generation Fuentes home should be considered a manifestation of Mexican culture, as clearly as that can be defined. Yet, as an immigrant family in the United States, the Fuentes home was neither monolithic nor static, and proved to be, initially and over time, adaptive in that it had to contend with interaction with and influence of American society.[4]

GENERAL MEXICAN TRADITIONS
IN THE FUENTES FAMILY

First and foremost, the Mexican culture manifested itself in the separate gender roles and language of the home. Mario and Manuela presented traditional Mexican gender roles of husband as provider and disciplinarian and wife as household manager and nurturer.[5] All the siblings recollected how their father was always working or looking for work. For example, Yvette recalled how her father would ride his bicycle many miles in the winter to work at a dairy, requiring him to be gone much of the day. Cristian, the second youngest, also claimed "his father was off working," so he never got to see him much. According to Michael, when Mario was away, the next in the chain of command as head male, was the oldest son: "Saul was a second father when Pop was away. If we did something wrong, he would report it to Pop."

In contrast to memories of their father, Fuentes second-generation children remembered their mother as homemaker and caregiver. Almost all Fuentes siblings stated that their mother was in charge of the activities in the home: cooking, cleaning, doing laundry, and mending for a family of twelve. Yvette described other daily or seasonal tasks her mother performed, such as making all their clothes with a foot-pedal sewing machine, embroidering and crocheting dishtowels and pillowcases, and canning peppers, fruit, cucumbers, and pickles in the winter. According to Cristian, everything was done by hand, like making tortillas for twelve, three meals a day, seven days a week.

Similarly, Manuela was adored and respected by her children for her kindness, generosity, and fairness. As children, many second-generation Fuentes' remembered how their mother governed with a gentle hand, as Michael describes:

> [She] never said, "Do this, do that." She'd always said, "Come on, let's do this. Make rice." . . . Mom always used to say, "One gets candy, everybody gets a candy. Or nobody gets a candy." So everybody was treated equally. No such thing as favoritism. Too many of us. Like she said. She had to be fair. She couldn't treat one better than the other.

Katarina relayed a story about how Manuela, exasperated with her sons' fighting, sought a more civil solution to the matter:

> They were always fighting and hitting each other. So one day my mother got [the idea,] "I'm tired of you guys [fighting]." She told somebody to buy her two sets of boxing gloves. So right when they were starting to fight, she'd say, "Okay you guys put on the boxing gloves and go at it." Hitting each other with boxing gloves they wouldn't be able to hurt themselves as much as punching. . . . So they got the idea and pretty soon the fighting stopped.

In the first-generation Fuentes home, children were also socialized to assume their parents' gender roles. Fuentes males tended the animals and garden. Cristian said that the chore of wood chopping was passed down from one brother to the next, a chore that began when Mario taught Michael how to chop wood. The two oldest daughters, Karatina and Yvette, recalled how they helped their mother with the cooking and cleaning.

Despite following the traditional gender roles in a Mexican family, the Fuentes family adapted to its American environment in a few ways. First, Manuela usurped her woman's role by assuming the role of family financier, a role associated with being the head of the household, which was typically held by men in Mexican culture.[6] Many second-generation members clearly recalled how their mother was in charge of the family funds and how to spend them. Samuel, one of the youngest, explained how his mother came to be the family financier:

> Later on as we grew up, my dad wasn't really the type to manage money. He probably didn't plan out for the future. . . . So, I guess, Mom, somewhere along the line, she kinda took charge of the money. How it was going to be spent. There always seemed to be money there for emergencies.

Along the same lines, Cristian described his mother as "the bank" of the family.

Additionally, there was contention between Mexican ways and the ways that Manuela wanted to do things now that they were in the United States. Samuel claimed his parents argued about discipline. Specifically, his father wanted to spank the children as a form of discipline, but his mother said "No." She would say, "We're not in Mexico. We're here." Another point of contention was socializing Florencia, the youngest, into her womanly role. According to her, Mario complained about Florencia needing to learn how to do household chores, and her mother disagreed: "I was the spoiled one. I didn't have to make tortillas. My dad would tell my mom to show me. And my mom would say 'No. No. She's got plenty of time.' I finally learned [w]hen I got married."

Similarly, Manuela deviated from typical Mexican gender roles by teaching her sons how to care for themselves domestically. She taught them to embroider, iron, mend, and cook. Michael, the third child, claimed that his mother taught him these skills as a form of self-sufficiency, and Manuela told him about how to use his domestic skills as a husband:

> I'll always remember her saying, "I'm teaching you this because someday you're going to get married and you're going to need it. I don't want you to suffer. I don't want you to come home, maybe you have a disagreement with your wife and her telling you that she's not gonna cook today. . . . You don't have to beg for her to cook." And she told the same thing to the women.

Florencia, on the other hand, claimed that her mother taught her brothers these skills, because she was trying to occupy their time from boredom, possibly trying to deter them from fighting. In either case, the Fuentes males learned these skills that were clearly associated with women's work.

The adaptive nature of gender roles was less pronounced with the Fuentes daughters. Neither parent encouraged their daughters to assume behaviors associated with male roles, to do so would seemingly reduce their chances of marriage. Katarina, the oldest daughter, claimed that her mother gave her daughters the following advice: "Be good wives, you know, faithful. Work for your family. Do the best you can for them. . . . Have your husband save money, you know and later on you can have something. Work if you can. . . . That's it." Clearly, this advice reinforces the woman's role as homemaker and caregiver, a Mexican woman's role. Nevertheless, it also suggests that Manuela believed that a woman could assume the role of wage earner outside the home if it complemented the goal of working for one's family.[7]

A more overt example of how girls were discouraged from assuming male roles can be seen in Florencia's tomboyishness. Florencia, the youngest Fuentes, described herself as a tomboy because she liked to dress up like a cowgirl with a toy holster and guns; she also liked to climb trees. At one point, Florencia and one of her nephews got into a physical fight over his teasing her. In the end, the nephew got a black eye and Florencia got a bloody nose. Believing Florencia asked for it, Manuela replied, "That's what you get for being a tomboy." This final remark suggests that Manuela wanted Florencia to see the detriment of stepping into a male role: One will not be treated as a lady.

Given the connection between language and culture, the Spanish language also socialized Fuentes second-generation children into Mexican culture. During the interviews, almost all of the members recounted consejos, a particular detail, or vocabulary in the Spanish language. For example, after his first interview, Cristian, the second youngest, showed me some of the family artifacts he had collected over the years. One was a high school yearbook from the year his oldest brother, Saul, died. In my notes I wrote, "We looked for Saul's picture in the yearbook only to find that it had been cut out. He [Cristian] said his mother did it, and when he asked her why, she said, *"Porque ya no existe"* ("Because he no longer exists"). More detail about the heritage language and English will be discussed in chapter 6.

The Catholic religion is considered an integral part of Mexican culture.[8] As a Mexican immigrant household, the Fuentes home provided religious direction and influence. First, Manuela, more than Mario, held a devout Catholic faith. Manuela always lamented that no Catholic church existed in close proximity to their home, because she could not raise her children with the presence of the church. At one time, an opportunity arose to have her children go to Catholic Sunday school in a neighboring town. Yvette, described attending Sunday school and her family's church participation:

> The only churches were ones in San Fernando and Canoga Park. There were no churches nearby. My parents took us to church in San Fernando or L.A. to be baptized. We went to catechism after school. Men would pick us up and take us to a different neighborhood where there were four or five families and the children were taught religion. It was the older ones that went. We didn't make communion. Catechism was just like school, they taught how to pray, the Hail Mary and all that for about an hour. We never said grace at home. We went to church together occasionally because my father always had to work. On special occasions like Christmas, Easter.

Manuela also practiced her faith at home, praying and doing the Rosary. With little resources, she encouraged her children to get religion where they could. In one case, she urged them to go to a summer program at the nearby Methodist church. Children were also exposed to religious rituals and practices through their mother's adherence to church traditions. When her oldest son passed away, her children recalled her being *de luto* (in mourning); Katarina stated that her mother stopped playing the radio for one year in observance of Saul's death.

Manuela and Mario's children were exposed to and experienced certain Mexican traditions, both religious and social. The most pervasive, binding them to other families in the community was the tradition of *compadrazco*. Without family nearby to fulfill this role, Katarina claimed that the barrio surrounding their home was named, *El Barrio de Los Compadres*, because of the baptism of children by adults in other barrio families. According to Michael, baptisms warranted special celebrations:

> Everybody was *compadres*. Some families would baptize who knows how many other families. Everybody was compadres. . . . And they'd be out there dancing. . . . Somewhere they got musicians from San Fernando. My godfather I remember he used to love to dance and dance. He'd get all the guys to play. The guitar. The violin. One saxophone. It would go on all night. Till the next day. There were no neighbors to complain.

Overall, it can be said that the Fuentes second generation clearly had a Mexican orientation to their socialization. Their parents reinforced gender roles, the Spanish language, food, lifestyle, and the religious and social traditions aligned with Mexican culture. Even still, as scholars have noted in other Mexican immigrant families, the Fuentes family remained an adaptive social unit. Males were taught and encouraged in domestic roles as a means of creating a distraction from the mundane or as a means of self-sufficiency, and women were encouraged to be wage earners as well as to accept the model of the women as family financier.

In the next section, this analysis becomes a backdrop for the discussion on the values system and beliefs that existed in the first-generation Fuentes home. Not surprisingly, this system resembles those of other Mexican families during the same period.

SECOND-GENERATION CHILDREN'S VALUES SYSTEM

The following set of values represents those exhibited in the first-generation home, a Mexican immigrant family establishing itself in a rural valley in Los Angeles County some time after the turn of the twentieth century.[9] This system is centered on five major categories: the value of *buena educación*, the value of family, the value of hard work, the value of schooling, and the value of saving and investment.[10] These values are represented here in no significant order and with no particular priority of one value over another.

Undergirding the value and belief system in the Fuentes home are Mario and Manuela's goals and aspirations for their children. The primary motivation for Mario and Manuela in coming to the United States was in search of a life less riddled with instability and unpredictability and a greater chance at prosperity. This sentiment emerged as a rationale for the goals and aspirations Manuela had for her children. In the first interview with Yvette, when I asked her what the most important thing was to her parents, she replied: "My mother was, most important to her, was to get ahead. To have a better life than what they had. That was the most important thing to her because she used to say so. My father never really, didn't say anything." Similarly, Katarina, the second child, refers to this desire to get ahead when she discussed good things about the Fuentes family:

> Well, I guess, we all did pretty good for ourselves. We all got married; we worked to improve ourselves more; we all have our homes. We all have good families, no drugs or anything like that. They're all striving to do better all the time. *I think that came from my mother's part in encouraging us, to work, do better than they did* [emphasis added].

Manuela, as the main caregiver, had other goals for her children, which relate to getting ahead. These goals usually revolved around the notion of being able to use one's resources to advance in life. Michael clearly recalled the advice his mother gave him about work and self-sufficiency:

> I used to do everything. We would all help. That's why we learned how to mend . . . we'd sew buttons, we'd iron, we'd cook, make tortillas. *That's how we know how to take care of ourselves.* We were taught. From the first day we started walking, we learned to do something, useful around the house. *We were brought up to do things for ourselves.* She used to tell us someday we'll need it. Sure enough, that's the truth [emphasis added].

In addition to wanting her children to be self-sufficient, Manuela valued her children's ability to use social resources or networks, in this case, family. In response to the question what were the important messages he received from his parents, Samuel, the third youngest child, said he learned from his mother that relying on siblings was a way to get help when he needed:

> We not only learned by being instructed to be brothers and sisters, but the dedication that my mom had toward us. She lived it. Her life is her family. . . . [She would say,] "In times of need, who can you turn to? Brothers and

sisters. In times of catastrophe, you got to learn to cherish one another because you are the same blood, you are the same family. This is what I offer you, because when you get older, there is gonna be some times when you need something. . . . You can always turn to your brother or your sister. . . . That's the way I want you to grow up. To consider their welfare and they in turn will consider your welfare. I want you to be close."

Nestled in the value of family is the desire for children to learn how to rely and depend on one another. Being self-sufficient is necessary for advancing oneself, yet having several reliable and dependable individuals with one's interest at heart can expedite the process.

One final goal that Manuela held for her children was for them to live an honest life. Coupled with her religious fervor, the horrible and cruel conditions of the Mexican Revolution most likely made Manuela conscious of the best way for an individual to live a prosperous life: to be an honest, law-abiding person. Cristian, who explained that the family's hectic life in his early years discouraged long sit-down conversations, claimed that Manuela started giving him advice in his adolescence:

"Don't do this, don't do that. Stay away from the bad people. [Don't] get in trouble. I don't want to see you in jail." It would kill her to see her son in jail. Stay out of jail, stay out of trouble. Basically, be good. Don't treat anybody bad or whatever.

In sum, Manuela primarily sought to guide her children to a life that was more prosperous and less strenuous than the one she had to live. Wanting her children to get ahead caused Manuela to stress that her children be self-sufficient, be reliant on family for help, and live an honest life.

The Value of *Una Buena Educación*

The first value in the Fuentes family derives from the Mexican cultural value of educación. Valenzuela (1999) defines this concept as follows:

It refers to the family's role of inculcating in children a sense of moral, social and personal responsibility and serves as the foundation for all other learning. Though inclusive of formal academic training, educación additionally refers to competence in the social world, wherein one respects the dignity and the individuality of others.[11]

In a Mexican household, a child is then raised with una buena educación (to be well-educated or well-mannered) if he or she performs respectful and respectable relations with others. Diaz-Guerrero and Szalay's (1991) description of an individual in Mexican culture clearly incorporates the notion of educación:

Mexicans, on the other hand, tend to regard "me" as a person with certain social attributes (understanding, helpful), roles (man, son) and functions (works). Their reactions seem to be connected to a "moral" way of being in the world. Life is a task of craftsmanship in attempting to live according to a set of values, which are essentially traditional.[12]

Griswold del Castillo (1984), in his review of Mexican and Mexican American families in the southwest, specifies what types of values and behaviors correspond to educación. Examples of these were mutual respect among family, *dignidad* (dignity), *respeto* (respect), obedience, and "firmness of character."[13] For second-generation Fuentes children, this instruction amounted to learning to be respectful, courteous, honest, hardworking, and dignified representatives of their family.

The term buena educación (or other derivations, *bien* or *buen educado*) did not emerge from second-generation interviews. Perhaps because these interviews were in English, the term did not come as readily as the descriptions of how they were raised. Nevertheless, Amanda, as Manuela's sister, shared the same goal in raising her son. Two years prior to the study, I interviewed Amanda on the topic of family and language, and this is what she said about how she wanted her son to grow up:

> [I hoped] he was a *good* young man . . . like all the rest . . . that he was *well-mannered* and did not come upon *bad habits* . . . he didn't *rob* or anything.[14]

On one level, this comment clearly implies that the objective of a child having una buena educación is for them to be good, well-mannered, and free of bad habits, like stealing. In fact, these were the things that second-generation Fuentes members claimed their mother had taught and encouraged in them.

Manuela encouraged her children to be good by warning them to stay away from bad people. We saw the advice she gave Cristian, and others expressed how their mother encouraged and discouraged certain behaviors to keep them out of trouble. For instance, Katarina stated that her mother encouraged her brothers to participate in sports to keep her sons "[f]rom hanging around the wrong kind of kids. Keep them off the streets and away from drinking." In addition to staying away from bad influences, Cristian's previous comment also suggests that he and his siblings learned not to treat people bad. According to Florencia, her mother was the example of how to treat others—"kind, gentle, friendly." Florencia also remembered how at least she and her younger siblings received "courtesy training" from their mother. She said, "[Mom] would show us how to welcome someone. And then she would say, 'How do you do?' and 'Hello.' She would coach us, how to treat a person."

Revisiting Amanda's comment, honesty seems to play a role in children having una buena educación. She claimed she did not want her son to rob or anything, suggesting that deceit or dishonesty was not desirable. Yvette, in discussing what some of the things were that she learned from her mother, replied: "[My mother talked] about being honest and not stealing, not yelling. She preached against drinking. To be honest, not to lie. Mostly. Not to argue. Do what we're told. Don't talk back." Yvette's comment also implies that deference to authority and obedience were expected of the Fuentes children. In Mexican culture, children defer to the authority of parents and other adult figures to preserve the social order (E. Martinez 1999). Manuela also held this expectation for her children. Several times in his interview, Michael noted this, which not only corroborates Yvette's comment but also indicates that violations of this code of conduct were disciplined: "[No back talk] was the law. We did what we were told and that was it. No questions. No nothing. That's the way we were brought up. . . . The rest of them behaved or else."

In the Fuentes' minds, being well-respected people, ones who are honest, hardworking, and responsible, and treated others courteously and respectfully were the types of people Mario and Manuela sought to raise.

The Value of Family

The value of family or *familism* has long and strongly been accredited to Mexican and Mexican American families and individuals (Baca Zinn 1983; E. Martinez 1999; F. Martinez 1993; Padilla and Perez 2000; Vega 1990). The Fuentes family, too, holds this value for its members in a variety of ways. Above all, the concept of family encompasses two types: family as close and together and family as support.

In her teachings, Manuela had certain expectations of her children in regard to how they treated one another. Second-generation Fuentes' claimed that she often told them that they needed to help each other as brothers and sisters; she immensely disliked it when the children fought with one another, especially the boys. Yvette and Samuel both claimed that they would be disciplined by their mother for picking on their siblings. In the preceding section, we have already seen the powerful message that Samuel received about the importance of family. Thus, for second-generation Fuentes children, there was an ideology of family togetherness that was implemented and emphasized in everyday life.

Despite their squabbles, second-generation Fuentes' described themselves as being close. In some cases, members recalled having a special closeness with a certain member(s). Carlos claimed that he and Rogelio were especially close as children (being the fifth and sixth children) and that that closeness followed them into their adulthood when they made concerted efforts to see each other frequently even after Rogelio moved away. Florencia, the youngest, recalled the special bond that developed between the three youngest Fuentes—Samuel, Cristian, and her. When I asked if she was close to her siblings, she replied affirmatively but acknowledged that she had the closest bond with her younger brothers, because they were closer in age. She said that Samuel was her defender and Cristian was the "teaser." "I think that's what kept us close together. [Chavez: the fighting. (*laugh*)] Yes, the fighting (*laugh*)]"

Both Yvette and Michael acknowledged that the closeness the Fuentes siblings enjoyed as children continued into their adulthood. Even in their advanced age, Michael said if they were not close they would not get together, and they tried to get together as much as they could Yvette conferred with Michael:

> Even though we don't see each other that much. You know, we still keep in touch . . . like some siblings, after they marry, they lose track of each other. We still keep in touch. [We get together] maybe once or twice [a year]. We just visit. This year were gonna get together to go up north.

In fact, during the summer of 1998, while I stayed with Yvette, Samuel, Michael, and Cristian visited at least two times each, and Yvette regularly went to Bible study with Katarina and Florencia. That same summer, second-generation Fuentes' also had a barbecue where they spent the evening at one of Michael's fish frys, eating and visiting. The notions of closeness and togetherness and helping and supporting one another are closely interwoven.

The Value of Hard Work

The value of hard work is deeply ingrained in the first-generation Fuentes home life. Above all, working hard was part and parcel of day-to-day life; every family member had to work, which usually required performing some physical task or labor.

Second-generation responses indicated that the value of hard work was modeled by parental example. For instance, Mario was the prime example of how hard work translated into practical results. Michael described how his father worked hard to provide for the family: "'Cause Pop was out there, he worked from sunrise to sunset. Ten cents an hour. That was the time given to him. Sunrise to sunset." Even after he began working as a construction laborer, Florencia also remembered how hard her father worked: "My father was working, construction. He worked hard. He worked long hours, a full day and over time if he had to. He worked on Saturday sometimes. He was always working."

Manuela was also an example of a hardworking individual. All second-generation members commented how hard Manuela worked to manage the house and the twelve-member family. Samuel, the seventh child, claimed that his mother carried quite a load to care for the family: "My mother always stayed home. She had so much work raising the family. Everything was done by hand. Heating up water, washing clothes with a washboard, cooking. Everything was done from fresh vegetables, sometimes canned." As the eldest female, Katarina claimed that once in awhile she would relieve her mother of her early morning duties to give her a chance to rest: "I also remember getting up early in the morning. I would say 'Mom, you stay in bed a little longer. I'll get up. And make lunch for my dad so he can go to work.' So that gave a little extra time in the morning to my mom [to sleep]."

Mario and Manuela's example set powerful precedents for the way their children were expected to work. Specifically, Michael claimed that he and his siblings were disciplined ("We'd get a whooping.") if they slacked off in their work. Cristian recalled how his father was a man of few words, but when he spoke he usually remarked something about work—"You're going to work, right?"

While Mario took a direct approach to promoting the value of hard work, Manuela used her caring and compassionate demeanor to encourage her children to work hard. Carlos recounted a time when he was chopping wood that his mother encouraged him to continue working hard:

> In those days, all the kids, they were, made to do things. You didn't volunteer (laughter). They were assigned, probably the mother assigned them to [do] certain things. Whether it was chopping wood. . . . I used to chop wood for the stove, because we had a wood stove. And my mother would give me all big credit, "Ay, Carlos, you are such a hard worker. Look at the big pile of wood you chopped for me." Then, I would really get going.

The value of hard work then became a direct connection to fulfilling the social responsibility to loved ones. During one of her interviews, Yvette explicitly recited a saying her parents told her and her siblings about hard work, and she believed it was the reason why she and her siblings were still active in their elderly years: "My parents' saying was that hard work never killed you."

In the end, the value of hard work was instilled in the Fuentes children as a natural course of a rural, immigrant family life. Furthermore, children were expected to work hard in fulfillment of one's responsibility at home as well as satisfying personal connections to loved ones.

The Value of Schooling

The term *educación*, which includes formal schooling, has been used previously to refer to the social education Mexican and Mexican American children receive. To differentiate it with the American English definition of education, *schooling* will be used to refer to education that ends in accreditation. In the interviews with Fuentes second-generation members, the notion of educación—being socially competent in dealing with others—emerged separately from the notion of schooling. In the first generation, the American concept of schooling was a notable strand of the family fabric. According to second-generation children, Manuela, more than Mario, felt that an education (schooling) would give her children a better life.

As stated in chapter 1, Manuela was forbidden by her grandfather to go to school, which was the greatest reason that prompted her to promote completing school. Four of the seven siblings stated this is why their mother encouraged them to finish high school, a level of education that was difficult to complete for most Mexican and Mexican American students of that time.

Moreover, Samuel expressed how his mother was devoted to her children's schooling and that he and his siblings took that to heart. When asked what his parents' attitudes were toward education, Samuel said his parents never wanted them to drop out of school:

> She always said to herself, "When I have a family, I will never allow them to work in the fields and spend their days in the fields because there is an opportunity over here." She would instill that in us when we were growing. . . . She always said, "You got to stay in school. Otherwise, you're gonna wind up not doing good for yourself." Some wanted to do that, some didn't.

It is apparent that Manuela understood the connection between schooling and opportunity; doing good for oneself meant graduating from high school. In her eyes, schooling could keep her children out of the fields she and her husband had to endure to support their family.

In fact, a few others mentioned that sending the children to school was a source of contention between their parents, as Katarina depicted the types of arguments her parents had over the issue of schooling. In response to a question about what her family was like growing up, Katarina immediately focused on the emphasis her mother put on school:

> First thing would be that my mom always said that we had to go to school. To learn to have a better, higher education than she did. My dad was reverse. He said that he wanted the kids to go to work to help the family. My mother said, "No. They're going to school. And they're graduating." And we did.

Katarina's comment implies that the family's need for income conflicted with the children's need for schooling. Yet, it seemed that Manuela had the final say about her children finishing school.

The Value of Saving and Investment

The concept of saving and investing one's earnings was a value that Manuela encouraged. Four of the seven second-generation participants expressed that their mother gave some type of advice about saving money. More often than not, the reason for saving money had to do with saving for the future and preparing for the unpredictable nature of life.

This comment made by Katarina clearly demonstrates that Manuela, and not Mario, held the value for saving money:

Chávez: Whose idea was it to save money?

Katarina: My mother. Because my dad was always thinking about going back to Mexico. "I'm going back to Mexico," he said. "Well, go. But go by yourself because I'm staying here," [my mother answered.]

Katarina continued by saying that her mother was really the go-getter in the family; Mario worked all the time, but Manuela saved the money he earned.

Manuela's children remember she had a vision for the family, which required saving money. Manuela clearly understood that money was one of the ways, if not *the* way, to advance in American society and thus perhaps urged her children to save. More succinctly, Michael described what his mother's vision was and where it originated. While describing the first house his parents bought, Michael interjected with this comment:

When [my mother] grew up, she grew up with her grandparents in Mexico. They were always moving somewhere, someplace. They never had a house. And that was her dream. She was the one who actually pushed for us to buy, buy, buy. She would tell me and the rest of the family, "Buy property. Can never go wrong. . . . You can lose money if you leave it in the bank." Because they lost everything in the bank, I forgot to tell you. In the 1929 Crash, everything that they had, they lost. For many, many, many years, she didn't believe in banks. . . . And that's why [she would say], "Some day, yes, Mario, look, one day we are going to have our own house. Some day. Ooo, you think you're rich [sic he used to answer.] Pop couldn't see it. . . . He thought he'd go out and just buy a house. No. It takes time. She managed somehow. She was the financial advisor, the bank; she was everything. She took care of the house inside and out.[15]

Michael's extensive reply identifies Manuela's personal vision to buy a house as a life goal after a life spent moving from one place to another. Buying a home is a way to set down roots and live a stable life. This personal desire coupled with her negative experience with U.S. banking perhaps led her to encourage her children to invest their money, not in a savings account, but rather in real estate, a more stable and less vulnerable type of investment.

As a result, the Fuentes children held this mantra close to their hearts as Yvette testifies: "One thing that we learned, because my mother always used to preach to us to always save for a rainy day. . . . Or don't waste your money because you worked so hard for it, don't throw it away." Like the other values described in this section, the value of saving and investment has had a profound effect on the state of the Fuentes family in the following generations.

NOTES

1. Given their thorough attention to the Mexican American family, Richard Griswold del Castillo, *La Familia: Chicano Families in the Urban Southwest 1848 to the Present* (Notre Dame, Ind.: University of Notre Dame Press, 1984) and George J. Sanchez, *Becoming Mexican American: Ethnicity, Culture and Identity in Chicano Los Angeles, 1900–1945* (New York: Oxford University Press, 1993) will be the primary sources for this analysis.

2. Griswold del Castillo, *La Familia*, 78, 79.

3. Griswold del Castillo claims that this behavior was associated with middle-class Mexican American families. It is not possible to determine Mario or Manuela's socioeconomic position in Mexico. Their life stories and educational level as told by their children suggest that at the least they might have been working class. This analysis suggests that this behavior may also be associated with a wider Mexican population.

4. Both Griswold del Castillo and Sanchez stress this point. Specifically, in *Becoming Mexican American*, Sanchez notes that variability was the norm, not the exception, in how Mexican American families adjusted to U.S. society: "Finally every Mexican that came to the United States made adjustments. Though most families did not disintegrate under the weight of changing circumstances, they certainly acclimated. The nature of this acculturation varied, depending on setting and different strategies were developed to fit the needs of the historical moment. A new identity was continuously being formed" (131).

5. In *La Familia*, Griswold del Castillo claims that both tradition and social pressure kept this Mexican sexual division of labor intact in Mexican American families. According to him, "the ideal wife and mother was supposed to be primarily concerned with the management of the *casa* (home) and the husband was to defer to her in mundane domestic matters. His sphere of responsibility lay outside the home as a protector and breadwinner" (29).

6. Griswold del Castillo claims that Mexican American women's biographies throughout history "suggest that there were socially acceptable ways in which women, particularly those of upper classes, could act outside the rigid limits of the patriarchal family. In reality women's roles were not always circumscribed by family obligations" (31). He further wrote, women (and men) in lower-class families also deviated from traditional roles out of necessity: "Among the majority of frontier families, however, men and women tended to share the labor of farming, ranching and household chores" (27).

7. Sanchez more pointedly notes what effect class had on whether women assumed the male roles and responsibilities as wage earner: "Both Mexican and American cultures designated men as the principal family wage earners. Whether or not a newly married woman worked for wages was often a source of discussion or consternation, although many families found the income generated by wives essential" (142).

8. For a more detailed discussion of religion and the Mexican American family during this time period. See Douglas Monroy, *Rebirth: Mexican Los Angeles from the Great Migration to the Great Depression* (Los Angeles: University of California Press, 1999). Suffice it to say, the Catholic religion shaped the roles and behaviors of men, women, and children in a Mexican and Mexican American family. Sanchez (1993) claims that the influence of the church on Mexican American families in urban Los Angeles in the first half of the twentieth century was weakened because of a loss of church control and lower presence in barrio communities where they needed to compete with other religions.

9. As stated in the preface, the assumption made here about the Fuentes Mexican and Mexican American culture is defined as their way of life as it relates to other Mexicans and Mexican Americans. It consists of food, language, values, and such, which they share with other Mexicans and Mexican Americans. In the past, culture has often been considered uniform and homogeneous; any deviations were often seen as unrepresentative. Recent scholarship (K. Gutierrez and Rogoff 2003; Mukhopadyay and Henze 2003) suggests a need to view the inherent heterogeneity in human cultures as well as the dynamic and multifaceted experience of cultures in contact, who tend to borrow and adapt features from one another. The Fuentes family is a case of the transformation of ethnic cultures in a U.S. context, in many ways describing Mexican American cultural transmission outside of the barrio scene.

10. It could be argued that the latter four categories could be subsumed in the first category. Because the Fuentes' did not make a point to relate these categories in this way, they are presented separately here. Each was discussed as a distinct value in and of itself.

11. Angela Valenzuela, *Subtractive Schooling* (Albany, N.Y.: State University Press, 1999), 23.

12. Rogelio Diaz-Guererro and Lorand B. Szalay, *Understanding Mexicans and Americans: Cultural Perspective in Conflict* (New York: Plenum Press, 1991), 56.

13. Griswold del Castillo, *La Familia*, 72–92.

14. Amanda spoke only Spanish; she said *[F]uera un jóven bueno . . . que toda la demás . . . que sea educado, jóven bien que no halla las malas costumbres . . . no fuera ha*

robado o algo. The data comes from a study on ethnic identity, conducted in 1996 that traced the use of and attitudes toward Spanish and English in a small sample of Fuentes members.

15. Manuela would say: *Algún día, sí Mario, mira, un día vamos a tener nuestra casa. Algun día." "Ooo, te crees rica tú."*

3

⁓〜

Home, Part II

Later-Generation Fuentes Homes

FUENTES PARENTS' ASPIRATIONS
OVER THE GENERATIONS

As described in chapter 1, overall second- to fourth-generation Fuentes' moved from their parents' homes to get married and to raise families. They did not endure the type of poverty that Mario and Manuela did, even though later-generation Fuentes families may have experienced times when their standard of living was meager or modest. Unlike the first generation, later-generation Fuentes parents tended to have dual-income families, women needing to work to supplement the family income. Once a home was bought, families generally had relatively stable lives in predominantly Anglo, working-class neighborhoods.

Generally, the goals that Manuela held for her children, to get ahead, to be self-sufficient, to rely on family and to live a clean, honest life, were also the goals and aspirations later-generation Fuentes parents had for their children. Parents in every subsequent generation made similar comments when asked what they wanted for their children:

Second Generation

I wanted my kids to be good, honest, decent, respectful, respectable people. We wanted to provide them with healthy, nutritious food. We wanted them to have religion, even though their mom let them choose what religion to belong to. We wanted them to be taken care of. (Carlos Fuentes, Manuela's fifth child)

Third Generation

Number one goal is education, as much as I can give them. . . . Love, knowledge and discipline and family. That is very important. When things don't work out, it is family that supports you, no matter what. (Monica Baca, daughter of Cristian Fuentes)

Fourth Generation

I want them to know that they can't just sit on their ass all day and expect money to roll in. You have to get out there and work for it. Me having three sons and me being their father, I want them to be strong. To be able to support their families. I want my daughter to recognize a strong man. I want to be that example. . . . I want them to be educated. (Simon Barrera, Sr., son of Noemi Young)

Getting ahead appeared to be a goal in the minds of Fuentes parents in later generations. In the second generation, Carlos claimed that he had wanted his sons not to be in their current profession (building contractors), because it was too physical. Being that he, himself, was a building contractor, it is likely that Carlos's desire to see his sons have a job where they do less physical, more white collar work is getting ahead.

Florencia, the youngest, made a similar comment about her children. In comparing her parents' aspirations to those she had for her children, when she replied:

Florencia: Maybe because I didn't finish high school and maybe that's why I encouraged them and pushed them that they should finish. Maybe that's why because I thought that was important to them. As I got older, I found that college, it was even more important for them. If I would have known then what I know today, I would have encouraged them to do more.

Chávez: What can college do for them?

Florencia: Get them a better, higher, better paying job. You know. For promotions.

This response further explicates the notion of getting ahead. A better job is one that pays more and allows for promotions, qualities that working-class jobs rarely offer. Hence, because she did not graduate, her children can do better by finishing high school. The previous concept of doing better appeared to be too little for what her children needed to compete as adults in the present labor market.

For the second generation, getting ahead then resulted in raising one's standard of living through attaining better jobs. Third-generation parents also hoped this for their children. Dora, Katarina's daughter, who had three children between the ages of twelve and twenty-six at the time of the study, explained her desire to see her children do better:

> You want to see your children do better. [But] it's a lot harder [now]. More competition, more people, more stress and everything. That you stress on your children to be more progressive and to do more for themselves.

Dora shares the desire for her children to do better, yet she clearly acknowledged that the change in the labor market makes it more difficult for them than perhaps it was for her.

Another member, Thomas, Rogelio's son, shared his aspiration for his children. Interestingly, Thomas is the only member to complete both a bachelor and a master degree. Married to an Anglo and father of two children, Thomas lives a more middle-class life as an owner of a bookbinding business. Be that as it may, he comments like other Fuentes about getting ahead:

> *Thomas*: Yes, I want them to be financially productive. For me, my belief is each generation should be better off than the previous. Does it mean that you're better? No . . .
>
> *Chávez*: What does *better* mean?
>
> *Thomas*: Better off economically. Because I believe if you are better off economically it gives you a better opportunity to be better off with your family.

Using the example of his large childhood family (seven children), Thomas continued to discuss how poverty limits the range of opportunity that parents can offer their children. The more money parents have, the fewer stressors there are on their income, allowing them to provide luxuries and opportunities, like college, which they themselves may not have had.

Finally, Francis, Noemi's son and fourth-generation member, characterizes how other members in his generation felt about their children getting ahead. Francis was upset that he never realized his potential early on and did not have a chance to pursue any of his interests. That being said, the following response reflects his understanding of how his children could do better than he:

> It's all about dreams. You have a damn dream and you go after it. . . . I'll be damned if they are going to become Latino statistics. . . . They're going to pursue their interest and they're going to make the best out of it. Whether or not they succeed as in they may become wealthy off their interest or whatever, that's not the point. I don't care about that. I just want them to pursue their dream. In whatever it is . . . that's my goal. That's my dream.

Thus, parents in each generation agree that getting ahead is an aspiration they had or have for their children. Each of the parents here has a similar, yet slightly different understanding of what getting ahead means to him or her. In particular, the era in which parents lived, as well as their individual circumstances, provided a point of reference by which they set goals for their children. Carlos and Katarina grew up in the Great Depression, an era different from Florencia who experienced the post–WWII period. Dora and Thomas came of age in the sixties and seventies, while Francis experienced the eighties. However, despite their differences in circumstance, these Fuentes parents have maintained aspirations set by Manuela some eighty years before: Parents want their children to do better than they did.

The second half of Francis's previous reply pinpoints the final goal that many parents mentioned: for their children to be happy or to live a good life. Francis's response suggests that following their dreams is a way for his children to be happy. This happiness is qualified not by monetary return or wealth, but rather by whether children do what they like and make the best of it.

Samuel's daughter, Laura, mother of four, specified this notion of happiness by explicating that she wants her children to be in a position to choose their fate:

> *Laura*: I try and tell my son or instill in him, *be whatever you want to be.* I'll support you emotionally and morally. Whatever way you need the support you need to do what you want to do. *Don't do something that you feel you are going to be forced into doing.* If it's education, go to school. For me, that's priority.

> *Chávez*: What does that mean for you? Does that mean, high school, to a trade school, to a college?

> *Laura*: Either, or. Whatever field that they feel comfortable doing. I don't want them to go, yeah, I want you to be a doctor, gotta be a doctor, you gotta be a lawyer. That's where the money's at. I just want them to feel that they are able to provide for themselves, take care of themselves and be self-sufficient. [emphasis added]

What appears most important to Fuentes parents in all generations is for children to decide what it is they want to do in life. That choice, parents hope, is not constrained by circumstances that force a child into living a life they did not choose. Similarly, while the idea that one can be whatever one wants to be can be traced to American ideals, Laura expressed how choice does not necessarily concern the acquisition of wealth or prestige. For her and other Fuentes parents, the motivating criterion for the decision is whether one can enjoy life or whether one can be self-sufficient. From this perspective, school is *an* option, but it is not the only option.

What is the origin of Fuentes parents' notion that children should find their own fate and happiness? One possible explanation is that like other values, it is derived from the ethnic culture. According to scholars, the concept of an individual in Mexican and Mexican American culture varies considerably from American culture. Diaz-Guerrero and Szalay (1991) claims that "[t]he Mexicans' central notion is 'me' as a person (*persona*), one *who is a unique human being* but who does not feel separated from others."[1] Sewell (1989), who studied the notion of a person in a Mexican American community, claimed that individuals are treated with regard to their unique and special attributes that the community has come to believe they possess. To force an individual to be different would be a social violation. Some Fuentes parents stated as much when discussing how they wanted their children to be as adults.

For example, Samuel claimed that he wanted his children to stay in school, but he knew that he could not force them to do it; otherwise, they just rebel. Ivan, Carlos's son, reiterated what his father said when talking about his own children: "I don't care no more. They're gonna do whatever they're gonna do. And if they're happy, then they're happy. You can't push your kids into doing anything."

Isabel, a third-generation member, mentioned she wanted her children to have a "nice family, [to raise] kids, [and to be] prosperous along the way." When it came to counseling them on careers, she replied: "We wanted them to go and do something, but I didn't know what they wanted. I suggested the bank. And Katherine [should] go into something financial. You know, but that's not them. So I can't force them." In the fourth generation, Lydia wanted her oldest daughter to "be happy with herself" and for her younger daughter "to know that she will be a positive effect on this world." When asked if having a lot of money had anything to do with these goals she replied, "No. Depends on how they want to live."

With regard to happiness, it appears that Fuentes parents expected and expect their children to choose what they are going to do in life, perhaps because they feel it would be a personal violation to make such a decision for their children. As a backdrop to this choice, children were provided the system of five values laid out in the previous chapter.

CONTINUITY AND CHANGE IN THE VALUE SYSTEM OF LATER-GENERATION FUENTES FAMILIES

In interviews with subsequent Fuentes members, four of the five values listed in the first-generation home were clearly present in the lives of later generations. Beginning with una buena educación, later-generation parents

have continued to instill the need for children to be respectable and respectful human beings. Children agreed with parents that this value was an
important part of their home life.

Fuentes members mentioned that children were expected to be respectful and respectable. To be respectful in a Fuentes way means to be well
mannered, to defer to authority, to respect and be considerate of others, to
show tolerance and empathy and to be friendly. To be respectable requires
a Fuentes to be lawful, self-sufficient, responsible, mature, presentable,
honest, fair, and moral. All these values concur with the definition of
buena educación as "a sense of moral, social, and personal responsibility
. . . [and] refers to competence in the social world, wherein one respects
the dignity and the individuality of others."[2]

How is the Fuentes value of una buena educación any different from
the American cultural notions of morality and personal responsibility?
What distinguishes the Fuentes family's notion of respectability from
other Americans is the level of prominence that these values play in their
lives. By comparing the total number of responses for each value across
generations by child and parent, the preponderance of the values becomes evident.

Table 3.1 indicates that both parents and children believed that the
greatest teachings they provided or received were tantamount with una
buena educación.

The Value of Una Buena Educación

Fuentes Parents

Given the status of buena educación in the Fuentes family, more compelling is the way each generation of parents and children speak of it. For
example, second-generation parents, Carlos and Florencia, provide two
powerful examples. As seen previously, Carlos desired for his children be

Table 3.1. Total number of responses per value by Fuentes parents and children[a]

Values	Total number of parent responses	Total number of children responses	Total overall responses per value
Buena educación	65	87	152
Schooling	48	52	100
Family	29	53	82
Hard work	16	45	61
Savings/Investment	6	10	16

[a]Note: Number of responses was determined by counting the expression of a value by separate turns. For
second, third, and fourth generations, responses were counted separately for child and parent recollections.

good, honest, decent, respectful, respectable people. Here, he explained what his approach was in raising his children:

> Trying to live by the rules, you know. . . . To earn, what's called nowadays, a straight living. Of course, as you're growing up in your teens, it's kinda you, get a little wild. . . . And, I think that had a little to do in myself kinda staying straight. *And trying to keep my children straight, which every parent does.* . . . Just trying to live by the law, the law of, *I don't mean the man-made law, I mean honest law. Trying to live a clean [life], even with what little you might have.* [emphasis added]

This response not only indicates Carlos's intent to raise his children to live a clean life, but it also acknowledges the continuity of his experience. He had been raised to earn a straight living; he strayed during his adolescence but returned to raise his children as he had been raised.

Florencia, the youngest child, also believed that her children should be raised to be buen educado. When she was asked whether she thought her children were successful, her idea of success revolved around the notion of buena educación:

> Yes, very good. Well, because they have a really close relationship with the family. And I can say, *they're cordial, they're very, how do you say, honest. They're good workers. My sons are good workers.* . . . *My daughter's an honest person. She's a friendly person.* . . . *So, morally I think that they're successes because (inaudible), morally. Good people.* [emphasis added]

Third-generation parents also professed that the traits and qualities children should have acquired should comply with those of respectful and respectable persons. Carlos's daughter, Tricia, revealed as much here:

> You hope that when they are younger that you bring them up with enough morals and rightness that they will go off and do well. They don't have to make a million dollars. They can be poor, I don't care as long as they live to be a good person. As long as they [can], be understanding and don't do things maliciously or purposely to harm people.

Likewise, Timothy also believed that his children should leave his home prepared to interface with the world in a respectable manner. Like Tricia, an acceptable life for Timothy's children is based on the edicts of una buena educación:

> I want kids to get a job where they could earn enough income to be self-sufficient, provide for themselves, live comfortably. Not rich. There are a lot of rich people that are lousy characters. . . . There are a lot of poor people that are great people. . . . We just want our kids to grow up to be honorable, to be responsible, to be good human beings. That's the bottom line.

Finally, fourth-generation parents spoke just as passionately about how their children needed to care for their reputation, especially how it was perceived by others. For example Lydia, Noemi's daughter, extolled the fact that her daughter's numerous social invitations were a sign of her daughter's success as a good person, something she took pride in:

> Randy's, like, really social. We try to explain to [her] "It's a compliment to you, Randy." I'm telling her. When the parents decided to have a small party and they always choose you. And they're doing that because their opinion of you is high. You have good manners. You're polite. And basically, a good child to associate with.

Natalie, Isabel's daughter, spoke of public experiences she had that clearly indicated to her that her children were good. Specifically, she talked about one instance when her daughter, Elisa, first went to kindergarten. Natalie claimed Elisa had a difficult time adjusting to the environment because "the other kids were meaner. . . . [They] had no manners, pushing and shoving and having mouths on them." In their apartment complex, Elisa caught a neighborhood boy trying to start a fire. She told both Natalie and the boy's mother and prevented a dangerous incident from occurring. Natalie took pride in the fact that her daughter did the right thing.

To ensure that children received una buena educación, Fuentes parents actively managed their children's lives by having rules that restricted children's behavior. Children had to tell parents where they were going and had to get permission to go places. When they were young, children had to stay in close proximity to home. As Noemi stated, "I was kinda strict with [my kids.]" In addition, parents had the final say with whom their children could and could not play. For example, after the fire incident, Natalie told her son that he was not to play with the boy who set the fire. Violations of these rules, as children attested, were punishable. These rules became the reins by which parents restrained their children from acquiring unacceptable behaviors (i.e., lying, stealing, and talking back).

Fuentes Children

Given their parents' attention to una buena educación, not surprisingly Fuentes' children learned to accept it as a fact of life, which eventually got passed on. For example, third-generation children recalled how their parents set strict rules that were to be obeyed Noemi, Yvette's second daughter, exemplifies this here:

> When [my] kids were growing up. [Things have] changed for the worse. When we were growing up, it was different. We didn't have to lock our

doors. We could go to one neighbor, tell our mom we're going to go over so and so's house. And be back at a certain time. Which we had to. But you know, we couldn't just wander.

Cristian's oldest daughter, Erica, explained what it was like to live with her parents. She and her sister had to be in bed at a certain time, even in junior high. Her parents expected them to do what they were supposed to, what they were told to do. They would say, "Don't talk back. Keep your hands to yourself." Ivan, Carlos's son, having some difficulty recalling specifics, claimed there were things he and his siblings were not supposed to do: "[Be] respectful. . . . Don't lie. I know I was told a lot of don'ts. . . . I'm sure like little things that I say to my kids. Don't do this. Don't do that. And they get in trouble for it." Ivan clearly articulates that he transmitted how he was raised to how he raised his children.

Fourth-generation children also remembered the types of behaviors they had to exhibit in their parents' homes. Katherine, Isabel's daughter, believed her parents taught her to respect others and they guided her in the right way, because she is not a "mess up." Paul, her brother, concurred with her, claiming that he and his sisters "had to have respect and act in a respectable manner." Lydia claimed she and her siblings had to "do what [their mother] told them" or otherwise get in trouble. She was "expected to tell the truth . . . and to learn life skills," how to take care of oneself. Gerald, Jr., also recognized the same types of behaviors as part of his upbringing: "Have good morals. . . . Don't treat anybody the way that you wouldn't want to be treated. Try not to be a smart ass. Then you won't be messed with a lot. Or people won't think of you in a certain way."

In the fifth generation, children articulated that their parents expected them to behave in accordance with una buena educación. Randy, Lydia's daughter, recalled how the last time she got in trouble was when she forgot the paper she needed to do her homework. Her mother then proceeded to give her a lecture on responsibility. JR and Francis, Simon Sr.'s sons, recalled how their father would tell them stories to get them to "act like him."

Francis's sons, Benjamin and Matthew, each recollected the kinds of things they got in trouble for. Benjamin had just been punished for "being bad," when he yelled and ran away from his teacher. Matthew claimed he would get in trouble for lying and saying bad things about the teacher. Matthew's most poignant response came as an indirect reference to una buena educación. Expressed with a mild repulsion, Matthew described why he does not like the children down the street: "They throw trash and don't keep their grass [looking good], all these beer cans and bottles and the cops come over. They're mean because they let their kids say bad words to anybody." At the age of nine, this reply clearly demonstrates that

Matthew had already acquired the values of cleanliness, lawfulness, and respect to evaluate his own and others behavior and character.

As a twelve-year-old fifth-generation member, Elisa was the most eloquent on the subject. She claimed that she "would like to hang out with the cool kids" at school, but she does not because "they get in trouble and talk bad." For Elisa, she acknowledged that her desire for being well-mannered is reinforced by her family:

> *Elisa*: I think most of our cousins are well-mannered. I mean because everybody in our family thinks the same, they think, they don't say, "Go ahead have what you want." Basically, everybody thinks like, "You better ask. Say please. Say thank you."
>
> *Chávez*: How do you know that?
>
> *Elisa*: Because we learn 'em here. We do. I mean it's like Derek (her three-year-old brother), he's concerned about himself, too. He says, "Thank you." "Please." . . . This is my opinion though, I think every parent should teach [these values], if they don't, their children have no manners. It's not nice. You can't just say, "Give me this." It's so impolite. I can't stand that.

At the ripe age of twelve, Elisa had already developed disdain for impoliteness. Remarkably, her response demonstrates the persistent importance of una buena educación in the Fuentes family through the fifth generation.

The Value of Family

Table 3.1 also indicates that the value of family, with the third greatest number of responses, has remained in the Fuentes family over time. Manuela's desire for togetherness and closeness and to use family as a resource has been passed on from one generation to the next. For many Fuentes members, togetherness referred to types of closeness and connections between family members, both immediate and extended. Family was also described as "being a priority," "being good to one another," or "no one being more important than another." Later-generation Fuentes parents commented that family was about being together and providing some type of emotional or other support, while children believed that the value of family was exemplified by parents' relationships with their siblings or other relatives. For some Fuentes members, family had been a moral guide when members were tempted by dangerous social influences.

Fuentes Parents

In the second generation, parents all acknowledged that family was an invaluable part of life. Some stressed this point with their children. Cristian, the second youngest, was one of the parents that specifically instructed his daughters about the importance of family as a source of help: "I wanted them to learn that family comes first. Don't run away from them because they are there to help you." Florencia also believed that having a close family is one of her successes:

We have a close relationship with each other. I think that's one of the things that comes to my mind now. . . . It's very important. I think if they have a close relationship with the parents that will help them. To be the people that they are, you know. I know because it helped me to be a better person.

For third-generation parents family closeness and togetherness were important to pass on to their children. For example, Dora, in particular, had assumed part of the responsibility for family gatherings by holding such annual family events as the Christmas and Fourth of July parties. She explicitly stated that she does this because of the loss of her grandmother, Manuela, as the cultural and family center. Dora holds the parties as a way for her children and other family members to have a place to meet outside their busy schedules; gatherings provided an opportunity to get to know family who may someday be in a position to help.

Generally, many of the parents were not as cognizant as Dora about the ways in which they promoted the value of family. In one case, during the accounting of her childhood, Noemi came to realize that the way she promoted togetherness with her children probably resulted from her own upbringing:

Noemi: I had rules when [my kids] went visiting with [their] friends. . . . They weren't free to roam the streets. Like some parents, you know, "Go. Go ahead." Or "Get out of my hair."

Chávez: Why were you like that?

Noemi: 'Cause I was afraid.

Chávez: Afraid of what?

Noemi: Something would have happened to [my] kid, (laughs) I was afraid if anything happened to one, one of [them] would be there or two of [them] would be there. To take care of each other. When I wasn't around. Mainly that was why it was. . . . You're safer when you're together. Than you are by yourself. Like I did with Grandma and Grandpa, too, when we were raised. We went that way. If I went, Isabel went. Or Beto. We did things together. . . . The same with Matthew and Benjamin (her grandson's). In the front, they have to be together or have one of the boys next [door], they can't be out there by themselves.

In this exchange, Noemi links second generation to fifth generation. She explained that the way she was raised, the way she raised her children, and the way her grandchildren are being raised are based on rules that promote togetherness and family.

Being in the process of starting their families and purchasing their own homes, fourth-generation parents had less to say about family as support and instead focused on the importance of family and togetherness. Simon, Sr., who lives in a midwestern state, was planning on taking his whole family to visit extended family in California that summer. Despite the fact that he felt somewhat peripheral to the Fuentes family for much of his life, he claimed he was doing this to help his children forge relationships with family members. When asked what things she and her husband agreed on when raising their daughter, Lydia stated that they wanted to teach Randy "family first, friends last." Finally, Natalie considered "family as part of a good life" for her children, making a concerted effort to teach this lesson to them by interacting with cousins who had children the same ages as hers.

Fuentes Children

Fuentes children responded more broadly and frequently about the value of family than their parents did. Few children recalled having their parents directly instruct them about family the way that Manuela did. It appeared that they learned about the value of family by example—from parents and other members—and the interaction they had with family through the years. Third- and fourth-generation children as adults tended to talk about family in terms of togetherness and support. Perhaps as an effect of their age, fifth generation had little to discuss about family with the exception of talking about how they spend time with one another.

An example of family togetherness arose out of the older third-generation cohort's distinctive memories of their childhood spent at Manuela and Mario's home. Isabel recalled how Sundays were the day her family visited her grandparents. Gerald, Sr., Isabel's younger brother by seven years, had fond memories of the time spent at his grandparents. When asked what he liked about those visits, he replied:

> I thought it was great. . . . I just felt safe. When you're a kid, you're sheltered a lot. . . . You have a sense of security when you're with family. . . . I'm not saying that it goes for everybody and every family situation. But I mean, in general, when I think of that time, that's the way I feel about it. You feel comfortable. I think that's what family is supposed to be.

Thomas, Rogelio's son, could not recall his parents ever talking to him openly about the importance of family. Having a large family taught him this lesson: "We never really openly discussed family even though all the kids knew we had a support system. We always knew we had someone to turn to."

As members of the younger third-generation cohort, Erica and Monica both recollected not wanting to attend family visits to Manuela's nor family reunions. Yet, their father insisted they go, claiming that "someday [family] will not be here," which implied that the passing of members is a passing of an opportunity to forge relationships. Laura, Samuel's daughter, claimed she was often reprimanded by her father for fighting with her sisters. He would say, "'You're sisters, [you're] supposed to take care of each other and you shouldn't fight.' . . . My dad used to say or tell what Grandma would do [in those situations]."

Fourth-generation members as children similarly expressed that context and not direct instruction had much to do with how they learned to value family. Paul recalled the same sense of security that Gerald, Sr., expressed about family: "With family, it was kinda of like, they were always there. They accepted you regardless. And that's the great thing about it. . . . It's that mutual respect." Similarly, Simon, Sr., expressed what he received from being with family: "Just being there as support, knowing that [family is] there. When life gets too rough, go with somebody [in the family] and [it] takes your mind off your problems. It's like a breath of fresh air. Nobody does it on your own."

As an only child, Gerald, Jr., felt he did not experience the close kinship he had witnessed with other family members and their siblings. He claimed that he learned of this type of closeness through the example of his father, his aunts, and uncle:

> I know my dad and his brother and sisters. I know that they will talk to each other about certain individual things. That they don't talk to their wife or husband about. I don't know what they talk about. But I've seen them you know, say, "Hey, I need to talk to you about this, this and that." [Or] "Have your mom or dad call me. I need to talk to them about something." . . . I don't have that kinship.

From a slightly different perspective, both Paul and Francis recounted times when family deterred them from getting in trouble. Paul told of a time when a friend of his was going to the store to shoplift and invited him along. At the time, Paul was with his family. When I asked why he thought he did not go along, he replied he did not want to get in trouble but also "probably just [to] stay with [his] family. [He] was having a better time and [he] didn't want to pick up and leave."

Likewise, Francis, in his teenage years, hung around with a few friends that got in trouble from time to time. In one case, they went cruising and were pulled over by the police. Sitting on the curb as police searched the vehicle, Francis claimed these thoughts went through his mind: "I was thinking like, 'The shame. What shame I had brought my mom. The shame I have brought my brother and sister. What shame have I brought them. You know. Everyone is going to look down at our family.'" For Francis, the consequences his behavior would bring to his family caused him to rethink his future; he further stated that that incident was the turning point to straightening out his life.

Fifth-generation children identified family largely as a group with whom they interacted at holidays and other informal gatherings. In the summer of 1998, Simon, Jr., and Francis came to visit for two months. Because they lived out-of-state, this was the only time that extended family had to visit with them. Again, Elisa described more succinctly, what it was like spending time with family:

> We go camping, and it's fun because all my cousins are there. There's no fighting, we're all cousins. And the adults don't have to worry about us. . . . We all have fun. Not just us have fun. 'Cause I know some times we can do something I know my parents don't really want to do. No offense. But they can drink and play cards and *Toma Todo (piranola)* and raffle prizes, dancing and DJs. They can do all that while we're having fun.

The separation between adults and children that happened in the first- and second-generation family interactions apparently still happen in fourth- and fifth-generation interactions. According to Elisa and other Fuentes, this circumstance allows children to develop the bonds of family that they will carry into their adulthood.

Much like the value of schooling, the value of family seemingly has survived the Fuentes family's interaction with American society. Over five generations, the reliance on family for togetherness and support continues to be part and parcel of the Fuentes family experience.

The Value of Hard Work

Fuentes Parents

For the Fuentes family, the value of hard work was integral in the first-generation home. For Manuela, Mario, and their children hard work went hand-in-hand with daily living without modern conveniences, caring for a ranch and providing for a family of twelve. Future Fuentes generations, however, had the benefits of modern living, including a stronger economy and varied labor market. Understandably, the concept of hard work in the Fuentes family has changed.

Overall, Fuentes parents and children of subsequent generations perceived hard work mostly through example and directives from parents. Examples of hard work derived from parents themselves who worked long hours at difficult jobs and some times at more than one job. Samuel mentioned how he worked at a full-time job while he went to night school to change his trade to obtain greater job security. In the third generation, Erica divorced and as a single mother, worked two jobs: "I worked and I picked up actually a second job. I worked at night for two years . . . for extra money . . . and [I] saved all of it."

Timothy, who is divorced and is now remarried, described how he was working to provide for both sets of his children: "I was working sixty or seventy hours a week. The Fuentes came out in me. And I was just working, working, working." Aside from describing himself as hard working, Timothy acknowledged that working hard is a key Fuentes family trait.

In the fourth generation, Lydia acknowledged that she derived her strong work ethic from her mother, Noemi, and wished to pass this trait on to her daughter. More importantly, she felt her daughter needed to know that working hard was valuable in and of itself, regardless of the level of appreciation or monetary return:

> And that even when your work isn't appreciated, it should have no bearing on the value you have on your own work. Because you can value your own work and take pride in your own ability, it doesn't matter how much you're getting paid or not getting paid. Because that's what it's all about.

Both Simon, Sr., and Francis believed that hard work not only had to do with effort but also had to do with a person knowing they were performing to the best of their ability. With reference to school, Simon "not only wanted his children to attend school, but that they do well. Not to just pass. It's the best that can be done." Francis expressed that he made an extra effort to ensure that his children followed through with all their endeavors, not allowing them to quit in the middle of anything.

Fuentes Children

Fuentes members as children saw their parents as the primary examples of hard work in their lives. Third-generation children described their parents, especially fathers, as "always working." Isabel, Yvette's daughter, described her parents as follows: "[My father] worked a lot. Then he would go outside and do something in the yard. My mom was always busy doing something." Likewise, when asked whether she thought her mother was successful, Dora answered: "Yes. She did pretty good for herself. She's a hard-worker. She worked all her life. She took care of us. She took care of herself. [She's] still working." Katarina, Dora's mother, was working part-time at the age of seventy-six.

Finally, Timothy, who possessed a special connection with his grand-parents, Mario and Manuela, spoke of hard work via the examples and consejos they gave him. Timothy described Mario as follows: "a hard-working man. He provided for his family when he was younger. So, I had a lot of respect for Grandpa because he was a man of responsibility." He stated later in the interview that his grandmother influenced him with the things she told him: "Grandma used to say to me: '*Mijo*, when you get older you make sure that you're an honest, hardworking, re-sponsible person. You take care of what you have to take care of. Don't be a bum.'"

Two of the Sanchez children, Katherine and Paul, agreed with third-generation members that their parents played a powerful role in shaping their value of hard work. Paul claimed that after high school he went to a community college and was unsure of whether he would work or not but conceded that he would probably decide to work:

> See I think from my parents, I don't know. It's part of our culture, we had more of a work ethic. Work hard, something will become of it. Yeah, 'cause I have never been fired from a job. I think that's mainly what our family's like is just, work. Work, work, work.

Resembling Timothy's reply, Paul believes hard work and a strong work ethic were closely associated with the family culture. Another example is Simon, Sr. After his mother separated from his father and they lived as a single-mother family, Simon, Sr., realized how hard his mother had to work to support them: "She was busy working two jobs and she had enough problems. I didn't want to give her a hard time."

Fifth-generation Fuentes were unable to express their understanding of their parents as hard workers, more than likely because of their age. What they did articulate was the fact that parents expected children to work around the house. As will be shown in the next chapter, the concept of hard work begins in the home, where children assume responsibilities and chores, first at home, then in the workplace.

The Values of Schooling

Fuentes Parents

In the Fuentes first-generation home, the importance of schooling ap-peared in the consejos Manuela gave her children. She stressed the need for schooling to get ahead.[3] Later-generation Fuentes families continued to stress the need for schooling. As table 3.1 indicates, parents and children had the greatest agreement (forty-eight from parents and fifty-two from children) on the importance of this value.

In general, Fuentes parents and children agreed that the value of schooling was communicated and emphasized in their homes, revealing that parents talked or lectured about the importance of schooling. In the second generation, Florencia commented on her encouragement of her children to go to school and to complete their high school education. Katarina claimed she "told [her] children the same as [her] mother did. To go to school. To be whatever they wanted." Carlos claimed he and his wife tried to keep his children in school by making them go every day. The result for him was that his two sons went to junior college and all four of his children graduated from high school. Both Samuel and Cristian wanted their children to go to college, suggesting they held high expectations for educational attainment.

Third- and fourth-generation parents also stressed and expected their children to "do" school. Thirteen of the fifteen parents in these generations mentioned that they directly instructed children about the importance of schooling or stressed the value of schooling. Gerald, Sr., claimed that "one of the things they stressed [with their son] was mainly getting him through school," which was particularly difficult because his son was diagnosed with a learning disability. Dora said she stressed school, because she had come to realize that she wished she herself would have "put more effort into it [so] she would have gone a lot farther." Cristian's daughter, Erica, claimed she reprimanded her son when he received bad grades: "To us, C or C-, it's like, 'Son, you can do better than that.' He would hear it from us. He doesn't want to hear it."

Fourth-generation parents also talked to their children about their schooling. Simon, Sr., said this:

> That's why it's important for me to be involved in what's going on with that [school]. 'Cause I want them to know, from the very beginning, that their parents, that it's important to us. Not only that they attend school, but they do well. Not just to pass, it's the best that can be done.

Natalie also claimed that she and her husband told their children that doing well in school was important to them, although her husband spent most of the time helping the children with their homework. Lydia, who reprimanded her daughter for forgetting her homework, also expressed how she and her husband set a high expectation for Randy's education:

> [That she wants to go to college] is in her upbringing because we ingrained in her that she was to go to college, since she was very small. You have to go to college. You have to go at least four years. [My] husband and I told her that

a high school diploma was not enough. By the time she graduates, more people will be in the job market and she will not be able to compete.

This response demonstrates how fifth-generation children have been instructed by their parents to do well in school from early on, for the purpose of being able to compete in a labor market, which, according to some
Fuentes members, appears to be getting more competitive.

Fuentes Children

As for Fuentes children, they remembered that they were told about the
importance of schooling in the home. Ivan recognized that his parents had
an expectation for their children to complete their education despite his
parents' low level of schooling: "I think part of it was they never had the
background in school[ing]. I think my dad only made it to the eighth
grade. And my mom, I think made it through high school. What I remember, they wanted us to go to school." Thomas stated that school "was
always an integral part of growing up. It was always mandatory. That
went without saying." Sisters, Erica and Monica, also acknowledged that
their parents encouraged them to go to school and praised them when
they did well.

Fourth-generation children remembered the emphasis their parents put
on education differently than the previous generation. They claimed that
education was mandatory, something that was expected for children to
do. Simon, Sr., claimed that in his home, schooling was not strongly encouraged but it was a requirement. He and his siblings had to go to
school. Gerald, Jr., considered the fact that his father evaluated the school
district in the new neighborhood as an indicator that school was important. He believed that "[college] was his parents' hopes and dreams. To go
for a good eight years and make something of [his] life."

In fifth generation, Randy explained how her parents tell her to get
good grades and how she is rewarded sometimes for getting good grades.
She further stated that her mother has high expectations for her high
school education, wanting her to go to a well-reputed, private, all-girl,
Catholic high school. Matthew and Benjamin both stated that their father
"wants them to do good in school." Matthew, at the time, was prohibited
from riding his skateboard for having poor grades. Simon, Jr., and Francis both agreed that their parents "say they have to practice harder and go
on and on in [school]."

In conclusion, Manuela's legacy of stressing the value of schooling on
her children in the early century continues to be an important feature in
Fuentes later-generation families. In most cases, both parents and chil-

dren remembered telling and being told that getting an education can help them to get ahead.

The Value of Saving and Investment

As indicated in table 3.1, the value of saving and investment received the least attention by later-generation members. A few of the aforementioned responses make reference to saving money. However, there was no overall pattern of responses, either across or between generations. Most of the responses came from second-generation members in reference to how their mother saved to live, eventually to buy conveniences and make real estate investments.

Rogelio's son, Thomas, made the most direct comment about how his parents instilled the value of saving into him and his siblings. His account of his first job as a paperboy explained how he was allowed to keep money he made on his own:

> Anything that we worked on, we kids, we got to keep. Then again, my parents did not direct us on what to spend and what not to spend. But savings was part of what we should do. . . . They helped in verbal counseling. They didn't help us in financial, "Here's a piece of paper and we'll put this much in every week."

Thomas was counseled to save the money earned and it was done in the form of consejos, like the teaching of other values.

Gerald, Jr., a fourth-generation member, remarked how investment was a way to make money so as to acquire nicer things, "but [one] [has] to make that money to invest it first." In this case, working for money, saving, and investing are tightly linked.

A fifth-generation member, Elisa, revealed that she knew savings accounts existed for her younger brothers. She described how she liked to spend time with her grandfather, Isabel's husband, doing various activities from which she learned. After helping her grandfather recycle cans he gives Elisa and her brothers the money, which went into savings accounts.

This was the extent of the responses on saving and investment by Fuentes members. One could argue that over time this value was lost. However, the descriptions of the family in the previous chapter beg to differ. Fuentes families have saved and continue to save money to purchase cars, homes, and other material possessions, which for a working-class family cannot be done without saving. This circumstance in and of itself proves that the value exists, despite the fact that family members did not readily consider its prominence in the family fabric.

SUMMARY

This chapter has shown that the Fuentes' have clearly held on to the values and beliefs set forth by Mario and Manuela Fuentes. These values began within Mexican traditions but have been adapted by subsequent generations of Fuentes members as they have forged lives in American society. All generations of Fuentes parents have desired their children to do better than they did—to get ahead—and to be happy in the lives they have chosen. Over five generations, parents have taught and children have learned the importance of leading a respectful and respectable life along with fulfilling their role in the social support system of family. Parents have preached the value of attaining schooling as a means of avoiding a hard life without it. Fuentes children have learned from their parents, either through example or directives, to work hard and that hard work will grant them satisfaction, greater prosperity, and security in life. Although the value of savings and investment has dissipated in the daily doings and sayings of Fuentes families, somehow, some way, Fuentes members continue to save and invest their earnings to acquire homes and automobiles and to provide a relatively stable life for their families. The Fuentes family's values of buena educación, schooling, family, hard work and savings and investment are alive and well in the twenty-first century.

NOTES

1. Rogelio Diaz-Guererro and Lorand B. Szalay, *Understanding Mexicans and Americans: Cultural Perspective in Conflict* (New York: Plenum Press, 1991), 53.

2. Angela Valenzuela, *Subtractive Schooling* (Albany, N.Y.: State University Press, 1999), 23.

3. The issue of schooling will be dealt with in greater detail in chapters 5 and 7. For the sake of efficiency, here the topic of schooling is limited to how it relates to whether schooling was promoted or stressed in Fuentes homes.

4

∼◡∽

Fuentes' at Work

Perhaps no other place is the effect of the Fuentes family's working-class status and racial categorization more observable than in the labor market. Before describing the Fuentes family's orientation to and activity in the labor market, I will discuss the history of the national and local labor market and economy, which the family has contended with over nearly a century.

THE LABOR MARKET AND ECONOMY

At the turn of the twentieth century, an economic boom in the nation resulted from the expansion of industrialization, exports and imports doubled and savings nearly quadrupled (Gordon 2004). This effect trickled down to major urban areas like Los Angeles, when "[t]he city had attained national prominence in manufacturing, distribution capabilities and marketing techniques."[1] From 1900 to 1930, Los Angeles grew by 900 percent from 100,000 to 1,000,000 inhabitants. Several factors contributed to the population and industrial boom during this period. For example, the building of the railroad in the 1860s, the construction of the Los Angeles Aqueduct, and the establishment of the Los Angeles Harbor all created jobs and demand for people to fill them. Regardless of class, most Americans experienced greater prosperity and a better standard of living, which, of course, made the Great Depression extremely catastrophic.

The American economy plummeted after the Stock Market crash in 1929, resulting in "as many as 60,000,000 people out of a total population of 126,000,000 were living hand-to-mouth by March 1933."[2] During the Depression, the working class felt the impact the greatest when companies and factories closed, and the sale of goods and services declined dramatically, by some estimates more than 50 percent. Minority and immigrant workers were more likely to be unemployed during the depression than white workers and "[b]lue-collar workers were three times as likely to be without jobs as white-collar workers."[3] The labor market circumstances, of course, established extreme and desperate living situations for working-class workers like the Fuentes.

During WWII, Osterman (1999) claims that companies set rules founded on the notion that "what was best for workers was best for the company." He stated, "[T]he ideology, of this period was that employment security was a desirable objective and that best practice to view the workforce as a community and to maintain that workforce in place whenever possible."[4] This ideology resulted in stable promotion structures and relatively equal wages across firms. Even when workers were laid off, such as in the recessions in the seventies and eighties, employees could expect to return when economic conditions improved.

However, not everyone benefited equally under this new labor market. Osterman (1999) acknowledges that the postwar system was "not of all one piece" in that a secondary labor market existed, which "provided unstable and low-wage employment and abided by few of the rules [he] laid out."[5] In the Southwest, race was one of the determiners of the segmented labor market; Mexicans and Mexican Americans were subjected to "colonial labor" from the time of annexation of the territory into the United Sates in 1848 to roughly the 1930s (Barrera 1979) and their labor was relegated to particular industries, such as agriculture and ranching, mining, railroad, and urban/industrial jobs.

This system parlayed into a "low-wage occupationally stratified system," resulting in a general hiring trend for Anglos as bosses and Mexicans and Mexican Americans as laborers. Employers were able to control wages, to control Chicanos against organizing, and to use minority workers as a labor reserve and "as a buffer to cushion the effect of economic downturns on other workers."[6] Other scholarship has noted the remaining effects of the segmented labor market, in particular the effects of discrimination and level of education, on later-generation and immigrant Mexican population in the middle and second half of the century (Reimers 1992; Sullivan 1986; Valenzuela and Gonzalez 2000).

Matters improved over time for Mexican Americans through the passage of certain laws that gave Chicanos more power over their employment circumstances, allowing them to organize and collectively bargain with employers. The segmented labor market that existed before and during the Great Depression has weakened over time but has not altogether disappeared. Chicanos have become more integrated into the American labor market but still experience some effect of the segmented labor market that prescribed their participation for several decades, with higher rates of unemployment, underemployment, and underrepresentation in white-collar and executive positions (Borjas and Tienda 1985; Grebler, Moore, and Guzman 1970; Groger and Trejo 2002).

What, then, is the present state of Mexican Americans in today's labor market? Post–WWII corporate rules and the subsequent labor market eroded in the nineties due to the advances in technology, a greater degree of competition, and new pressure from stockholders for short-term profits (Osterman 1999). These new pressures prompted U.S. companies to lay off workers more frequently in times of prosperity and to dislocate workers for the purposes of restructuring, without regard for their livelihoods. Now, jobs are insecure, and American workers are understandably preoccupied about their futures in the workforce.

Although these are the general conditions for American workers, certain workers have more to fear than others. Specifically, dislocation has been greater for noncollege employees than for those who have college degrees. This fact most strongly affects blue-collar and lower white-collar workers who do not require a college degree to do their jobs. Young people also have much to fear from the state of today's labor market. Even in the prosperous economy at the end of the twentieth century, gains in earnings had only affected some 20 percent of workers. "For most people who are dislocated the consequences are quite negative. It can take three years to regain employment levels and when jobs are found, the earnings stay on the average much lower than in the lost jobs."[7] Furthermore, wages for the working class, who tended to be high school graduates, actually declined in the 1980s and 1990s: "The increase in the high school wage penalty between 1979 and 1995 varies from one labor force group to another (from around 30 percent to 60 percent)."[8]

Mexican Americans have experienced some social mobility because there are more white-collar workers who are Chicanos than ever before. This increase in occupational mobility occurred most strongly during the sixties; but (after 1973) eroded.[9] Realistically, regardless of mobility and coupled with the legacy of colonial labor, these statistics demonstrate that Mexican Americans are concentrated in those jobs (blue-collar and low white-collar), which are most vulnerable to the new economy and labor market. In this light, the Fuentes' have had an upward struggle despite America's prosperity in the twentieth century.

Los Angeles and the Valley's Economy and Labor Market

The national economic and labor market trends trickled down to the state and local level. In Los Angeles County, the population grew 45.5 percent between 1950 and 1960 and experienced rapid commercial and industrial growth. From the seventies to the nineties, the defense and aerospace industries, television and movie industries, manufacturing, biotechnology, professior..i service, and banking made up a new diversified economy (Acuña 1996; Grant 2000). Blue-collar jobs dried up as more lower white-collar work became prevalent.

Locally, in Los Angeles County, and in the Valley itself, this system of segmentation provided the environment for Chicanos work. Overall, in the sixties, minorities (African Americans and Latinos) increased 113.7 percent and were 20 percent of the six million inhabitants. The Spanish surnamed population increased 100.5 percent, its largest sector between the ages of five and thirty-five, and were overrepresented as field workers, laborers, and service workers (9 to 4 percent) and underrepresented as managers, clerical workers, craftsmen, and professionals (2.9 to 7.7 percent), whereas Anglos had largely blue- and white-collar occupations (County of Los Angeles Commission on Human Relations, 1965).

Additionally, regardless of comparable graduation rates, unemployment was an issue between Anglos and Chicanos in Los Angeles County at the time. Unemployment for Spanish-surnamed residents was almost 3 percent greater than for the Anglo population (5.8 percent). Of those unemployed, the majority were Chicanos between the ages of 14 and 24 and 75 and over. These data suggest that, even when the economy was flourishing in the sixties, Chicanos were more likely to be unemployed than their Anglo counterparts. The County of Los Angeles Commission on Human Relations reported that "discrimination seem[ed] to prevent minority group members from obtaining jobs and salaries similar to the majority group members with the same educational attainment."[10] It is likely that Barrera's (1979) notion of colonial labor has left a pervasive legacy in Los Angeles and the Valley.

Two factors strengthened the Valley's economy during this period. The railroad, which extended from Los Angeles to the Valley in 1876, provided the Valley access to markets in the East, and the Los Angeles Aqueduct, completed in 1913, provided water for irrigation of crops. Between 1915 and 1917, the Valley became the jurisdiction of Los Angeles County when it was annexed. According to the Security First National Bank report (1967), "the passing years saw continuing development in the valley as it was transforming into a place of cultivated fields, fruit, orchards and luxurious residential tracts."[11] This economy generated the agricultural job market that received Mario when he arrived in 1921.

With the introduction of the automobile and a freeway system, parts of the Valley grew in population between 81 and 122 percent from 1950 to 1955 (Durrenberger, Pitt, and Preston 1966). Beginning in approximately 1945 and lasting through the 1960s "large tracts of land once used for agriculture stood vacant, awaiting conversion to urban uses."[12] The postwar activity, both in industry and population, generated huge increases in the major industries in the Valley in the fifties and sixties, especially in government, manufacturing, trade and service occupations, and movie industry (Roderick 2001; Security Pacific National Bank 1967). Manufacturing increased in 1966 by 84 percent since 1955, adding over 51,000 jobs; trade and government combined increased by 40 percent during the same period; and construction grew by 10 percent; but agriculture and forestry declined. Service industries were the third largest employer in the Valley, as 20 percent of all workers were employed in some type of service industry (Bearchell and Fried 1988).

After the boom in the sixties, the Valley's economy crashed in the seventies and eighties with the recessions. The deindustrialization of the manufacturing industry nationally also effected the manufacturing industry in Los Angeles and the Valley. Even though the defense industry was thriving on government contracts, the auto and machinery companies laid off many employees, and commercial and residential building all but halted. Technology and aerospace industries expanded while the service sector experienced the greatest growth (Pastor 2001). The hardest hit by the recession in all of California, Los Angeles County also had a drastic increase in unemployment in the early 1990s: "suffering 70% of California job losses between 1991 and 1993" with racial minorities experiencing a decline in wages and household income.[13] All this to say, during the last part of the twentieth century, to those with high school education or less, the Valley economy offered its inhabitants largely manufacturing and service jobs and to those with better qualifications, higher paying aerospace and technological jobs.

Without the advantage of race and education, the first, second, and third generations of the Fuentes family fit the need for workers in the manufacturing, construction, and service industries, while fourth generation members are contending with a crueler labor market, which favors corporations, companies, and shareholders.

THE CONNECTION BETWEEN
HOME VALUES AND THE WORLD OF WORK

As we saw in the last chapter, the Fuentes family instilled the goal of getting ahead and the value of hard work into its members. The idea of getting ahead is relevant here in that parents wanted their children to attain better jobs to be more economically stable—not to have to struggle like they did. The notion of getting ahead promotes the need to get well-paying jobs to raise one's standard of living.

More directly applicable to the working world is the Fuentes family's value of hard work. Explained in the previous chapters, this value urged children to be conscientious workers. At a young age, children were expected to be responsible for chores, and the negligence of chores was most often a punishable offense. In many cases, parents believed that chores or working taught other qualities necessary for life. Yvette, specifically, viewed these qualities as work-related abilities:

> I thought [working] was good [for my children]. It made them dependable and responsible. . . . I always think it's good for young people to work. . . . I still feel that way. I think it teaches them responsibility. How to be there, on time. Some kids never learn that. Always late; never prompt.

According to Yvette, working reinforced some of the values obtained with una buena educación: dependability and responsibility. In addition, children learned to be punctual, a quality often associated with being a good employee.

This practice did not just affect older third-generation children. In fact, Samuel, a second-generation member, and Isabel, a third-generation grandparent, claimed that their children had asked them to "put [their grandchildren] to work." When her fifth-generation grandchildren came to visit, Isabel stated that Natalie asked her to have Elisa work in the kitchen while Isabel's husband worked with Elisa's brother, Nicholas, in the yard. Likewise, Samuel was also instructed by his eldest daughter to "put her sons [fourth-generation members] to work" around the house when they visited. In these cases, Fuentes values extended beyond the parent-child relationship and were reinforced by grandparents.

Another way that Fuentes members signified that work played a crucial part in their lives was the way they talked about success in their adulthood. Of the twenty-six adult second- through fourth-generation members, eight members identified themselves as successful because of some aspect of their work situation. For example, Cristian's daughter, Erica considered herself a success because: "[She's] working. [She] enjoy[s] what [she] do[es]." Timothy, Florencia's son, stated that he was successful "because [he] could provide for [his] family. [He] generated enough income to support [his two sets of kids]."

In the fourth generation, members were still establishing themselves in careers; hence, in their minds, success had yet to be attained. Nevertheless, they gauged their future success on their jobs. Paul said that he was

Table 4.1. Fuentes members' criteria for a good job

A good job provides . . .

- Enjoyment.
- Compatibility with one's personality.
- Work that is challenging or interesting.
- Some degree of mobility in terms of promotions and raises.
- Full benefits (medical, dental, and retirement).

"mentally [successful]," because he had not created any major personal crises in his life. Yet, he "still ha[s] to make it monetarily." In his view, he would accomplish this by "more or less hav[ing] a job that [he's] happy with, giving [him] a sense that [he is] building something . . . [by] mak[ing] himself] rich and not the company." In Paul's case, as with others, sole proprietorship is a vital feature of success, a socially notable type of success. Yet, it was not the only feature in that members had to also be personally satisfied with what they do.

The Fuentes' goals of getting ahead and job satisfaction procured the search for a good job, which fulfilled the criteria shown in table 4.1.

Table 4.1 indicates that enjoyment, opportunity for promotion, fulfillment of personal goals, and access to medical and dental benefits were primary criteria for Fuentes' determining whether a job had merit. From this perspective, Fuentes' look for work that is both satisfying and challenging but also protects against the harsh economic situation of the working class.

First, members across generations expressed how they were satisfied with their jobs because they found them enjoyable. For example, Gerald, Sr., and Ivan replied how they liked the work they did. Gerald stated, "I make a living at what I'm doing. I'm happy. I like what I do." Ivan expressed a similar level of satisfaction: "I don't do it for the money. It does pay good. When I'm working. It has to do with enjoyment." Ivan, later, expressed that he quit a factory job because "[he] likes the outdoors. [He] likes to be free," implying that construction was more suitable for him.

Fourth-generation members, who were still in the process of finding careers, spoke with less certainty about satisfaction with work. Gerald, Jr., who was working with his father, in addition to trying to start his own pool-cleaning route, claimed he "felt fortunate to know two trades." Katherine liked her present job, because she was in a "float pool" of medical clerks that allowed her to work in different areas. This floating kept her engaged in having to learn new aspects of the field.

A second feature of a good job for Fuentes' was one that offered a promotion ladder. A few Fuentes members mentioned that they looked for jobs with the possibility of advancement. Monica claimed that, "whenever [she and her sister] applied for positions, [her] parents always inquired about promotions, insurance [benefits]."

All but two of third-generation members and all but three of the fourth-generation members recalled being promoted on the job, usually for a challenge or an increase in wages. Included in job advancement are members who opened their own businesses. In the second generation, Michael owned his own restaurant for a few years, and Carlos became an independent contractor. In the third generation, three members began their own businesses. Both Gerald, Sr., and Ivan were mason and building contractors, respectively, and Thomas used his experience with a bookbinding company to start his own company. Paul, in the fourth generation, started his own neon sign company for a year. Fuentes women, on the other hand, tended to stay within companies or organizations, climbing the promotion ladder.

The final criterion, obtaining full benefits, only appeared once in the interviews, where Erica recalled what types of questions her parents asked whenever she got a position. The basis for this criterion emerged from field notes and my own personal experience with the family. First, I observed several gatherings where work was a topic of conversation. In each event, I was privy to at least one conversation about work, talk about a member's new position or discussion about available work. In all these conversations, medical and dental benefits were questioned or discussed—"The job has full benefits." In my experience growing up among Fuentes', I specifically recall that the value of a position was to be determined by wages, scheduled hours, and benefits. The company's assuming of medical and dental costs frees up personal income to be used on other expenses or investments; it provides a level of security against injury or illness for oneself and one's family.

Fuentes' motivation for work is linked to the values promoted at home, providing and caring for one's family as well as having a strong work ethic. Valuing the uniqueness of an individual may be linked to their desire to find work that is enjoyable and challenging. However, as members of the working class and as a racial minority who experience the effects of a segmented labor market and those who are most vulnerable, they are preoccupied with attaining secure jobs that will help their families meet their basic needs—a steady income and health care.

ENTERING THE WORKFORCE

After learning the importance of work in their childhood, Fuentes members actually entered the labor market, formally or informally, in their adolescence. Either in formal employment (employment in businesses or organizations) or informal employment (private citizens), a trend emerges across generations. The second-generation members began to work between the ages of fourteen and twenty-nine as factory workers or laborers. In the third generation, Fuentes members began to work as early as twelve (usually with a paper route) and as late as eighteen. They were babysitters, retail clerks, factory workers, housecleaners, and food service workers. By the fourth generation, Fuentes' were taking on paper routes, house cleaning, food service, and prop-making. What we see here is Fuentes members working young but also working mostly in unskilled occupations. The economic prosperity in much of the twentieth century did little to improve when and where Fuentes members began to work.

Reflecting on the period in which they started to work, Fuentes members expressed that going to work was either ordinary or necessary. In most cases, Fuentes children had to purchase the extras their parents could not afford. For many, money earned from work was used to pay for records, fashionable clothing, and socializing (dances, movies). Some members earned and saved money to buy a car and car insurance. In fact, many members claimed that they received some kind of directive from their parents to get a job, perhaps reinforcing the practical values associated with working (responsibility and promptness).

For Fuentes members, the pivotal juncture for determining a career came after graduating high school. Faced with the completion of their education, most Fuentes' expressed ambiguity and uncertainty about what their lives would entail after graduation. With the exceptions of those who went to college, few others were academically prepared to enter a four-year tertiary institution. College not being an option, Fuentes generally tended to rely on the jobs they attained in adolescence.

Regardless of cohort, second-generation members had the fewest options available to them in choosing a career after high school (even though they were U.S. citizens). For Fuentes men in particular, the availability of work was a vital feature in determining employment, as well as the tendency for "over three-fourths of [sic] Mexican American male employees [to be] [sic] in [blue-collar] occupations" in the 1960s.[14] Yvette, the only Fuentes woman who worked outside the home early in her marriage, attests to the conditions of the segmented labor market:

Yvette: I was going to look for a job. And get a job doing whatever I could find. In those days there weren't that many opportunities or work. Or anything like that. Usually if you went and applied for telephone operator. Usually they didn't hire Mexicans.

Chávez: So there were only certain jobs you could do?

Yvette: Yeah. I don't know why. They just didn't [hire Mexicans]. And a lot of employment and lot of work [did that]. Factory works, you know. Sewing. Construction hired Mexicans [sic]. Mostly, there was a lot of construction then. Hardly anyone by then [was working in the fields] because by then they had brought the men from Mexico during the war. I'm talking about after the war now. They [Mexican men] did all that. The Mexican Americans did not go out and do that anymore.

According to Yvette, the segmented labor market excluded Mexicans and Mexican Americans from certain jobs, which became abundant after the war. Furthermore, the Bracero Program, which began in 1942, pushed Mexican Americans out of the fields and into the service sector, labor sector, and armed services.

In the third generation, Fuentes members had a different experience from the previous generation. First, more third-generation members graduated from high school (nine of eleven) and seemingly had more education with which to navigate the labor market. Yet, when the time came for Fuentes members to find work, many of them expressed a high degree of uncertainty as to what exactly they were going to do. This varied by both gender and cohort. The older third-generation female cohort (Isabel and Noemi) followed in their mothers' footsteps by marrying and having families. Isabel expressed how she and her husband married two weeks after she graduated, claiming that in those days "girls went to school, graduated, married and had kids. [And became] Suzy Homemaker." For her, the social norm that women became wives and mothers legitimized her decision not to work after high school.

On the other hand, the younger cohort, growing up in the seventies and eighties after the height of the Equals Rights Movement, more often than not had jobs before they got married as well as when they were married. By the time they were starting their families, it had become more acceptable for women to work. Both Dora and Tricia commented how women went to work without much contention. Dora claimed that it was a "sign of the times. . . . [You] get a job and support your family."

Unlike the older third-generation women, these younger Fuentes women responded with indecision about their futures, whether they graduated or not. Erica claimed that she "didn't have any goals, [she] just went to school. There was nothing in particular [she] wanted to do." After graduating, her parents came to her about her future and offered to pay for whatever schooling she wanted. Having enjoyed her office assistant job in high school, she decided on a private business college. Without the strict guidelines of social norms, these younger third-generation women received little to no guidance from parents or society about choosing a career beyond the encouragement to get a job.

In accordance with traditional gender roles, third-generation males, on the other hand, did not have the option of not working because they were expected to be the main providers. Interestingly, regardless of cohort, they received the same lack of guidance as younger women, and had little knowledge about what line of work they were going to pursue. Gerald, Sr., Ivan, and Timothy all claimed that they did not know what they were going to do after high school—they had no idea. Although Timothy was already working at a grocery store, "working forty hours a week [meant that he] did not really plan to" realize his dreams of traveling abroad as a merchant marine. This lack of guidance encouraged Ivan and Timothy to remain in the grocery jobs that they had during high school. They made the most of their decision by working hard and moving quickly up the promotion ladder.

Fourth-generation members were most like third-generation Fuentes'. When deciding what to do with their lives, all members had little guidance and little notion about their futures. Females were less explicit about this than males. Males, on the other hand, were more vocal about their lack of guidance and uncertainty about their futures, perhaps because there was greater pressure on them to provide. The oldest male, Paul, replied that after high school he thought he would continue to work while he attended a local community college because many of his friends did the same. He took "just . . . general education classes and had basically no direction." Although Gerald, Jr.'s parents wanted him to attend college and become a professional, his struggle with a learning disability and his naïveté about life led him to wander the labor market: "I looked at it [finishing school] as, I graduated with my diploma and I can do whatever I wanted. That was the stupidity in me. Being naïve."

Regardless of generation, Fuentes members, like other working-class individuals, appeared to have had tremendous difficulty moving from school to work (Hamilton and Powers 1990; Rubin 1987; Weis 2004). Fuentes homes fostered a strong work ethic but little in the way of career guidance. Fuentes parents' lack of imposition on career choices resonates with their desire to not force children into lives that would make them unhappy, a coercion that violates an individual's uniqueness. Even still, had parents wanted to guide children in their choice, their own experience in the segmented labor market (and the changing face of the economy) shaped their restricted knowledge about the range of options that truly existed for their children, a consequence that snowballed in later generations. Because school also did not fulfill this need, as will be described in the next chapter, members tended to rely on their most powerful and natural resource—family.

FUENTES' RESOURCES FOR FINDING WORK

In determining work after high school, Fuentes members did not directly use their school and work experience. Few Fuentes second- and third-generation members claimed that school provided the experiences that illuminated the types of work they wanted to do after high school. For males, these experiences came from industrial art classes. Samuel remembered how he was directed by a counselor to take industrial arts courses[15] and later realized he liked doing things with his hands:

> [The counselor said,] "Well, maybe you should take industrial or this." Wood shop or things like that. . . . I liked industrial things because I always grew up using my head to try and make things, toys and games. I liked to work with my hands.

Only one female recalled schooling having some bearing on the type of work she did as an adult. In the third generation, Erica stated that her classes in business prompted her decision to enter a business college after graduation: "All along in school, I guess, 'cause I had business classes. I enjoyed them [a so-so intonation] . . . 'cause I wanted to know more about working in the office. That field."

Contrastively, fourth-generation members made no mention of schooling helping with their career choices. It is likely that two factors can explain this difference: change in school curriculum and change in the labor market. First, by the time fourth-generation Fuentes arrived in high school, many of the vocational and industrial arts programs had been eliminated or reduced considerably. In Los Angeles County schools, this curricular change lowered the number of classes offered, as well as the quality of instruction of those that remained. Second, males in this generation of Fuentes' witnessed how the recessions in the seventies and eighties severely impacted Fuentes men in the construction trade, who had a difficult time holding steady work because of the slowdown in construction and the weakening of labor unions. This possibly indicated to Fuentes males in this generation that the skilled trades were too unpredictable as a livelihood.

Besides schooling, work experience also influenced career paths. A few third-generation males experienced working with their fathers or other male relatives, which became a reference to deciding on a career. Gerald, Sr., claimed that he and his older brother, Beto, learned masonry techniques "by working with [his] dad on weekends and side jobs." Gerald eventually became a masonry contractor himself. Thomas, the college graduate, also mentioned that he went to work with his father:

Oh yeah, I went to work with my dad. Summers and weekends if he needed help. Once we got old enough. We would go with him and play when we were younger, on the sites. We would actually be required to help, if he needed it. He would pay us. But it's like, "I'm short-handed; I need you."

Later, Thomas claimed, despite helping his father, it was his lack of understanding of the trade that may have possibly prevented him from going into the business:

I also recall not having an interest in going into the construction industry. That decision was based on what I knew of it. Had I known that I could have been trained to be a general contractor or something, I might have gone that way. My dad never really introduced me to that. He was focused just on his business.

In the fourth generation, Simon, Sr., was the only member to mention working with his grandfather and uncle, Gerald, Sr., during the summers. For Simon, however, this experience did not parlay into a career in the construction trade.

Furthermore, in the fourth generation, work experience offered negative examples of what work Fuentes members wanted to do as adults. Only two fourth-generation members referenced how the work they did as adolescents steered them away from doing service jobs. Paul, who started to work at fifteen in 1980 at a fast food restaurant, explained that he went to work for one day and never returned because he found the work degrading. Lydia, three months younger than Paul, recalled how her first job was helping her mother clean houses and take in ironing. She believed that this experience gave her a sense of what types of jobs she did not want to do:

Because that's part of, at least for me, but cleaning house and ironing, really got me to thinking, "Do I want to do that for the rest of my life?" Got me to thinking, "What can I do?" If I don't know, I'm gonna find out. What am I good at. . . . To give myself more options.

For both Paul and Lydia, working helped them to look for positions that better suited them.

Another type of work experience that resulted in insight into potential careers was service in the armed forces. According to McNamara (1957), Mexican American men in Los Angeles after WWII used their training in the armed forces to obtain jobs on their return. Two members, Samuel, a second-generation member, and Ivan, a third-generation member, both used their experience in the service to direct their employment after discharge. Samuel, who was coaxed by friends to enlist in the reserves when he could not find work after graduation, trained in the Army in automotives for six weeks and then worked in the motor pool. He claimed, "It was good for what I did later, because I learned a lot about how machines were put together."

Regardless of generation, Fuentes members received little guidance in choosing a career. Neither school nor home helped them sift through the options that were available to them. Work experiences seemed to be the most compelling evidence for pursuing or not pursuing a type of work. The result of this situation is that all generations of Fuentes' had to navigate the labor market through unskilled, semiskilled, and skilled labor in search of a good job.

GETTING CERTIFIED TO GET QUALIFIED

The definition of higher education excludes vocational education that many working-class jobs require for certification and licensure. Any form of education other than a university degree is assumed to be less valuable, less rigorous.[16] Therefore, the types of postsecondary education working-class people acquire are never counted. In truth, any working-class individual knows full well the value of these certificates and licenses, because they are the determiners of higher wages and positions and can make the difference between a job and a "good" job. For these reasons, I argue that while the Fuentes family may not have high rates of college attendance or completion, schooling, in the form of vocational courses and programs, plays a vital role in the standard of living Fuentes' provided their families.

Once they acquired good jobs, Fuentes members used schooling and certification as a means to promotion or to finding a career. Table 4.2 depicts a partial list of the Fuentes members' schooling and certification they obtained for work.

In actuality, four of the seven second-generation, eight of eleven third-generation, and five of seven fourth-generation members have some schooling associated with work. These numbers indicate that Fuentes members actively engaged in formal schooling and certification to obtain jobs and promotions and raised their occupational status from semiskilled to skilled.

However, schooling did not always result in certification or promotion. At its least, schooling resulted in obtaining employment (i.e., Noemi worked as a data processor for a period after her training) or providing experience used to decide to move into another field (i.e., Laura worked as a medical assistant and quit because of the health risk to her and her children). Third- and fourth-generation members supplemented their vo-

Table 4.2. Partial list of Fuentes members' occupational schooling and certification

Members' name	Schooling	Certification
Yvette Romano	Blueprint and schematics night school	Certificate in blueprints and schematics
Carlos Fuentes	—	Building contractor license
Gerald Gallo, Sr.	Contractors' school	Masonry contractor license
Dora Dominguez	Computer classes Beautician school	—
Erica Herrera	—	Business school degree School district exam
Timothy Perez	—	Civil servant exam
Lydia Lopez	Business administration courses	Business administration certificate
Gerald Gallo, Jr.	—	Pool cleaner's license

cational schooling with community college courses, whether or not they were work-related.

SUMMARY

Invariably, I have heard from others in conversations how, despite their immigration and socioeconomic status, Mexicans (immigrants) are very hardworking, agreeing with how scholars have described them (Dohan 2003; Weaver 2000). Weaver characterizes Mexican Americans as "productive, cooperative, and networking, with a strong sense of work ethic and job satisfaction."[17] For the Fuentes family, this orientation begins at home. As a way to fulfill being bien educado, Fuentes children learned how to work and learned the importance of working, thus learning to be a productive member of the family and society—"Don't be a bum." Parents directed children in adolescence to the labor market to learn the importance of responsibility, dependability, promptness, and to earn money to supplement their working-class income.

Regardless of generation, the Fuentes members began working in unskilled jobs in their adolescence. Due to official and unofficial policy and practice based on race, which created a segmented labor market, the first two generations encountered obstacles in raising their socioeconomic status through work, not being able to attain work that would earn them significantly more than their parents. Although the third- and fourth-generation Fuentes' had a less restricted labor market and moved more quickly from unskilled labor to semiskilled labor, the working-class legacy handed them by the first two generations affected the degree to which these members were able to make career choices. That is, Fuentes parents limited knowledge of the current range of jobs and their qualifications, likely affected the way they advised their children in choosing careers. The end result has been the Fuentes family possessing largely working-class jobs over four generations.

As a credentialed society, where one's educational certification determines one's social status and access to resources, the Fuentes' need higher education to move to middle-class standing. Like other blue-collar workers, Fuentes members have used formal schooling to gain certification and promotions (Fussell 1983; Shostak 1969). Although not all schooling and certification were used to attain employment, it was a means to an end—to get a good job to support oneself and one's family—a challenging task for later generations given the change in the economy and labor market. From this perspective, the idea of a college degree is that much more removed from a working-class life than from a middle-class life predicated on college education as a minimum qualification.

NOTES

1. Richard Romo, *History of a Barrio: East Los Angeles* (Austin: University of Texas Press, 1983), 3.

2. Ronald Edsforth, *The New Deal: America's Response to the Great Depression Problems in American History* (Malden, Mass: Blackwell Publishers, 2000), 77.

3. Edsforth, *The New Deal*, 79.

4. Paul Osterman, *Securing Prosperity: The American Labor Market, How It Has Changed and What to Do about It* (Princeton, N.J.: Princeton University Press, 1999), 25.

5. Osterman, *Securing Prosperity*, 67.

6. Mario Barrera, *Race and Class in the Southwest: A Theory of Racial Inequality* (Notre Dame, Ind.: University of Notre Dame Press, 1979), 82.

7. Herbert A. Applebaum, *The American Work Ethic and the Changing Work Force* (Westport, Conn.: Greenwood Press, 1998), 207.

8. Osterman, *Securing Prosperity*, 89.

9. The issue of Mexican Americans' mobility in the labor market is complicated by the continual influx of Mexican and Central American immigrants in the latter part of the twentieth century. Some studies have attempted to tease out the various factors on foreign-born and native-born Mexicans (Borjas and Tienda 1985; Browning and De la Garza 1986; Hart 1998; Valenzuela and Gonzalez 2001) and have found that there is an increase in wages between the former and latter, but the population as a whole experiences a job ceiling in low-skilled white-collar jobs. The presence of immigrants can undermine Mexican American wages and employment in certain sectors as well as affect overall statistics. Briggs, Fogel, and Schmidt (1977), for example, attempted to explain that the entry of lower skilled

Mexican workers was why California in the 1960s experienced wage decline for Mexican American workers when other states showed an increase: "[T]he high absolute and relative incomes in California have attracted large numbers of less qualified Chicanos from other parts of the Southwest (especially Texas) and from Mexico (through legal and illegal immigration), who must start at the bottom of the job structure" (60).

10. County of Los Angeles Commission on Human Relations, *The Urban Reality: A Comparative Study* (Los Angeles, Calif., 1965), 37.

11. Security First National Bank, Economic Research Department, *The Growth and Economic Stature of the San Fernando Valley and the Greater Glendale Area* (Los Angeles: Author, 1967), 42.

12. Robert Durrenberger, Leonard H. Pitt, and Richard Preston, *The San Fernando Valley: A Bibliography* (Northridge, Calif.: Center for Urban Studies & Bureau of Business Services & Research, San Fernando Valley State College, 1966), 15.

13. Richard E. Preston, *The Changing Landscape of the San Fernando Valley between 1930 and 1964* (Northridge, Calif.: Center for Urban Studies, San Fernando Valley State College, 1965), 7.

14. Fred H. Schimdt and Kenneth Koford, "The Economic Condition of the Mexican-American," in *Mexican-Americans Tomorrow: Education and Economic Perspectives*, ed. Gus Tyler (Albuquerque: University of New Mexico Press, 1975), 90.

15. It should be noted that during this time schools in the Valley were largely advocating for students to take industrial arts classes given the increased demand in manufacturing and trade occupations.

16. Mike Rose in *The Mind of Work: Valuing the Intelligence of the American Worker* (New York: Viking, 2004) makes a case for the valuing of skills and intelligence obtained through working-class jobs. He claims that physical work requires special mental skill, perception, judgment, and memory; it requires great amounts of literacy and numeracy. The subsequent skills and abilities working people gain provide workers with great satisfaction in what they do. His work "illustrates other spaces in the picture of human cognition and gets us to consider why we so often view this picture partially—and the effect that partial perception has on the way we think about mind, work, school and social class" (213). With regard to the vocational track in schools, Rose notes that schools have been at the root of the low educational outcomes and low perceptions of students in this track: "We charge the school with cognitive development, yet in the very curriculum that places work at its core, we find a restriction of intellectual growth . . . [sic vocational education in the United States diminishes] the intellectual dimension of common work and of the people who do it" (170).

17. Charles N. Weaver, "Work Attitudes of Mexican Americans," *Hispanic Journal of Behavioral Sciences* 22, no. 3 (August 2000), 275.

5

School, Part I

Fuentes' in Schools

As mentioned in the last three chapters, school has been a focus of Fuentes family endeavors at home and in the workplace. This chapter looks specifically at the way the value of schooling intersected with Fuentes' actual school experience. In the end, the promise of schooling as a means to raising one's standard of living was dulled by the legacy of social policy and practice to treat Mexicans, Mexican American, and working-class students differently from white middle-class students.

LOS ANGELES COUNTY AND VALLEY SCHOOLS

Since the Valley's annexation in 1915, Valley schools have been subsumed in the larger Los Angeles Unified School District. From the beginning, what was the rule for downtown urban schools became the rule for rural schools in the Valley. The first school in Los Angeles County was built in 1850. It was not until 1872 that more elementary schools were built, followed by the first high school in 1873. The first schools in the Valley—three elementary schools, one junior high school, and three high schools—were built in 1915, slightly predating the Valley's annexation into Los Angeles County.

The increase in the immigrant population caused the sudden need for schools. When attempting to absorb the influxes of immigrants, schools in Los Angeles and the Valley were segregated like other parts of the Southwest. According to Raferty (1992), as early as the 1930s, Los Angeles (presumably White) "residents exerted pressure to segregate schools" because they felt threatened by nonwhites.[1] For the Valley, the increased number of immigrants comprised mostly Mexicans who came to the United States after the start of the Mexican Revolution in 1910; as a reaction American citizens intensively segregated public spheres by race. One such case of segregation in schools happened in the Valley circa 1921. Although segregation was against the law, the school board circumvented an infraction by allowing (Anglo students) on an individual basis to relocate to outlying schools. Having already established a dependable transportation system to service schools, Anglo families moved their children to more remote schools. Only Mexican children remained in these central schools, which resulted in the creation of de facto Mexican schools.

Like African Americans and Native Americans, segregated schools have been a factor in Mexican and Mexican American students' education. When their numbers were large enough and districting created segregated residential areas, Mexican American students throughout the southwest experienced de facto segregated schools, where facilities, materials, and teachers were substandard (Donato, Menchaca, and Valencia 1991; V. Ruiz 2001). While many communities complied with these separate but unequal facilities, a few were legally challenged, as in Lemon Grove, San Diego, and Westminster in Los Angeles, which became foundational legal precedents for the desegregation movement in the 1950s.

Like other parts of the nation, Los Angeles "[reformers, educators and service groups] worked to mitigate the hardship of the immigrants and at the same time assimilate them into American society."[2] As a result, Americanization programs were initiated in Los Angeles public schools in the 1920s, and by the 1930s, schools became Los Angeles's main institution for assimilation. For Mexican Americans and other minority populations, school became the site for learning the ways of Anglo Americans while subordinating the ways of their heritage culture, especially subtracting the Spanish language (G. Gonzalez 1999).

In addition to the Americanization programs, Los Angeles schools also prescribed curriculum for minority students. In 1937, Los Angeles County produced an informal report to its public school patrons, stating that elementary schools offered the basics in reading, writing, and arithmetic. In junior high school, the curriculum became more extensive, offering courses such as health and physical education, social living, math, art or music, industrial arts (boys), homemaking (girls), and remedial work. Other possible electives were drafting, auto shop, floriculture, journalism, ceramics, science, Latin, and library practice. The district justified this industrial or vocational curriculum by claiming that "[i]ndustrial surveys ha[d] made it evident that employment [was] not too remote to make [industrial] training practical."[3]

In turn, the district abandoned the accumulation of credits in junior high and focused on preparing students for the types of jobs available in the county. Given the effects of the segmented labor market as well as racial attitudes, this curriculum then became a mainstay for minority students' school experience. According to Romo, "over the years, the vocational classes would become the principal course of study in the working-class communities of Spanish-speaking and Black residents of [Los Angeles]."[4]

In the informal report, the plight of contemporaneous Mexican American students emerged. The report presented the enrollment rates of Mexican Americans versus Anglos in the district. In elementary school, Anglos outnumbered Mexican Americans by 61 percent, by 86 percent in high school, by 78 percent in adult education, and by 98 percent in junior college. These figures indicate that Mexican American students in Los Angeles schools were enrolled in elementary more than in junior and senior high. Additionally, postsecondary education for Mexican Americans included college (2 percent) and adult education (12 percent) for a select few. Some claimed this may have been because schools did not provide appropriate curricula to keep Mexican Americans males interested in school (Los Angeles Board of Education 1937), while others believed that the families' poverty necessitated children to leave school for work (Carter 1970; Lyon 1933).

Although exceptions existed, Raferty (1992) implies that lives of immigrants were focused not on higher education but rather survival and it was not until the second or third generations that high school became an aim. In any case, in the 1930s, most Mexican and Mexican American students did not remain in Los Angeles County schools past elementary school; those that managed to graduate from high school did not go on to college, resembling Mexican Americans in general at the time (Casso 1975). This educational attainment would have been the historical context for second-generation and older third-generation Fuentes.

With new coats of paint and minor changes to the curriculum, the Los Angeles school system described above remained relatively intact through the fifties and most of the sixties. Given the prosperous economy, huge increases in technical and skilled jobs were projected. As a result, some called for a closer connection between school curriculum and the need for specific types of workers, resulting in school counselors more actively urging high school students into industrial and vocational tracks (Dauwalder 1961).

In the spirit of the Civil Rights Movement, court cases throughout the Southwest questioned the way the system treated Mexican and Mexican American students (Carter and Segura 1979; Donato 1997; San Miguel 1987). A large impact on the schooling of Mexican American children was

the emergence of a Chicano Movement on university campuses that fil-
tered down into the streets of many barrios in Los Angeles. The attention
to Mexican American student needs resulted in providing appropriate
language instruction for Mexican immigrant children through bilingual
education, while the scholastic needs of English-dominant and later-generation Mexican Americans were addressed through the establishment of
federal compensatory programs like Head Start, Upward Bound, and Affirmative Action (Pearl 1991).

Another major educational issue that faced both Los Angeles and the
Valley arrived in the seventies—integration and bussing. Los Angeles
County's residential segregation was pervasive (Bobo et al. 2000), and Los
Angeles and Pasadena school districts, in accordance with lower court rul-
ings, attained some racial balance through bussing programs causing
many white families to move to suburban areas fearing the subsequent
lower quality of local public schools (Helfand, Merl, and Rubin 2004). With
the exception of two Valley areas, (San Fernando and Pacoima) the other
nine-tenths of the Valley had predominantly Anglo schools (Caughey
1971). To comply with the court mandate to desegregate schools without
building any new schools in minority communities, Los Angeles Unified
schools bussed inner city "Black and Brown children to Valley schools."[5]
African Americans and Mexican Americans that lived in Anglo communities in the Valley were lost in the crossfire.

In the eighties and nineties, bussing faded as a major issue while the increase in immigrant populations came to the fore. Between 1999 and 2003,
Latino students increased from 70 to 73 percent, Anglo students decreased
from 10 to 9 percent, and African American and Asian decreased slightly,
from 13 to 12 percent and 4.2 to 3.7 percent, respectively.[6] With the move
toward accountability, the central issue became California schools' poor
standings, spurring the state government to remedy them through imple-
menting numerous school reforms (i.e., class size, back-to-basics, *No Child
Left Behind*). Furthermore, the abolishment of bilingual education and the
implementation of Proposition 227 demonstrated a concern for academic
achievement of newly arrived Latino immigrants and the school's role in
assimilating them. At the same time, through Proposition 209, a major
compensatory social program to later-generation Chicanos, Affirmative
Action, was repealed. As a racial group indistinguishable from other
Latino immigrants, Mexican Americans are likely to be affected by the
racial and ethnic tensions exhibited in the changing demographics.

Historically, in Los Angeles and the Valley, Mexicans and Mexican
Americans (by extension) have been targeted by reforms (Americanization, vocational education, or bussing) intended to improve their academic
performance, and schools have been the major site of implementation.

SCHOOL EXPERIENCES FROM
KINDERGARTEN TO HIGH SCHOOL

Overall Fuentes' School Experience

In American education we have a bias toward thinking that a child's school experience should be rich with a love for learning. That is, students should develop a thirst for knowledge and an intrinsic gratification from its pursuit. While this notion is that which teachers should aspire for all their students, it neglects to account for the multitude of students (not all of whom drop out) who do not experience schools as hopeful, meaningful, and life affirming. Many studies have shown various populations have less than favorable perceptions and experiences in schools (D. Foley 1990; Michie 1999; Quiroz 2001; Rolón-Dow 2005; Romo and Falbo 1996). In the Fuentes family case, members' overall sentiment about school is best described as mixed, resembling the Mexican American student group, characterized by Matute-Bianchi.[7]

Initially, all second-generation members attended the same school, Halstead Elementary, which was a one-mile walk through orchards from their home. In the tradition of one-room rural schoolhouses, Halstead Elementary was a single brick building that housed approximately one hundred students from kindergarten to eighth grade, the majority of whom were Anglo. The older Fuentes members attended this school until the eighth grade, and then were bussed to high school in San Fernando and Canoga Park. Only the younger second-generation members attended junior high schools before high school, as they were not built until the 1940s.

Older third-generation members also began their school careers at Halstead Elementary because the hub of family activity still centered on Mario and Manuela's home in the nearby barrio. In the beginning, once Fuentes families moved into largely Caucasian working-class communities, their children attended local elementary schools, and then the larger district junior and senior high schools.

Perhaps as an effect of the Elementary and Secondary Education Act of 1964, some fourth- and fifth-generation members started school at an earlier age than their parents or grandparents in either Head Start or private preschool programs. While most members went to school in the Valley, a few exceptions existed. Rogelio's son, Thomas, went to schools in Ventura County, approximately forty miles north of Los Angeles County. Noemi's children (Lydia, Simon, Sr., and Francis) attended elementary and some junior high school in Arizona. Simon, Sr.'s children, JR and Francis, went to primary school in the Midwest, where they have lived for the last seven years or so.

Fuentes' Perceptions of Their School Performance

One measure of the Fuentes' school experience is how well they felt they did as students. In the second generation, only three members graduated from high school. While in today's context this may seem tragic, according to trends of the time, the second-generation Fuentes' performed like other Mexican Americans who did not complete high school, often leaving school after elementary school. Yet, even those Fuentes' who did not complete high school attended some high school, which far exceeded the general trend described in the first section.

Table 5.1 shows Fuentes' attitudes toward school in relation to the number that finished high school or that dropped out. The general trend across generations is that despite their lukewarm attitudes toward school, Fuentes members completed at least high school.

In table 5.1, of the twenty-two adult members who responded to this question, little more than half (twelve) clearly had a positive affinity toward school, while about one-third (six) had mixed experiences (at some point both liking and disliking school), and about one-fifth (four) disliked school all together. First, if Fuentes members liked school, they tended to stay in school longer (eleventh grade) or receive a diploma or GED. Of the six with mixed attitudes, that is both liked or disliked school at various points in their scholastic careers, only one dropped out. Of the four members that disliked school, three received either a diploma or GED, while the other dropped out. It seems that, regardless of their attitude toward school, Fuentes members earned diplomas or GEDs, suggesting a strong influence of the value of schooling in the Fuentes family.

Additionally, I asked Fuentes members how they did in school to determine their sense of themselves as students. With a few exceptions, those who stayed in school longer or completed high school were more likely to rate themselves at least as average or passing. Those that disliked school were inclined to rate themselves as poor students at some point. Interestingly, with the exception of two, a second- and fourth-generation member, respectively, no student rated himself or herself as excellent.

Table 5.1. Overall attitudes of Fuentes members in school compared to high school completion and dropout rates

Attitude toward School	Total	Total who completed (Diploma or GED)	Total who dropped out[a]
Liked school	12	9	3
Liked/disliked school	6	3	1
Disliked school	4	3	1

[a]Those members in this column that liked school or disliked school but dropped out (4) were second-generation Fuentes, who were the least likely to complete high school.

One may be inclined to say that modesty played a role in their self-assessment. I do not completely accept this interpretation given how members discussed their work performance in the previous chapter. Some members shared the fact that they received high marks on job-related exams, placed high in rankings, or received promotions. However, with regard to school performance, some members followed up their assessments with comments to the effect of "I didn't do as well as I could have" or "I wished I did better," suggesting that Fuentes members believed that they performed beneath their potential.

These descriptors highlight the experience Fuentes members have had in school, yet also raise certain questions. For example, why, regardless of generation, have members had mixed attitudes about school and low perceptions of their performance? What were the school features that may have contributed to forming these attitudes? The remainder of this chapter will serve to answer these questions.

The Role of Race and Ethnicity in Fuentes' School Experience

Regardless of generation, issues related to race and ethnicity loomed large in Fuentes members' recollections of school experience, more than likely because there were few Mexicans or Mexican Americans in their communities or schools. For one, discrimination, both in and out of school, was mentioned by second- through fourth-generation members. For second and third generations, discrimination began in the elementary years. During their interviews, no second-generation Fuentes' mentioned outright or blatant cases of discrimination. However, it was not until interviewing Dora, Katarina's daughter, at least one memory surfaced. While Dora recounted how she experienced open discrimination in her school, Katarina confirmed and concurred the same was true for her:

> *Dora*: There was a lot of prejudice at that time; I remember being called names.
>
> *Katarina*: It was like when I went to school.
>
> *Dora*: Yeah, they used to make fun of my mom's burritos when she was a child.
>
> *Katarina*: They called us, "You dirty Mexicans." And we would say, "You dirty white trash."

In combination with the literature that verifies the blatant discrimination of Mexicans and Mexican Americans during the thirties and forties (Acuña 1984; O. Martinez 2001), this remark clearly indicates how second-generation members must have experienced discrimination from Anglos.

It is important to point out, however, for whatever reason, most second-generation individuals interviewed chose not to raise the issue of discrimination.

Third-generation members (six of eleven) were more inclined to discuss discrimination as part of their school experience. Some recalled acts of discrimination that coincided with moving into their new white working-class neighborhood or attending a new school. In her interview, Isabel began describing in vague terms her recollection of moving into her new neighborhood: "There wasn't too many Mexican kids. I remember that. Just the kids from our own neighborhood. I don't even remember even having kids in my own class that were Mexican."

Discrimination in school was not limited to a single branch of the family. Ivan and Laura had similar recollections. For example, Ivan often got in trouble for defending himself against his classmates' teasing:

Chávez: What were the kids like then [in elementary]?

Ivan: Ooo, shoot, I was always fighting. . . . Always getting called names. . . . All kinds of names. They used to call me, "Blackie" [or] "Nigger." I used to stick up for my brother.

Chávez: He never fought?

Ivan: No, not really.

Chávez: Did they call those names to your sisters?

Ivan: No, not really. . . . My mom would always go to school, you know, and bail me out. That's why I was always in trouble.

Ivan, who is a child of Spanish and Mexican parentage, had the darkest complexion of all his siblings; his sisters and brother who inherited their mother's light complexion, dealt with discrimination to a lesser degree than he did.

Laura also claimed that her awareness of color began in elementary school, when a male classmate she had played with all her years called her, "brown like coffee." She claimed that the comment could have been innocuous, but it was the seed that made her realize she was different from her Anglo friends.

In elementary school, fourth- and fifth-generation members were less likely to mention blatant discrimination as second- and third-generation members were. Perhaps, open discrimination did not occur, given the unacceptable nature of these acts after the passing of civil rights legislation. In addition, schools changed the manner in which they responded to the diversity of students, using rhetoric encompassing culturally appropriate instruction and introducing aspects of multicultural education, which may have minimized these comments. Nevertheless, later-generation members experienced more subtle and different types of discrimination than previous ones. Regardless of generation, these acts of discrimination and other experiences heightened during the major transitions into junior and senior high school.

Fuentes' Coming of Age:
Navigating a Turbulent School Landscape

Research claims that Mexican American and Latino students' social affiliations in school can determine their level of engagement and academic performance (Bettie 2003; Flores-Gonzalez 2002; Matute-Bianchi 1991; Vigil 1988). According to Matute-Bianchi (1991), Mexican American social groups in adolescence range from Mexican oriented, Mexican American oriented, and *cholo* or *chola* (ganglike/affiliated). The two former types have high- and low-performing subgroups, while the latter considers low performance as a group marker. These groups (among others) form the social landscape in school that Fuentes children navigated through adolescence.

Because the ethnic makeup of Fuentes' elementary schools reflected the predominantly Caucasian communities in the parts of the Valley where they resided (sparsely populated by Mexicans), a major factor in secondary school experience for second- and third-generation Fuentes' was race or ethnicity. More often than not, this resulted in an awakening of ethnic identity that they had not experienced in childhood. Cristian recalled how going to Sutter Junior High in 1951 or 1952 "shocked [him to see so many Mexicans since] there were so few at [his] elementary [school]." Samuel made a similar comment about starting high school and "realizing there were other Mexicans" in the Valley.

In the 1960s, older third-generation members, too, encountered a larger number of Mexicans and Mexican Americans in secondary schools. Gerald, Sr., stated: "[In elementary school,] there were a few Mexicans in the whole school. . . . When I got to high school, there were a couple hundred Mexicans and a handful of blacks." In the 1970s, Monica, Cristian's daughter, also expressed a new connection with her ethnic group:

> *Monica*: It was different, since I hung out mostly with Anglos. But it was something I adapted to really quick.
>
> *Chávez*: Did [the Mexican students] accept you?
>
> *Monica*: Oh yeah. Definitely. I liked them because they were just cool. They spoke differently. They spoke, like Spanglish, and since I didn't speak Spanish, I picked up a lot there. It was different in the very beginning, but after that it didn't faze me anymore.

In general, for fourth and fifth generations, Valley demographics dramatically changed since their parents' and grandparents' childhood and adolescence. By the time Paul was in middle school, there had been large influxes of not only Latino immigrants but also many Southeast Asian and other Asian immigrants to the Valley (Grant 2000). Schools were then more diverse, yet, fourth-generation members found a need to affiliate with Mexicans and Mexican Americans, as Paul explained:

> There were rumors about getting scrubbed. For protection, I hung around with the Mexicans. I didn't get in trouble with them, but it was the backup I had, that no one's going to bother me and nobody did. Other friends from grammar school, many went to another school. . . . I did it out of necessity. I met another guy that was Mexican and we were buddies. We became tight.

For Paul, his affiliation with members of his own ethnic group became a necessity to navigate the potential social turbulence that existed for incoming freshmen.

Second-generation members had the least to say about social groups in school. In general, they tended to refer to a circle of friends or particular individuals. In talking about how she met her first husband, Katarina explained how she and her circle of female friends would sneak off to Reseda Park to meet boys, but she mentioned nothing about these friends in relation to school. Florencia also mentioned a good friend she had in junior high who was Native American with a Spanish surname.

On the other hand, Samuel recalled how his fellow Mexican students viewed him as "whitewashed," calling him *mosca en leche* (a fly covered in milk) for performing well academically. Samuel did not specifically mention who his friends were in high school, but it is likely that he knew Caucasian students because he participated in extracurricular activities, having lettered in cross-country track and been elected senior class representative. Cristian, too, claimed he had a Mexican circle of friends from whom he put up with a certain amount of teasing for having good grades. Yet, his participation in the Audio-Visual Club and in Track and Field suggested that he interacted with Anglo students, too. In this comment, he indicates how this contact may have isolated him from his peers socially:

> Also at that time, you had, I guess, what you knew or that they had different classes for different people. If they knew more, or to read better, they put you into a different class. Readers at your level. So then I started noticing there were a lot of Mexicans, they were all in one class. So they'd make fun of me because I was in all different classes. I could read better, and I could write and I could communicate in English and everything else.

Cristian raises a keen point about the type of schools that Mexicans and Mexican American students attended then. As was noted previously, Mexican and Mexican American students have traditionally attended Mexican schools, segregated from their Anglo counterparts, where both the quality of instruction and facilities were substandard. For better or worse, Samuel and Cristian's attendance at a remote rural school with predominantly Caucasian students perhaps buffered them from the effects of these social practices. In this light, the structural inequities between Anglo schools and Mexican American schools placed a wedge between the Fuentes' and their peers.

Entering senior high school in the sixties, third-generation members were more inclined to discuss the fact that many of the people in their social groups were, in fact, Mexican American or Chicano. Especially for older members, pride associated with socializing with other Chicanos is attributed to an increase in the Latino population in the Valley and to the increase in ethnic solidarity, a result of the Chicano movement. For instance, Dora experienced an ethnic awareness and pride given the greater presence of Chicanos on school campuses. She described her experience along with the new formation of a Chicano "style," which led to a group of them hanging out together, some of whom were Fuentes':

> I went to Sutter Junior High, more Mexicans there. It was great. . . . I still had my Anglo friends. . . . I met more Hispanics here. It was a really good experience in junior high. Then, it continued in high school, where I hooked up with Gerald, Tricia's sister, Ivan, Beto and Ivan's brother. It got to a point where people were afraid of them [Chicanos]. Maybe because of the ways they dressed with khakis. . . . People were more afraid of us. Even though, there was a lot less of us. I guess appearance. I don't know. . . . Tables had turned but we were in our own world by then. We stuck together.

Clearly, Dora expressed how the tables had turned, where Chicanos were not afraid to hang out together as a show of unity. Their numbers and their struggle for rights brought about an ethnic pride which Mexican American students exercised at school through associating with their peers.

Timothy, who went to a different high school from other members in this generation, appeared to fall into a similar type of social group as Dora's. In talking about the transition from lower grades to upper grades, he, too, connected with Mexican Americans:

> Most of my friends were Anglos. I did not start hanging around Mexicans until my junior year in high school. I would get teased by my white friends [about starting to hang with Mexicans]. I [also] got teased in tenth grade from guys in Van Nuys, "Why you hanging around those white guys? You should

be hanging around with us." They called me *falso* (imposter). This is when I really started to see racial issues. . . . Some of my [Chicano] friends did not graduate. But they were good guys because you could count on them. It was kinda like family. It was close-knit.

Although he experienced more racial tension for his affiliations, Timothy navigated between his old friends and new, who liked going to ditching parties and hanging out. Nevertheless, he took care of business and graduated on time.

The youngest third-generation members went to junior and senior high in the late seventies and early eighties. This was after the height of the Chicano movement, when the association with Chicanos was not necessarily related to a show of solidarity. By this time, certain Mexican Americans had become known for their gang-like behaviors and dress—cholos or lowriders. This group became a viable social affiliation in schools and communities across California (Moore 1985; Vigil 1988). They, more than the Chicanos during the time that the older cohort was in high school, had also developed a reputation of being underachievers. For Erica, Monica, and Laura, this group presented a possible social affiliation.

Erica and Monica, who both experienced an ethnic pride with entering junior high school, seemed to fall into this social group. Although they never described their friends as cholos or cholas in the interviews, my encounters with them at family events during their junior and senior high school years indicated that they socially associated with them (not necessarily in gang activity). At these events, they wore khaki pants, Hush Puppy shoes, Pendleton shirts, and excessive makeup—all signifiers of chola wear. What did play out in the interviews was the connection to low academic performance and friends. In Erica's case: "[In high school,] it was more of a chance to get into trouble. Driving and a lot more freedom. Doing that was not necessarily more appealing, I just wanted to be with my friends. I didn't want to miss out." She claimed that her friends ditched a lot of class, and wanting to be a part of the group, she did, too. As a result, her grades dropped:

I was at a D level and I had to bring my grades up to at least average. My parents and I knew that I was capable of doing better. I did not apply myself because I thought my friends were more important. . . . I think I saw my friends not doing well. . . . And they just thought, "I'll just go to summer school. Not important to graduate." Then I saw [graduation] coming. . . . So, then I felt I better go to school or do something.

According to Erica, the combination of her parents' intervention and her own realization that school was necessary for her future led to her eventually graduating.

Laura came about her ethnic awareness and affiliation uniquely, having volunteered to be bussed to East Los Angeles. As a means of satisfying the desegregation laws, Los Angeles County schools resorted to bussing inner-city youth to Valley schools. Many, mostly white, Valley parents were greatly concerned about the quality of education lowering to accommo-date inner-city students. After one of her friend's parents pulled her friend out of school to attend a private school, Laura's parents wanted to do the same. However, she refused then transferred to Stevenson Junior High School in east L.A. From that experience, she learned: "The purpose of in-tegration was to bring the white students, [to] integrate them to East L.A. None over here that were riding the bus, they were all, the majority of [the bus], were Mexican."

Laura returned to the Valley school the second semester of her seventh grade year. For her, that experience ignited a connection with Mexican Americans she had not had prior, which led her to stay affiliated with Mexican Americans for the rest of her schooling: "When I came back I stayed with the same people I got bussed with. I think I came back a bit resentful; defensive for the things I experienced, that the color of my skin mattered." Laura claimed that her circle of friends was more interested in "hanging out and not going to school." Despite her affiliation, Laura graduated.

Moving into junior and senior high school about the same time as the youngest third-generation members, fourth-generation members had to contend with similar issues. Paul, Natalie, and Katherine stated that their parents moved them from Canoga Park to Bixby Meadows, because they feared what would become of their schools now that African American and Latinos were being bussed into the Valley. Thus, they spent their ju-nior and senior high school years transitioning into life in a middle- to upper-middle-class semirural community. Part of this adjustment was fitting into social groups at school.

Paul, who described how he had begun to associate with Chicano stu-dents in a Valley junior high, attended Bixby Meadows Middle School, and characterized it as follows:

> I wore jeans and a T-shirt then as part of my identity. No big deal, people wear it now. Back then, eighth grade in middle school, people were not ac-cepting of it. It was more of an issue with them than it was for me. It was just who I was. When I was in the Valley, growing up in all those schools, there was no name-calling. I didn't have to deal with that.

For Katherine and Natalie, Paul's sisters, they had little to say about the type of social groups they associated with during adolescence. One thing that both girls confirmed is that during their high school years, once Natalie had a car, they would drive into the Valley to meet boys of "their own culture." The criticism that they received for the type of music (Oldies) and dancing (break dancing) they liked established a discord between themselves and their peers in their new neighborhood.

On returning to the Valley from Arizona after their parents' separation, the Barrera siblings experienced different types of discrimination and disorientation in schools. All three recounted how the social landscape in school was more than they cared to participate in. The discrimination and harassment did not come necessarily from other Latinos or Caucasians, but seemed to be an attitude reflective of the whole school system. Simon, Sr., described it this way:

> It was a whole other system of school, you know. They're (students) disrespectful. Teachers didn't have control of the classrooms. I respected the order we had in Arizona. . . . Now, [in California], I could take it or leave it. . . . In California, it's about getting high, who would have sex with [whom], what girl does what. What was *that* all about? I went along with the program, just to fit in. Then I felt stupid trying to hang out with those idiots.

For Barrera children, who had experienced schools in Arizona, which were shaped by Mexican and Mexican American families that promoted una buena educación, fitting into Los Angeles schools meant lowering their academic standards, irrespective of their racial or ethnic association.

As Fuentes members moved into the more socially complex system of junior and senior high schools, ethnicity figured largely in their school experience. While second and third generations experienced blatant acts of racial or ethnic discrimination in elementary school, most later-generation members experienced it in secondary school. Discrimination tended to come from majority members as well as other Mexican Americans. Positively, although ethnic groups tended to perform poorly, ethnicity gave some members a strong sense of ethnic pride and consciousness, a feeling of family in an environment where they were outnumbered and where they felt different. School experience for Fuentes' appears to be contradictory. Despite these turbulent transitions and affiliations, the majority of members finished school.

TEACHERS, MENTORS, AND CLASSES

Looking for Guidance:
No Teachers, No Mentors, No Connection

Part of students' school experience is the teachers and classes they encounter day in and day out. In general, Fuentes members had little to say about teachers. In some cases, general comments were made like: "Teachers were pretty good;" "Teachers were okay;" or "Teachers were mean." Some members recalled specific teachers, commenting on personal characteristics or traits a teacher possessed. Like other Latino students (Abi-Nader 1990; Chávez 1996; Espinoza-Herrold 2003; Hayes 1992; Valenzuela 1999) good teachers were described with some degree of affection, admiration, or respect for the care they gave and the personal concern they showed to students, while bad teachers were mentioned with disdain, because they treated their calling like a job.

Similar to encounters with teachers, mentors are another reason students do or do not perform well (Keating, Tomishima, and Foster 2002; Stanton-Salazar 2001), providing necessary information and motivation and support to succeed academically. Thomas and I are two examples of the importance and effectiveness of mentors. Generally, most Fuentes' could not recall having any person within school that they called a mentor; with few exceptions, members were cognizant of the fact that no school personnel, teachers, or others were available to them. One reason for this has been the way in which Mexican and Mexican American students have been perceived and treated by teachers and administrators, historically being thought to be unintelligent, unambitious, and uninterested in and incapable of learning (G. Gonzalez 1999; Marx 2004).

Gerald, Sr., claimed that high school was "okay" except for the fact that school had too many rules he did not like. Gerald expressed that he often got in "disputes with teachers," in turn, giving him a bad reputation with the school staff: "I didn't want to conform and I felt as if teachers were picking on me. There were not very many Mexicans in the school at that time. I felt like I was being made an example of and I didn't like it." At one point, Gerald had been "thrown out of class" by a teacher and sent to the vice principal's office:

> Only reason I stayed [in school] was because of the Boys' VP. . . . I always admired the VP, Mr. D'Amico, for what he did for me. He gave me a job working for him for credits. I would give tickets to jocks and other people for parking in "no parking" places. It was a positive incentive. . . . All the jocks and those guys would park wherever they wanted to. So, here comes a 135-pound Mexican guy over there, I put a sticker right on their windshield. I had power to roam the campus as long as I did my job.

This account of Gerald's experience typifies an adult figure who took interest in a troubled student and gave him an empowering role in school, which resulted in a sense of purpose and belonging. Although the incentive was disconnected from academic material, Mr. D'Amico saw beyond Gerald's trouble and race and gave him a chance to contribute purposefully to the school community.

Thomas, Rogelio's son, who entered a state university, also experienced mentorship. Because his parents' lacked knowledge about the school system, Thomas heavily relied on his college counselor: "[My counselor] help[ed] me with school selections . . . helped me with the application process, application deadlines. Pushed me, 'You're coming up on two months. You gotta get those in.'" While Thomas's counselor gave him extensive and invaluable advice about college, it did not come freely. Later in the interview, Thomas recounted how he had found out some years later through his mother that his father had approached the counselor about how she treated Thomas: "One time my dad was very dissatisfied with my counselor. And pulled her aside and had a few words with her. My mom said after that point she was like, '*Thomas Fuentes.*' When he called, she answered type of thing." Although Thomas had access to an adviser, she required a nudge to be more vigorously involved.

These were the only cases of mentors in school. The majority of Fuentes members contended that there was no one in school that attended to their academic or personal needs. Although most had counselors, these interactions often amounted to the nuts and bolts of advising. Ivan gave an example of this:

Chávez: Did you have anyone approach you about what to do?

Ivan: No. It was just a counselor. [He'd say,] "Well, what are you interested in?" [I'd say,] "Well, I'm interested in this." "Well you have these options of classes. You take these certain classes. And as the years progress, you get your AA and then you can get your BA. Then you have to think a little more seriously on a major," [he'd say]. . . . Nothing real serious because I wasn't really sure what I was going to do.

While the counselor provided Ivan with information about the overall process of an academic career, it was much less than Ivan felt he needed. Perhaps looking for good teachers, Ivan required someone who knew and related to him and could help him figure out what he was going to do— he needed a true mentor.

A Marker of Race and Class:
Low-Level Classes and Low-Level Expectations

Given the association with schooling and the economic structure (Blau and Duncan 1957; Bowles and Gintis 1976), school track affects students' school experience and performance, and subsequently influences their attitude toward school and their futures (Anyon 1980; Oakes 1985; Willis 1977). Students in higher academic tracks (i.e., honors, advanced placement, and college prep) tend to go to four-year universities whereas students in lower tracks (general, remedial, special education) tend to join the workforce after graduation (Oakes 1985; Parnell 1985). Studies have shown differentiated curriculum and instruction between these tracks shape students to be workers needed in the labor market. For example, working-class students, expected to fulfill blue-collar jobs, are placed in general and vocational education tracks that focus on rote memorization, information literacy, discipline (obeying authority), and following directions, while middle-class students work independently, think critically, and solve problems (Finn 1999; Linkon 1999).

Demonstrating overwhelming similarity across generations, the Fuentes family's case supports the fact that, as both Mexican American students and working-class students, members were placed in general and vocational tracks. First, fourteen of the twenty-five Fuentes' claimed that they were in the regular track, neither remedial nor college preparatory. Of the remaining eleven,[8] three, all in the fourth generation, identified themselves in special education. Only one in the third generation was in college preparatory courses. It appears that the majority of Fuentes had largely a general high school education, indicative of their racial or class classification.

Fuentes members' school track correlates with their perceptions and accounts about classes, especially in high school. Interestingly, members used race as the basis for their placement. In the second generation, given that Samuel was the first participant to complete high school, his experience is somewhat fundamental to the family's general experience. When I asked about racial issues in school, Samuel replied that he had little experience with this:

> The only time I remember, trying to, I guess, assimilate, I tried to take Algebra classes in junior high and the counselor's all, "You don't need that." [I said,] "Well, I wanna learn, other than math." "Well maybe you should take industrial [class,]" [he said.] Wood shop or things like that. I never realized maybe what the intention of that was and I never asked, "Well why not? Why can't I?" I was kind of following along with what they guided me.

Samuel's statement demonstrates a few points. First, when he wanted to take more challenging classes, he met with resistance from the school gatekeepers—counselors—who are believed to overlook one's race and other affiliations to help students meet their full potential. Second, Samuel, perhaps without parents or other siblings as advocates, was inclined to believe that the counselor knew best. What Samuel did not know was that his faith in the system constrained his scholastic opportunities.

Third-generation members gave few specifics about the classes they took. Those that did, presented a stark view of the classroom, which was associated with racial classification. As American citizens, Fuentes members were English dominant. Gerald, Sr., Yvette's son, described his high school experience in the late sixties and noted how his Spanish surname resulted in his placement in remedial courses:

> They did put me in a remedial class, and I was the best reader in there. Probably because of my surname. I didn't know no different. . . . [My] parents didn't know any different. There were people in the class who couldn't read. I think, in those times, if you had a Mexican or Spanish surname, they used to put you in those classes. Automatically they would. . . . My other classes were regular; I made it to ALG 1 or 2 in math.

The gross incongruity between a remedial reading class and an upper level Algebra class would these days surely have caught someone's attention (but perhaps not). During this period, unfortunately, for Gerald, the legacy of school practice that designates Mexican American students to remedial tracks persisted.

Thomas, who was fortunate enough to have a parent intercede on his behalf, also recognized the type of treatment Mexican Americans were getting roughly some years later in the late seventies. During one interview, he recounted a story about a Hispanic friend of his who told Thomas he did not receive the same treatment Thomas had in his college-prep courses:

> [My friend] hated [his counselor] for steering him toward only industrial professions. [The counselor] just assumed that this kid was not academically capable and steered him in one direction. And this guy is extremely smart. If somebody would have steered him toward math, he would have excelled because he knows engines, he knows equipment. He would've been an engineer. . . . [Now, my friend] oversees operations for an oil rig in California. . . . He was unfortunately robbed of an opportunity he could have had.

In his friend's case, Thomas has come to realize that race figured into his friend's treatment by his counselor, which was a gross injustice in his eyes.

Other Fuentes' coursework more clearly indicated a working-class orientation, courses designed for students to assume working-class jobs. The younger third-generation members, Laura and Erica, stated that they, too, had regular classes in the eighties. Laura detailed her schedule, claiming she spent a lot of her time in horticulture and floriculture: "In high school, I went four hours to regular high school and then a class at West Valley Occupational Center for cosmetology [I went with my friend]." Laura's comment also describes a vocational track, a program where students took courses at local vocational schools for high school credit.

Erica also had this experience. She claimed that she was enrolled in the Retail Opportunities Program (ROP), which gave her retail merchandising experience; she did not like it and now thinks she should have done something more business oriented. Like Samuel and Gerald, Sr., Laura and Erica's unawareness of the tracking system and the lack of knowledge of their right to choose from among courses caused them to defer to the school's choice of direction for them—filling a working-class job trajectory in cosmetology and retail.

Attending high school in the eighties, fourth-generation members similarly described the courses they took. Diagnosed as dyslexic in elementary school, Gerald, Jr., was in special education. He claimed that in high school he took one special education class in conjunction with regular classes, where he brought his day's homework to his resource teacher where he got more hands-on with the content.

At one point, Gerald approached his math teacher about changing his class to one that was more challenging, only to meet resistance:

> Even like, I started in general math and I told the teacher this is too easy. And she looked at me like, "Oh okay, whatever." Looking at my school schedule at the beginning of the year, [the teacher said,] "Well, you have this class [RSP]." I say, "Well, just because I have this class doesn't mean I'm stupid in everything." I was kind of angry at that time.

While Gerald's interpretation of the situation did not directly cite race as an explanation for his experience, perhaps he felt it was associated more with his learning disability. Like Natalie below, he had not made the connection between his special education designation and the correlation with race (Hosp and Reschly 2003; Rueda 1991). However, his experience in Bixby Meadows consisted of racial profiling as he complained how the police frequently stopped him and his friends asking for identification, while nearby groups of Caucasian youth were not harassed equally. Luckily, Gerald resisted and managed to get out of the general math class.

Natalie, who had the same resource teacher as Gerald when she went to school three years before, expressed that in high school she had only three special education classes: "Math, English and Social Studies and the rest were regular courses." When discussing how she now struggles to help her own children with homework, Natalie described her schooling as follows:

> We had the same notebook. It was a workbook for all three years. If we had time at the end of class, [the teacher asked,] "Did your pages?" "Yeah, whatever," I'd say. "Okay, you're done for the day, go home, you can leave early." That's how school was to me. That was Math, English and Social Studies. Those I had all three Special Ed. Spanish was very hard for me. I passed P.E. I took some electives. . . . Ceramics, metal, woodshop.

Although her mother (a high school graduate who likely believed the school knew best) placed her in special education upon counselor's request, Natalie's characterization of her high school coursework implies lower academic standards, which has made it subsequently difficult for her to help with her children's schoolwork.

One point must not be overlooked with regard to the latter fourth-generation members: Gerald, Jr., and Natalie's experience contrasts their Valley cousins. Both sets of parents moved to Bixby Meadows precisely to escape the poor quality of instruction in Valley schools as a result of bussing, perhaps believing that a more affluent community provided better schools. Ironically, all three of these members described a school experience that was less than challenging and wanting in many aspects. In a previous interview, Natalie discussed her high school experience. When I asked her what other students were like in those classes, she responded: "Come to think of it, everyone in those classes were Hispanic or Black. There were a few white people."

This reply clearly identifies a covert school practice to place minority students in remedial and regular tracks. While it may be argued members were less than prepared to handle regular or college-prep classes, one has to raise the question: How could these Fuentes members ever be expected to rise above the school's preconception of minority students without the necessary incentive and involvement from school personnel to help them?

This section depicts that the Fuentes' school experience was lacking a strong connection to school because of the manner in which school received them. Teachers were not available to students; Fuentes members had no mentors in teachers, counselors, or administrators. Lastly, despite their English monolingualism and citizenship, schools funneled Fuentes members into lower and regular tracks likely because of their race and/or class affiliation, which provided them with an experience base that had few marketable skills and no preparation to pursue a college education.

FUENTES' IN TROUBLE:
DRIFTING AWAY AND DROPPING OUT

This section focuses on the Fuentes members who did not follow the overall pattern of high school graduation and instead attained a GED or altogether dropped out. I decided to deal with these individuals separately given the effect that dropping out had on their futures and how dropping out has persisted into the fourth generation, when the effects of immigration have supposedly all but vanish. For those Fuentes who struggled to complete a diploma, schools became overwhelmingly unappealing and dissatisfying even though they spoke English and were American citizens.

To begin, the reasons members dropped out varied by generation. In the second generation, especially, the older Fuentes' futures were less rooted in the completion of school given the importance entering the labor force had in contributing to the family's financial well-being and the social standard for Mexicans and Mexican Americans to drop out. As the eldest child (once her older brother passed away), Katarina claimed she dropped out in eleventh grade "so she could work to help the family." Michael dropped out in the eleventh grade to enlist in the Navy to fight in WWII, "so his other brothers would not have to."

Carlos, who dropped out in eighth grade, never really felt like school was the place for him:

> I got some of the worst grades any kid could get in school. In fact, I think I stayed in the same grade one or two years because I was getting bad grades. Because my hands were too busy doing something. Sometimes I ignored, you know, doing my work, so I did flunk once or twice. In the very early years.

Carlos was also prone to playing hooky. He claimed that he "had too many other interesting things on [his] mind that [he] would be thinking [he] would want to do after school. A lot of projects, building slingshots, bow 'n' arrows." In the second generation's time, the consequences of dropping out were not severe and were justifiable.

In the third generation, matters changed. Second-generation families had established a more stable life allowing third-generation members more opportunity to get involved with school without the obligation of contributing to the family household. Only three members either received a GED (Gerald, Sr.) or dropped out (Noemi and Monica), while a few others struggled to graduate.

Noemi was the first third-generation member to drop out. At the time, being a woman may have buffered her decision to drop out given that there were many Mexican American women who did not finish school to marry and start a family. Nevertheless, with Noemi's bleak description of her experience in the classroom, it is no wonder marriage was more appealing than graduating:

> I remember that I didn't ask many questions. I remember they did not pick on me either, the teacher. The teachers didn't answer questions or anything and I didn't ask any questions. I felt like I was more in the background than anything. . . . It just seemed like I was there because I was supposed to have been there. I'm supposed to be there because I'm supposed to go to school. That's it . . . not because the teachers wanted me to learn anything.

Noemi characterizes her presence in the classroom as merely part of the background, seemingly invisible, and school was an obligation and not a path to learning.

Likewise, third-generation families were relatively stable, where both parents worked to ensure a life for children to go to school. All fourth-generation members that received a GED (Lydia) or dropped out (Simon, Sr., and Francis) were siblings, Noemi's children. Most remarkable was their recollection of returning to California only to dislike the new school system. They all experienced a general lowering of learning expectations and became unmotivated. Simon, Sr., and Francis gave an austere depiction of the process of dropping out. As Simon already explained, he returned from Arizona to have to participate in a school system he did not like—no respect for teachers nor learning. Nevertheless, the low expectations school held took its toll on his desire to finish:

> By the time I got into high school . . . I knew I didn't want anything to do with school anymore. I just saw it as . . . because the teachers didn't teach, students didn't learn. . . . I'm the kind of person that needs to have a lot of motivation. I need to be motivated. . . . And school was, all it was, just nothing, full of idiots, man. . . . It was so ridiculous for me. I just didn't want to be part of it.

Later in the interview, he continued with this: "I felt like I was invisible. And at the time, I didn't know how to ask for help, you know. I didn't really quit school, I just kind of drifted away."

Francis's story is much like Simon's only that he felt disenfranchised from school from the beginning. He claimed that having parents who were not academically oriented influenced his slow start in school. Coupled with his quiet nature, he got little attention from teachers:

> I had no idea why I was in fifth and sixth grade. . . . I didn't learn anything. I learned nothing. . . . I mean you're going to learn the basic stuff in school, unless you're retarded, man. . . . In junior high, my pattern was, don't do the homework, don't participate in class, screw around, when [I] had finals, study for a week, just study and just pass, get a D.

Often how Francis was treated in class or how he experienced school was at odds with his intellectual ability: "Everything I learned about history, science, I taught myself. But I never exercised it. I never displayed it in school." In his senior year, Francis finally decided to leave:

> I went to twelfth grade and dropped out in the middle of the year. I couldn't finish. . . . I went to a counselor. I said what do I need to graduate. My counselor couldn't see me, so I had to go see some other counselor. And [he] just basically laughed and asked me, "How come no one, has anyone spoken to you yet about this?". . . I took responsibility for it. . . . They said I would've

had to repeat another year. There was just no way; there was no time in the world. . . . I was working.

Like his brother, Francis's options were limited by the fact that he did not have anyone in school looking out for his academic development as well as the fact that bureaucratic red tape made it all but impossible to return to school. In addition, he had already redirected his life toward the workforce. As a result of his scholastic history, Francis, as a parent, provides a more productive and constructive scholastic environment for his children.

It is not surprising that these fourth-generation males had such negative school experiences that caused them to drop out. It is entirely understandable given that Noemi is their mother, a woman who herself felt grossly alienated from school. Although this is perhaps the worst case scenario in the Fuentes family, coupled with issues of single-parent family and divorce; this experience is not far from how other Fuentes members experienced school in special education and regular tracks, an education of little use to members once they graduated. The schools' role in the process of dropping out is clear: they provided no advocates; they provided unchallenging classes in conjunction with a school environment that distracts students from the goal of learning; and they provided poor guidance counseling and established rules that are more highly valued than students' circumstances.

Overall, Fuentes parents could not provide more help with schooling than they did, because their abilities directly reflected their own experience in the school system. What is salient is the fact that these individuals had a safe place to fall. Their saving grace was family, where parents verbally counseled them to stay in school and where the family values of getting an education and working remain as internal homing devices.

THE FUENTES' FUTURE:
THE FIFTH GENERATION IN SCHOOLS TODAY

As mentioned in the introduction of this chapter, the schools the fifth generation attends today are drastically different from those of preceding generations. The issues that have plagued the schools they attend are often seen in the news: overcrowded classrooms, poorly trained teachers, and dwindling school budgets. Only one member of this generation attends a private parochial school, a system that has been criticized for similar issues.

Unlike previous generations, four of the six members in the fifth generation began their scholastic careers in a pre-K program, either private or Head Start. Perhaps as an effect of their age, fifth-generation Fuentes' were unable to recall what school was like when they first started, yet their parents claimed they had mixed experiences starting school. Some embraced school, while others had trouble for various reasons. One example was JR, whose parents, Simon, Sr., and Ofelia, rationalized his beginning as difficult "because it was so far from home." When I asked if there were any memorable experiences they had about JR starting school, his parents explicated the following incident:

Simon, Sr.: What about the time he would not apologize to that kid.

Ofelia: Oh yeah, that was in Head Start. They had really rough kids there. One of the kids there, he didn't like to share. So one time JR came up to me and said, "Mama, this kid is bothering me." [I said,] "You know what JR, you're going to have to take care of it because I'm not there." Even if [JR] would tell him, this kid would not quit. So JR got it up to himself to [kick the kid . . .]. He has always been a really calm kid. It's not in his character to hit or to attack.

Fifth-generation members did not mention why they liked or disliked school, mostly commenting on favorite teachers or subjects. Matthew said school was "okay," following his comment with a statement about liking his teacher who was funny and who lets them play games to learn. Randy claimed she liked "Bellwork" (error detection exercises in English grammar), Art, and Science. Benjamin said he liked recess and games that his "fun" teacher gave them for math practice; he also liked journals because he was usually the first one to finish. JR liked playing in the after-school care program.

Elisa, the oldest at twelve, and the most verbal, remembered more of her experience in elementary school. She began school at a private Montessori preschool in Bixby Meadows while she and her mother lived with her grandparents. During this time, her mother met her stepfather, and they eventually moved away to Azusa while he finished his bachelor degree in business. Elisa attended kindergarten at the local public school. The following year her parents married, returned to the Valley and rented a condo. She started first grade at the local elementary school when problems arose:

During that time I got C's and D's, no B's and an F. I got in trouble. It wasn't that I wasn't doing my homework. I was just having a hard time understanding how to do it. In the old school, I was not used to homework. The school where we lived in Azusa, they did not give me homework. But when I went to Dalton they gave me lots. So I was way behind in first grade.

Despite her early introduction to school, the difference in academic expectations between one school and another complicated Elisa's school performance.

Brothers, Matthew and Benjamin, also remembered details about their school beginnings. Matthew, for reasons to be explained in the next chapter, began school a year late, thus, making him the oldest student in his third grade class. He did not attend a preschool, because his father could not afford it, starting kindergarten at the elementary school where Noemi worked as a cafeteria manager. Both Noemi and Francis have received compliments about Matthew's well-mannered behavior, yet reports also came home about his difficulty learning to read. Matthew discussed his schooling until third grade as "easy . . . [because] . . . you get to do easy stuff and all these people help you." In third grade, Matthew felt school was harder:

> *Matthew*: 'Cause you had to do a lot of stuff. There wasn't a lot of stuff to play. . . . You didn't have time to play with something, you had to do all this math.
>
> *Chávez*: And your Dad didn't teach you that at home?
>
> *Matthew*: No. 'Cause he was always working. He was never there. I had homework, working on my homework with no one helping me. I did it by myself.

School was hard for Matthew because the shift from play in school to academics was unexpected for him. In addition, his father was working the night shift at the time and was not available to provide the help Matthew needed. Once Francis got on the day shift, Matthew claimed that he "liked it when his father teaches [him]."

Benjamin had less to say about academics and commented more on starting school and getting in trouble for his misbehavior. Unlike his brother, Benjamin attended preschool for half a year at his aunt Lydia's recommendation; Francis enrolled Benjamin in the preschool that Randy had attended. When I asked Benjamin what is important for him to do at school, he replied with the following:

> To not yell or run away from the teacher. I ran away from the principal and Nana (Noemi) was the one who caught me. I did it because I was really mad. I did not tell anyone because kids would laugh at me. If I tell a grown up, they will ask the teacher why and she will say because I was being bad. I *was* being bad.

In first grade at the time of the study, Francis also received reports of Benjamin's difficulty learning to read. When I asked Benjamin whether he liked school, he stated "Not really, I'm bored on it a little bit." Aside from this type of experience, Benjamin claimed he liked recess, playing basketball, freeze tag, and dodge ball.

Since her beginning in school, Randy has always been an exceptional student. In fact, in her preschool, where she began at age three, she was part of a small select group of students that had a close relationship with the teacher and would sometimes visit the teacher's home. She began kindergarten in the same Catholic school as her older sister and started to read at four years old. When I asked her how school was she merely stated, "Okay." She was also well aware of the fact that public school did not "teach as much" as her school. Nevertheless, she was hoping her mother would allow her to go to Matthew and Benjamin's school, because she thought it would be good to "see family everyday."

Francis and JR have not experienced the same schooling as their cousins in that their parents moved them to the Midwest as they were starting primary school. The only other Mexican Americans in the school they first attended happened to be their cousins on their mother's side. The initial experience of fifth-generation Barrera children is the starkest compared to their California counterparts. Both boys were identified as having difficulty learning to read and were placed in an ESL classroom with English language learners, even though their mother tongue is English. At one point, the school approached Simon, Sr., and Ofelia with the option of retaining their sons. Figuring repeating the year would allow them time to catch up, Simon and Ofelia had their sons repeat third and second grade, respectively. When I interviewed JR and Francis, they were experiencing the repercussion of having to repeat a grade, being teased for "being dumb." JR had a girl repeatedly tease him, saying, "JR's dumb because he's in the Barrera family." Low performance had already begun to be associated with their difference in race. JR claimed he liked school because repeating a year for him meant he could get more work done. The younger of the two, Francis, however, found school "boring," although he liked his teacher. When I asked them if they got in trouble at school, they claimed they did for not finishing their homework, which meant they had to stay in at recess to do it.

The major transition for previous generations of Fuentes', junior high school, is yet to come for fifth-generation members. How these Fuentes members' will experience this transition is dependent on how schools or if schools have changed, and what fourth-generation Fuentes parents' orientation toward their children's schooling is.

SUMMARY

Mostly attributed to their ethnicity, two common perspectives why Mexican American students' achievement do not succeed academically are that they are only interested in working or not motivated to learn; from these perspectives, the responsibility for their performance rests entirely on them, and by extension, their families. The Fuentes family's school experience demonstrates how race, to a lesser degree class and ethnicity, has clearly played a role. Even when discrimination legislation had been passed, race has shaped how peers, teachers, counselors, and administrators have received Fuentes' on campus and in the classroom. As Pizarro (2005) notes the research on Chicano or Chicana students has had its limits because "[sic it has] almost always [been] based on the assumption that there is institutional and systemic interest in making change when in fact the majority of Chicano or Chicana youth attend schools in districts that have little interest in moving in the suggested directions."[9]

Looking at four generations of the Fuentes family's school experience, Pizarro's point (2005) has an astounding ring of truth. Not having been served directly by many of the legislation and policies meant to help Latino students, the success in educational attainment belongs to Fuentes members and families and not to schools.

NOTES

1. Judith Rosenberg Raferty, *Land of Fair Promise: Politics and Reform in Los Angeles Schools, 1885–1941* (Stanford, Calif.: Stanford University Press, 1992), 5.

2. Raferty, *Land of Fair Promise*, 13.

3. Los Angeles Board of Education, *Your Children and Their Schools: An Informal Report to the Patrons of the Los Angeles City Schools* (Los Angeles, Calif.: Author, 1937), 4.

4. Richard Romo, *History of a Barrio: East Los Angeles* (Austin: University of Texas Press, 1983), 137.

5. Duke Helfand, Jean Merl, and Joel Rubin. "A New Approach to School Equality: Fifty Years after Brown Ruling," *Los Angeles Times*, May 15, 2004, A1.

6. See Los Angeles Unified School District Website, available at: www.lausd .k12.ca.us/lausd/offices/bulletins/5_yr_review.html.

7. Maria E. Matute-Bianchi, "Situational Ethnicity and Patterns of School Performance among Immigrant and Nonimmigrant Mexican Descendant Students," in *Minority Status and Schooling: A Comparative Study of Immigrant and Involuntary Minorities*, ed. Margaret Gibson and John U. Ogbu (New York: Garland, 1991). Matute-Bianchi claims that Mexican American students do not fit into her immigrant/nonimmigrant continuum. These students appear to be unique to any of the descriptions she provides: "the students in this category are more ambivalent and uncommitted in their ethnic orientation . . . are active and successful in school but many appear to drift, to be disengaged and withdrawn from much of what the schools offers. They can be found in all curriculum tracks in the school, but are probably more likely to be found in the general to low tracks. They are more likely to be seen and not heard," (242). It seems the Fuentes' provide an insight into the ways and reasons why they are like and unlike Mexican-oriented and Mexican-descent students. Their experience provides another dimension to bicultural orientation.

8. The remaining seven consisted of five second-generation members who did not complete high school. The two in the third generation did not identify their track.

9. Marcos Pizarro, *Chicanas and Chicanos in School: Racial Profiling, Identity Battles, and Empowerment* (Austin: University of Texas Press, 2005), 20.

6

~~⌒

School, Part II
Fuentes' Homes, Language and Literacy

Latino academic failure has been attributed to Latino families and homes. Some believe the presence of the heritage language at home deters the acquisition of English and thus contributes to difficulties in academic learning for immigrant and second-generation individuals.[1] Unfortunately, this assumption of English language difficulty is loosely extended to later-generation Chicano students who speak English (albeit, who are likely to speak a nonstandard variety, Chicano English influenced by Spanish) as a first language.[2] Similarly, the language and cultural barriers that disallow Mexican immigrant parents to participate in their children's schooling are also extended to later-generation parents, despite the fact that their families have been U.S. citizens for generations and have themselves experienced being students in American schools. Based on these assumptions, Latino families are continually and perpetually seen as linguistic and ethnic others despite their American citizenship. In the eyes of the mainstream, Latinos' desire to hold onto their ethnic ways jeopardizes their success at becoming full-fledged Americans.

While much research and academic conceptualization still promotes that Latino families' inability to affect Latino student failure is closely, if not completely, associated with their difference in culture (including language), the Fuentes family's situation suggests otherwise. Over the course of five generations, the Spanish-dominant home of the first generation gives way to predominantly English-speaking homes by the third generation. Families cultural and language adjustment diminish, and literate practices and orientations, which are aligned with working-class families, play a role in whether Fuentes children were or are prepared to meet the high literacy skills demanded by schools and valued "in the U.S. economy [sic as] a key resource in gaining profit and edge."[3]

While race or ethnicity and class may explain why Fuentes have been historically relegated to general and vocational high school tracks, their class position more adequately signifies why the family's educational resources (derivative of their education experience) do not provide the know-how to secure the fifth generation's entrée into higher education.

LANGUAGE PATTERNS

The Place of English and Spanish in Fuentes' Homes

Spanish was primarily spoken in the original Fuentes home as Mario and Manuela learned little English over the years. Given their residential isolation, second-generation Fuentes members had little contact with either English or Spanish speakers other than their parents until they were exposed to English when they began school. The younger cohort, however, had more access to English because their older siblings and the neighborhood children spoke to them in English.

The effect of Spanish as an L1 (first language) on schooling for second-generation Fuentes' resembled the effects of other immigrant children who struggle to learn the language while they learn academic material (Rumbaut and Cornelius 1995). Katarina, the eldest member, stated this about how she and her siblings started school: "When we started school, we couldn't speak English. All the family spoke Spanish and not English. . . . We had rough times, but we learned it. . . . We had difficulty making ourselves understood." Michael also attested to the need to adapt to his new language environment: "Kids could learn [English] in school. I learned it. We learned it. The other kids learned it. We had to learn it. Because the teachers, they would not allow Spanish to be spoken."

Michael's response raises the fact that schools enforced the "No Spanish Rule" which was enforced in much of the southwest during roughly the first half of the twentieth century. Believing that speaking Spanish impeded children's acquisition of English and American culture, this rule did not allow Spanish-speaking children to use their mother tongue anywhere on the school premises (G. Gonzalez 1999; Hernandez-Chavez, 1995). Other possible rationales for this rule is that school personnel saw that speaking Spanish might allow children a way to subvert their authority as well as corrupt the learning environment for Caucasian students.

Fuentes members, like other linguistic minorities in American history, paid a price for the political and public war that was waged against their mother tongue. In younger second-generation members, it resulted in language loss. Florencia recalled how the prohibition of Spanish affected her ability to speak her first language:

> Mostly, it wasn't permitted really in school. When I was in elementary school, most students were all white so I did not speak Spanish. Not many Spanish-speaking people. Not like it is now. I did not see speaking Spanish as a hardship. I do think that being in an all-English-speaking environment helped me [with my English], but it also affected my Spanish. . . . Because as I got older, I really didn't know that much Spanish.

Although extolling the virtue of having to speak English to learn it, Florencia poses that the coercive nature of learning English impacted her first language ability and her connection with members of her community.

As a result of spending much of their time with Mario and Manuela, the older third-generation members, namely Isabel, Noemi, and Ivan, recalled being Spanish speakers as children. By the time they went to school, however, no one recollected being prohibited from speaking Spanish, suggesting that they were already English dominant. Here, Noemi's recollection as a Spanish speaker sets up a contradiction:

> *Noemi*: [My mother] spoke English to us and we spoke Spanish to our grandmother. She [grandmother] spoke to us in Spanish. But somehow we understood her.
>
> *Chávez*: And how did you talk back to her?
>
> *Noemi*: English. We spoke back to her in English.
>
> *Chávez*: You don't remember speaking to her in Spanish?
>
> *Noemi*: No.

This response implies that older third-generation members at least developed receptive skills in Spanish, and that older generations accommodated the younger generation by allowing them to respond in English. However, Noemi initially identifies as a Spanish speaker. Noemi and her family lived in the barrio and also in migrant camps for about four years where Spanish speakers were predominant, making it unlikely that they did not also develop productive skills. Ivan's recollection illuminates this situation:

> When I was little I was told that's all I spoke was Spanish. And then we [his older brother and he] went to a hospital for a while. We contracted TB. And then from what I was told that we were punished if we spoke Spanish [in the hospital.] Yeah. We were punished. I was told when my parents would bring us something, if we spoke Spanish, they would take it away from us and give it to the other kids.

Although this remembrance is a secondhand account of Ivan's child-hood, it makes two points. First, second-generation members recalled older third-generation members as Spanish speakers. Second, third-generation members have obscured memories of heritage language proficiency. Once these members moved into their new family homes in Anglo working-class communities and spent less time with their grandparents, English became dominant.

Contrarily, most younger third-generation members clearly remembered not having acquired Spanish language ability. Erica, Monica, and Laura all recalled how their fathers had to interpret for them when they visited their grandmother. Erica said: "We could not communicate with [Grandma] because we did not speak Spanish. My dad always interpreted. I remember being young and not being able to understand what she said. I felt kind of awful, but that was the way that it was."

The only younger third-generation member that maintained proficiency in Spanish was Timothy. As a postal worker in a large Spanish-speaking community, he welcomed the opportunity to use the Spanish he acquired in childhood. Having lived with his grandparents for a few years when his family was going through hard times, Timothy learned Spanish to communicate with them. Although one of the youngest third-generation members, he has a clear memory of being a Spanish speaker:

> I learned Spanish very young, from the time I started walking. I remember one of my uncles from Mexico, when I was eight or nine years old, saying that I spoke both languages well. I think I spoke Spanish before English because I was around my grandma so much. . . . [After my parents moved,] I would spend weekends with my grandparents and speak only Spanish, then go home and speak only English. I was able to get the best of both worlds.

For Timothy, the close connection he maintained with his grandparents, even after he moved to his new neighborhood, helped him maintain his Spanish.

Like the younger third-generation cohort, fourth-generation Fuentes members also remembered being English-dominant with no access to Spanish in the home. Having grown up in California with Noemi's family, the Barrera children (Lydia, Simon, Sr., and Francis) struggled to acquire Spanish after moving to a border town in Arizona. Now, in adulthood, each has variable proficiencies in Spanish as a result of living his or her childhood on *la frontera*. The Sanchez children (Paul, Natalie, and Katherine) made comments about how they had experienced discrimination from Spanish-speaking people for being English dominant. Gerald, Jr., also claimed that he did not "grow up" speaking Spanish. As adults, some third- and fourth-generation members were or are in the process of reacquiring or acquiring their Spanish language abilities as a way to preserve their ethnic identity—"As Mexican Americans, we should know it."[4]

Four of the fifth-generation members (Elisa, Randy, Francis, and Benjamin) did not acknowledge that they speak Spanish. Matthew claimed he did not speak Spanish but understood a little bit. In my experience with him, however, I have never known him to understand Spanish that is spoken around him. Simon, Jr., claimed he spoke a little but understood more. Both he and his brother, Francis, visited their mother's relatives in Mexico for several months prior to beginning school. Lydia, his aunt, claimed Francis returned speaking nothing but Spanish. Since they reside in the Midwest, the Barrera brothers now have little contact with Spanish speakers, despite their contact with their mother's family, who accommodate their children by speaking to them mostly in English.

With one exception, what we see with the Fuentes' is Joshua Fishman's general rule that the heritage language (Spanish) is lost by the third generation (Fishman 1989). It must be acknowledged, however, that there are fourth- and fifth-generation members with varying proficiency in Spanish, suggesting that a complete and total shift to English is neither linear nor absolute.[5]

What then is the reason for the shift from Spanish to English? Scholarship (Hornberger 1998; Portes and Hao 1998) claims there are many reasons immigrant or heritage language (HL) shift to the dominant or host language. One, in particular, is the power differential between the HL and the dominant language, such as fewer uses for HL in public life, lack of input for HL acquisition, language accommodation by older generations to younger ones, negative affective reactions to speaking the HL, and HL loss (Kouritzin 1999; Krashen 2000; Schecter and Bayley 1997; Tse 2001). In the Fuentes case, English dominance in the lives of the second generation can explain part of the shift. In Dora's interview, her mother Katarina stated that she had intentions of raising her children speaking Spanish, but her English speaking ability interfered:

Chávez: Did your mom speak to you in Spanish when you were growing up?

Dora: No.

Katarina: I swore that I was going to speak to them in Spanish. I would start in Spanish and because I was so used to English, I went into English [laughs].

Dora: My brothers speak it. I don't know how they learned it. I guess they learned it on their own.

Katarina: No. [With] Grandma and, you know . . . at that time there was more English speaking, Spanish speaking, too.

This exchange ascertains two circumstances. First, Spanish language ability for the older third-generation cohort is associated with the number of Spanish speakers in the community. By the time Dora came around, people had moved out of the barrio; soon after, her family followed. Second, there was an intention for second-generation members to teach Spanish to their children but that the predominance and prominence of English in their lives interfered with their decision to do so.

Only one second-generation member, Yvette, claimed she made a conscious decision to speak English to her children in the home. When I asked Yvette why she did not raise her children speaking Spanish, she replied: "I didn't think [it was important] because when I was in school we were prohibited to speak Spanish. [So I felt it wasn't important.]"[6] For the Fuentes family, the power of school (and public) policy to suppress the mother tongue has had a lasting effect. In today's climate where immigrant languages have more value and power than they have had in the past, later generations are often blamed or pitied for not having maintained the heritage language (Duarte 2007; Krashen 2000). In the Fuentes case, it highlights the role that anti-Spanish or English-only laws have had on the family and the role that public policy and social practice played in causing language shift (Crawford 2000). More importantly, it dismisses the family's pride and success at being able to fully participate in American society as Americans precisely because they are English dominant.

Literacy Patterns in Fuentes' Homes: "We are What We Read and Write"

Given that the Fuentes' were English dominant by the third generation, the HL cannot be considered a factor in the schooling for later-generation Fuentes'. Then, what factor mediated how well members did (or did not do) in school? From Fuentes' accounts, once English language acquisition was complete, literacy practices emerged as a factor.

The research on families and literacy can illuminate another possible explanation for the Fuentes situation. We know that the way families teach and use literacy in the home circumscribes the type of experience children will have learning to read in school. Children from upper-middle- and middle-class homes tend to have an easier time learning to read compared to children from working- and lower-class families, because their homes have access to the literate material and language structures and practices necessary for becoming academically literate (Heath 1983; Lareau 2000).

Upper-middle- and middle-class parents' college education, social networks, and political power grant them unfettered access to school resources and personnel in support of their children's schooling. The educational level of lower- and working-class parents (Anglo and African Americans) tends to provide them with little access to the types of learning and literacy experiences prominent in schools. Although few studies exist on the literacy patterns of Latinos, it stands to reason that working-class Chicanos' educational level and subsequent resources affect their children in similar ways with regard to literacy acquisition and access to a variety of literacy types and practices. Nevertheless, the Fuentes family dispels the myth that these families have no literacy in the home; rather, they possess the types of literacy that have been present in their childhood homes and in their schooling.

Despite the time-consuming life of migrant agricultural workers, Spanish literacy was present in the original Fuentes home. Second-generation Fuentes members claimed that their parents read when they had time. According to Michael: "[My parents] read in Spanish, *La Opinión*, the Bible. I taught myself to read in Spanish by reading my parents' newspapers. They had comics and I wanted to know what Tarzan was saying." Samuel further stated that his parents also read magazines, and his mother read Spanish "novels that [his] aunt [Amanda] bought and handed down to her." Florencia claimed her mother read magazines when "[her parents] went to San Fernando and got stories and news from Mexico. Sometimes unsolved mysteries."

Cristian was the only member to remember his parents' writing activities. Cristian was uncertain how well his mother read but knew that when she wanted to write a letter she called on his father: "I don't know how my father learned to read and write. He had nice handwriting and used to write letters for my mother. She would yell to him, '*Mario, escríbela esta carta*' (write this letter). My mother dictated and he wrote." In the Army, Cristian was on the receiving end of this activity, as he communicated with his family by letter: "When I was in the service, I taught myself to use a Spanish-English dictionary to write letters to my mother, because she only knew Spanish." Like Michael, the need to communicate or to understand written material prompted Cristian to acquire literacy skills in Spanish.

With regard to Spanish language literacy, only Florencia remembered being directly instructed by her parents to read in Spanish:

> My dad taught me to read. I remember, as a little girl, he would teach me the ABCs in Spanish. So, he was the one that taught me to read. My mom was always busy in the kitchen, but my mom would tell him "Mario, teach her the ABCs. Because if you don't teach, you know, she's not going to learn." So, my dad would pick me up crying, (pretends to cry like a child) and teaching me the ABCs. I'm glad he did because I sure need it now. Because there's a lot of Spanish-speaking people.

Because Florencia was Mario and Manuela's last child, more than likely she, and not her other siblings, received this instruction because Mario and Manuela were more financially stable and had time to give to her because the older adult children relieved some of the household workload.

At least one other member recalled how family played a role in learning to read, this time in English. Samuel claimed he had trouble learning to read, which developed into a dislike for school and led to his playing hooky to avoid the issue:

> At one time, I didn't want to go to school. I didn't want to go to school, but I didn't want to tell anybody. And finally my brother-in-law, he got my confidence. [I told him,] 'Well, I don't know how to read. We're studying these reading books and I don't know how to read. And I'm embarrassed.' I was in grade school, first grade. Second grade. Every morning the bus would come and I would take off running and no one could figure out why. [It was my brother in-law that] sat with me and taught me how to read.

It is not difficult to imagine, given the times, why Samuel's reading problem was not a concern of the teacher. Mexican and Mexican American students who missed a lot of school to follow the crops were written-off, because they fell behind in their academic work (Carter and Segura 1979). The remedy, however, in Samuel's case, seems to have been simple. The intervention of a family member (and perhaps any adult figure would have sufficed) who cared enough to ask why and who spent the individual time he needed to acquire the skill.

Even though the issue of frequency of literacy practice is not clear from these descriptions, Mario and Manuela's examples as readers and writers resulted in their children becoming readers themselves. Five of the seven second-generation members claimed that they enjoyed reading when young. Katarina expressed: "I used to love to read. I would get complaints from mom, 'Turn out that light (kerosene lamp) and go to bed.' I checked out books from the school library." Florencia, too, stated: "I liked to read fairytales. I would go to the library and read the books. They had a bookmobile and I got books from there. . . . I read a lot back then, but then got away from that as I got older."

Florencia was the only second-generation member that recalled that her mother encouraged her to read: "My mother encouraged me to read. She would tell me that it was very necessary for me to read, you know. She did not really give any reasons. That I would learn a lot by reading." Although other members did not make this comment, it would seem the example of their parents as readers extended to second-generation Fuentes' desire to read.

Parents as readers became more obscure in the third generation. Only five of the eleven members mentioned that their parents read. Three of these were siblings, Isabel, Noemi, and Gerald, Sr., who stated that their parents read newspapers, novels, and magazines. Isabel specifically remembered that her father read history books, and her mother read novels and dieting books. Monica, Cristian's daughter, remembered that her parents read *"Reader's Digest, Time,* [and] *National Geographic."* Thomas had the most to say about how his father, Rogelio, who read to learn: "My dad had an interest in Chinese history. I think through reading history maybe he acquired some opinions [that] throughout life people should have certain things. Education. A hard working attitude. A willingness to go beyond." Thomas went on to say his father was always reading the newspaper and history books. The family had encyclopedias and at one point Rogelio encouraged Thomas and his siblings to read the church missal on Fridays.

The children of other second-generation parents made no comment about their parents' reading habits, possibly attributed to the separate realms parents and children often inhabit. Another possibility for this is the fact that both parents had busy work schedules. Many of the mothers stayed home with their children in the early years, but, once children were school-aged, they went or returned to work. Additionally, a few parents (Katarina and Florencia) whose children did not respond claimed that reading was not an active part of their adult lives. Carlos, Ivan and Tricia's father, claimed that his lack of schooling (eighth grade) meant that he did not like to read much but that he got all his knowledge from the Discovery and History Channels.

As children, a few third-generation Fuentes' identified themselves as readers. Thomas was the only member who recalled being encouraged to read. The Gallo children, Isabel, Noemi, and Gerald, Sr., did not remember anyone encouraging or "forcing" them to read. Nevertheless, Isabel stated that as an adolescent she read a magazine called, "True Stories," which was dedicated to telling the life stories of women. She did not recall her parents reading to her, but she remembers reading to Gerald, Sr., (who concurred) when he was young.

The fourth generation commented even less on literacy in their homes. Francis was the only one who recollected his parents reading anything. He claimed that his family had a set of encyclopedias because "[his] dad was into studying this and studying that." Francis lamented that his father never shared his love for learning by reading to his siblings and him. Natalie said that her father was not a reader but that her mother, Isabel read a lot of novels. She also claimed her siblings and her were never forced to read. Lydia was the only fourth-generation member that read to her siblings when they were small.

Second- and third-generation parents' working-class lives provide a backdrop to why they may not have read much or read to their children.

Both parents were working; fathers in particular were frequently out of the house. Families averaged three children, and parents focused on meeting their children's basic needs. Although the first-generation Fuentes, Manuela and Mario, read and somewhat encouraged their children to read, reading was still more associated with schooling than with home life, implied by the Fuentes idea that one must be "forced" to read at home.

Without the know-how necessary for stimulating strong academic performance, it is likely that Fuentes parents did not understand the connection between reading and school performance, indicative from the few parents who expressed opinions on reading. In the second generation, Florencia remarked that her second oldest son had trouble learning to read, so "[she] started taking him to the library. [She] felt [her] responsibility as a parent was to make sure he read. He started to do better." Gerald, Sr., regretted that he had not been "forced to read," claiming "reading helps with learning vocabulary." His older sister, Noemi, said as much when she talked about how she was showing Benjamin, her grandson, to use the dictionary to look up words he did not know. When I asked if it was important to encourage someone to read, she replied:

> *Noemi*: Yes. Because you need it. . . . Your vocabulary is better. As you grow up, you're reading more, you learn different words. A person who reads gets more information.
>
> *Chávez*: From *True Stories*?
>
> *Noemi*: I'm not talking about *True Stories*. I'm talking about the newspaper, history books.
>
> *Chávez*: Did you encourage that in your kids?
>
> *Noemi*: What I remember about my kids, that I used to buy them a lot of records (albums) and a lot of books.
>
> *Chávez*: Did you read to them?
>
> *Noemi*: Well, maybe, not very often. I remember when they were younger. I used to read to them when they were younger. Lydia used to read [to her siblings]. Really it's so important. And understanding and comprehension that you get out of reading.
>
> *Chávez*: Did you know that when you were younger?
>
> *Noemi*: No. No one told me. When I got older, [I learned].

These comments from Fuentes' members indicate an understanding about the usefulness and mechanics of reading. Florencia's comments imply that, when reading is difficult for a child, exposing her or him to books and increasing the time he or she spends reading improves reading. Gerald saw reading as a matter of increasing one's vocabulary. Noemi agrees with her brother and adds that reading is about acquiring information and comprehending what one reads. As education professionals, we all know these insights have bearing on how and how well a child reads. A more poignant point about Noemi's comment is the fact that she was not instructed to know these connections; she did not learn these aspects until she was older. More than likely, Noemi and other Fuentes', may not have known these important elements about reading while they were raising their children, because they did not have the advantage of learning this from highly educated parents or from completing a college-bound education.

According to field notes, books were seldom discussed in the large or small family gatherings. If books were mentioned, they were spoken with reference to the stories they told. Often topics of conversations and discussion were facts or issues associated with current events, from local newspapers or news programs. In these discussions, participants tended to express personal opinions and attitudes, which generally most participants shared. On occasion, information or a fact from a book may have been shared, but it was often treated like new information rather than used to segue way into a broader discussion. Despite the relative silence about reading and books, literacy was clearly present in Fuentes homes, even if only on an individual and casual level.

While the Fuentes' literacy was restricted to everyday use and information, one extended reading circle illuminates how literacy was used to link members with their ethnic identity. The reading circle existed in Yvette's family. At one gathering, Isabel expressed that she was going to reread a book that had been passed on to her from Lydia, Villasenor's, *Rain of Gold*. In her first interview, Noemi claimed that Lydia passed on M. Ruiz's (1997) book, *Two Badges*, an autobiography about a Latina cop working in a Latino community. Simon, Sr., stated that Lydia gave him a book by Ana Castillo (1995), *Massacre of the Dreamers*, and reading it had changed his perspective on the female presence in his life. Although he could not remember the title, Gerald, Sr., claimed he was reading a book that "Lydia had lent [him]." As an avid reader, Lydia had become somewhat of a family librarian, passing down the books she read to other family members. It appeared that Fuentes members were drawn to reading about the stories of other Americans who may have experienced life in America as they had—Mexican American—stories which are seldom seen in mainstream forums, including schools.

Contrary to the stereotype, Fuentes' were not averse to reading. Mario and Manuela performed and encouraged literacy activities in their home, reading and writing personal and informational materials when time permitted. Second-generation children recalled their parents as readers to a greater extent than third- and fourth-generation children. As children, few Fuentes members from each generation considered themselves read-ers, and most all members did not recall their parents encouraging them to read as children. Yet, reading occurred, even unbeknownst to many Fuentes', as literacy became more of a private endeavor than an element of the family's social interaction.

THE SIGNIFICANCE OF LANGUAGE AND
LITERACY IN FUENTES' HOMES

Fuentes homes have experienced the language shift to English that char-acterizes many other immigrant experiences in the United States. Unlike those of European descent, however, they have not been able to escape criticism for their language situation or perception, despite their Ameri-can citizenship. Fuentes' over time have become keenly aware of the need for English language and have raised children to speak this language ex-clusively. Yet, members' English language acquisition has not guaranteed academic success, as others have noted (Macgregor-Mendoza 1999). Also members' racialized perception as Spanish-speaking "Mexicans" (identi-fied through phenotype and surname) has continually placed them at risk of being identified as newly arrived Spanish-dominant immigrants and subsequently misplaced and mistreated by school officials accordingly. Their Americanness is seldom recognized, and subsequently, their success as a productive working-class American family is institutionally under-mined and ignored.

With regard to literacy, the Fuentes' tendency toward certain uses and practices of literacy can be seen as a result of the racial segregation and so-cial discrimination they experienced in schools as they have been continu-ally tracked into general and vocational education. Brandt (2001) claims that schools act as sponsors, "agents, local or distant, concrete or abstract, who enable, support, teach, and model, as well as recruit, regulate, suppress, or withhold, literacy—and gain advantage by it in some way."[7] As a sponsor, schools "are delivery systems for the economies of literacy, the means by which these forces present themselves to—and through—individual learn-ers."[8] Given that schools assumed the major role for literacy, the Fuentes members in good part are what schools have made them.

According to Finn (1999), one of the major detriments of public school-ing for working-class students is the type of literacy to which they are ex-posed in their school experience.[9] In his estimation, working-class stu-dents possess high levels of performative literacy, the ability to read aloud at the word and sentence levels, and functional literacy, the ability to use reading and writing for everyday purposes. On the other hand, these same students have inconsistent or limited experience with informational literacy, the ability to read, comprehend, and write about academic material, and powerful literacy, the ability to analyze, evaluate, and synthesize school material.

From the above description, Fuentes literacy patterns tend to resemble performative and informational literacy—reading and comprehending magazines, novels, and newspapers. Language is often confined to the word or sentence level—learning to use a dictionary, reading more fluidly, increasing vocabulary. Even in cases where members are reading complex texts—history, nonfiction, cultural studies—these texts are less likely to be shared in family discussions. Members may mull ideas and concepts over in their own heads but presenting, analyzing, evaluating, and synthesizing literate texts are not enacted in the family environment, as occurs in middle-class homes (Lareau 2003). Equally important is the fact that the Fuentes', schooled in general, vocational, and remedial tracks, have had little experience with sharing and discussing their own opinions and insights about literate material. The literate practices in Fuentes homes appear to have aligned themselves with those of other working-class individuals in the schools they attended and the places they worked.

Therefore, a clear link exists between what Fuentes' have learned (or not learned) in school and how they share those experiences in their families. Thus, the Fuentes family literacy environment has not prepared children to contend with the more complex literate material and related academic skills. Unlike middle-class families who have the benefit of powerful social networks and academically enriched schooling, Fuentes', like other working-class Americans, are meant to resort to their class-affiliated education and personal networks (Bettie 2003; Diamond and Gomez 2004; Lareau 2000).

This interpretation suggests that the Fuentes family has been wrongly expected to acquire the literacy habits associated with middle-class families, solely based on the fact that they are now English-speaking Americans. Many laypeople believe that citizenship automatically provides unlimited access to opportunity and resources for high academic achievement. However, research claims that one's class, individually or in combination with other social factors, affect the type of resources one has at one's disposal (Lareau 2003; Rist 2000), thereby delimiting one's life chances (Willis 1977). In other words, at best, schools have made Fuentes members' successful literary consumers of the working class.

NOTES

1. See Henry Trueba, *Latinos Unidos: From Cultural Diversity to the Politics of Solidarity* (Lanham, Md: Rowman & Littlefied, 1989) and Lucy Tse, "Resisting and

Reversing Language Skills: Heritage-Language Resilience among U.S. Native Biliterates," *Harvard Educational Review* 71, no. 4 (2001): 676-708, for a fuller discussion on the perceptions of linguistic minority student failure. Tse clearly demonstrates that this assumption is false, noting "[a]lthough there is some variation in performance across ethnic groups and the originating country, immigrant children perform remarkably well overall both in terms of English-language proficiency and in academic achievement and progress" (21).

2. The documentation on Chicano English (Fought 2003; Ornstein-Galicia 1988; Penfield and Ornstein-Galicia 1985) is less studied than African American Vernacular English (Mufwene et al. 1998; Norment 2003), a much more accepted spoken dialect by a racial group. The controversy lies in thinking that Chicano English is either a true dialect of standard English or an interlanguage of immigrant parents' acquisition of English, an imperfect form of standard English spoken by later generations (Fought 2003; Santa Ana 1993). More study must be done on the various linguistic and sociolinguistic features of Chicano English before a definite conclusion can be made.

3. Deborah Brandt, *Literacy in American Lives* (Cambridge; New York: Cambridge University Press, 2001), 4.

4. This data was collected from a 1996 study of Fuentes family's ethnicity and language attitudes.

5. This data derives from a 1996 study of Fuentes family's ethnicity and language attitudes. In large and small gatherings, English was the predominant language of communication; however, Spanish emerged around telling jokes and making side comments that Spanish speakers did not wish English monolinguals to understand or as a sense of closeness. There also was a cachet of remaining Spanish vocabulary (i.e., *hijole* [oh boy], *mijo/mija* [my son/daughter], *Mira* [Look]), which members used in interaction with one another.

6. Also from 1996 study of Fuentes family's ethnicity and language attitudes.

7. Brandt, *Literacy*, 19.

8. Brandt, *Literacy*, 19.

9. Patrick J. Finn, *Literacy with an Attitude: Educating the Working-Class Children in Their Own Self-Interest* (New York: State University of New York, 1999), 124–26.

7

~⁀ᵔ⁀ᴐ

Fuentes' Homes and School

Parental Involvement

In today's society, despite the fact that research on the effectiveness of parent involvement is mixed (Gándara 1995; Mattingly, Prislin and MacKenzie 2002), the trend is for schools and teachers to expect it, which has not always been the case. Initially, schools were solely responsible for children's academic development. As schools became more bureaucratic, they began to demand parent participation; parents, however, contested and protested this demand (Cutler 2000). Since the early 1900s, parents' role in the schooling of children was never passively and unanimously accepted, while parent involvement, as we know it, as a vital part of a children's education, was roughly established in the 1960s. Be that as it may, today, in conjunction with their numerous other responsibilities, parents are expected to play a highly active role in their children's schooling. Parents who do not are criticized, and their love and concern for their children is questioned (de Carvalho 2001; Kravolec and Buell 2000).

Few educators and policymakers, however, seldom acknowledge the literature that identifies how significant social factors affect parents' level of involvement. These studies recognize that the cultural, social, and educational capital parents possess determine the ways in which they interact with school (de Carvalho 2001; Lareau 2003; Marjoribanks 2002). Specifically, similar to the discussion on class and literacy, upper-middle- and middle-class families have an edge over working-class and poor families because their language, literacy, and social interaction styles match those of schools. In regard to Latinos, their lack of parental involvement is often associated with Latino families' cultural devaluation of schooling (Gaitan 2004; Moreno and Valencia 2002). Valencia and Black (2002) argue, however, that Chicanos devaluation of schooling is a myth given the community's litigation record for better and equal schooling. Chapters 2 and 3 testify to the Fuentes family's value of schooling as a major family value, perhaps linked to the cultural value of una buena educación; however, in this chapter, we will see that a lack of or low parental involvement is linked to the family's working-class or racial classification.

FUENTES PARENTS' PERCEPTIONS OF CHILDREN'S PERFORMANCE AND SCHOOLING

Parental involvement in the Fuentes family mirrors the change in schools' expectations of parents. In the beginning Mario and Manuela's language and cultural barrier prevented them from taking an active role in their children's schooling, acknowledging, of course, that American parents at that time were not being asked to do so. Parent involvement can be identified here as those traditional activities enacted in the home that promote or reinforce children's academic performance. The one considered here is being aware of and monitoring children's school performance.

Despite their lack of example, second-generation parents, however, were aware of how their children were doing in school. For example, Katarina, Yvette, Cristian, and Florencia all claimed that their "kids liked school." More specific assessments often referred to Fuentes children having trouble (behavioral or attitudinal) in school. Katarina mentioned how her oldest son had a hard time in school because "he cried when he had to go." Likewise, Florencia commented that her children came home and told her about "problems they had with other children." Samuel talked in the most depth about his youngest daughter who had trouble in school and eventually dropped out: "My youngest daughter dropped out of school in the eleventh grade. She was one that never liked school. She was in with the wrong crowd for a couple of years, but when she got in trouble once, I think that changed her mind and she got straight."

Later in the interview, Samuel articulated how he responded to his youngest daughter's difficulties by being more active in her schooling: "I was involved with her studies at the time of elementary and junior high. I went to school to talk to the teacher. It was that she just didn't do her assignments." In this recounting, Samuel understood his daughter's problem with school as an aspect of personality—"She never liked school"—as well as a bad choice in friends. Although second-generation Fuentes parents could talk about their children's trouble in school, they did not have the detailed evaluation of their children's academic performance that may have resulted in swift and effective intervention of children's scholastic problems. By the same token, other parents of the time, roughly from 1940s to 1960s, were probably not much more aware than these Fuentes parents.

Like their parents, the older third-generation members, parenting roughly in the 1960s to the 1980s, tended to remark in general terms about their children's schooling, specifically about problems in school. Isabel mentioned that her children liked school initially, noting a change in her daughter's attitude toward school but did not give any specific reason for the change: "They did well [in elementary]. Natalie didn't like high school, but Katherine did. She always went to school. Natalie wasn't one to study, didn't like to get up [and go to school.]" Isabel contrasts her daughters' good performance in school with their attitudes toward school, implying that disliking school can lower one's performance. Her perception of her daughters' school performance revolved around attendance and not being school-oriented, "not one to study." It is important to recognize that Isabel's assessment does not contain Natalie's sentiment that school was "boring and unchallenging," suggesting that she did not know that this might have been a possible reason why Natalie checked out.

Noemi's estimation of her children in school derived from the subjects her children liked (i.e., math, history, and art) as well as other abilities they exhibited ("She was good at [art])." After claiming he stressed for his son to finish school, Gerald, Sr., referred to his son's personality as a factor in the struggle to get him to complete high school: "He was stubborn not wanting to finish." Ivan mentioned that two of his daughters either "got good grades" or "[was] doing better than the others." With some explanation about school tracking from me, Ivan was able to recall that one of his daughters was in a magnet school in high school. Evidently, older third-generation parents were no more prepared to evaluate their children's performance than their parents were.

This changed, however, with the younger parents in the third generation, roughly parenting in the nineties. With the exception of Monica and Timothy, whose children were in the early grades, the younger third-generation parents made specific comments about their children's performance or schooling. After expressing her daughter's interest to be a veterinarian, Dora stated the following:

> I want to get her into a magnet program next semester. My brother says if my daughter goes into magnet I will have to hire tutors. My daughter attended Kumon for two years. It was hard to do school and after-school academics. It's like doing double school. [But,] you have to.

Relying on her brother's advice, whose daughter had graduated from Princeton that same year, Dora knew she needed to place her daughter in a higher track and to enroll her in extra academic activities outside of school. However, the die had already been cast for her daughter's chances of entering a magnet program at this late stage, because they tend to select students based on their previous placement in magnet schools.

In this same cohort, Laura, whose children were in elementary school and who is a single parent, also discussed her children's performance in specific terms. In accordance with public service announcements, she expressed vehemently that it was important for parents to be involved in their children's schooling, even though it may be hectic at home. She continued with the following:

> Believe me, when I have the older two home and their homework, you know, I slacked off for one semester for my oldest, just to see if he's taking the initiative to do it himself. And I'd ask every day, "You done with your homework?" "Yeah, I'm done," [he'd say]. . . . Then I'd be with my second on her homework. So come report card time, he didn't do good this third one. The teacher's, like, "Well, he really hasn't been turning in his homework. And he hasn't been participating in spelling test, blah, blah, blah." I kinda fell off the wagon and because I thought he's trying to take a little initiative and be responsible for his homework. So I told him, "We're gonna be on you again." That's a priority. And dinner's all late. Homework's going to be a priority.

Laura demonstrates with this response that she played an active role in helping her older children with their homework, monitoring her son's performance by paying attention to report cards and communicating with the teacher. Realizing that her son was not assuming his responsibility to take care of his academic work, Laura intended to work more closely with him again. As a consequence, though, the well-being of this single-parent family may have to suffer—"Dinner's all late."

Like the younger cohort, fourth-generation parents also had much to say about their children's schooling. Of the four fourth-generation parents, only one, Natalie, had minimal information about how well her children were doing. Natalie's husband, a college graduate in business, was in charge of the children's academics (confirmed by her daughter, Elisa). She attributed this to the fact that her special education experience had not prepared her well to undertake this task. Nevertheless, Natalie knew Elisa was doing fine, and her son was having some problems reading. At a Thanksgiving gathering, she revealed that Elisa had been part of a select group of Hispanic students who were taken to the local state university for a tour.

Lydia, of all fourth-generation parents, was the most articulate about her children's academic endeavors. Beyond the interviews, we have had many conversations about Randy's school performance and Lydia's interactions with teachers about assignments and curriculum. In the interview, she recalled aspects about her children's study habits, schoolwork, and abilities:

Randy reads more to me than to my husband. She is now reading a 200 to 300 page book. She's doing it in place of the three book reports she has to do for school. . . . [For my older daughter,] class size was a problem. [My oldest] would not get the time she needed in class and my husband and I had to work with her at home. . . . Randy puts a lot of pressure on herself to succeed. She has to overdo. If they want a three-page report, she will do eight. . . . My oldest never volunteered information about school. Only talked about social relations and gossip. Randy talks about her lessons and things. Tells me that she had a bad day.

In conclusion, the younger third-generation and fourth-generation parents were more likely to demonstrate specific knowledge about their children's schooling and performance compared to older Fuentes parents who spoke about whether their children liked school or what their favorite classes were. The older parents were more inclined to refer to children's school performance in general terms regarding personality or character, while younger parents were able to discuss children's classes, study habits, and academic performance.

This change in Fuentes family parental involvement was not random but rather roughly corresponds to the change in parental expectations schools have established, which are aligned with white middle-class behaviors and values (Berger 1991; Coleman 1987; Cutler 2000). In this excerpt, Francis clearly indicates this:

I think me being angry for a lot of years, I forget that we came along in an era when times were changing. . . . Because, you know, lifestyles. Households. We're going into the seventies, the schools, the state, the city, the government. Wanted the parents to take a bigger role in the household than just going to work and providing food and a house and clothing. Where the State said, "We're not going to be raising your friggin' kids anymore. You take the responsibility now, you step forward and start raising your children." . . . We came along in that time where the parents were being asked, *told* really, to take a forward approach. And ours didn't. And now that I have children now, it's like a must. You have to do it because the schools are not going to do it. They either don't have the capabilities of doing it or they just don't want to.

Francis's response characterizes the change in standard for parental involvement, which was set to align with meeting the will of the school and the government and not with parental choice or need. More importantly, it suggests how this change affects the generation of children who were now being asked to be involved in their children's schooling without having had parents who demonstrated how to do this. Equally important is the fact that schools and the powers-that-be have not offered the types of parent education that would give Fuentes parents the educational capital they need to improve their children's academic performance, because the types of programs that exist tend to be geared toward immigrant non-English-speaking parents and centered on parenting style (Trumbull et al. 2001) rather than parent involvement strategies and how and why they are likely to work. Nevertheless, as a testament to the Fuentes family, each generation of Fuentes parents has risen to the occasion by being more involved in their children's schooling.

FUENTES PARENTS' ROLE IN THEIR CHILDREN'S SCHOOLING

The second aspect of Fuentes parents' involvement is the specific role(s) parents played in regard to school. Table 7.1 displays by generation both the parents' and the children's perceptions of the parents' role in schooling.[1]

In table 7.1, the encouragement that members received from parents reflects the value of schooling as a core Fuentes family value (see chapters 2 and 3). It consistently appears across all generations by both parents and children. Noteworthy, however, is the relative disagreement between third-generation parents and fourth-generation children. This is likely attributed to the fact that the fourth-generation Fuentes' interviewed were among the eldest and associated with older third-generation parents, who were less involved than the younger cohort. They were not on the receiving end of the change in parental involvement. Interviewing younger fourth-generation members may have produced greater agreement.

Table 7.1 also demonstrates that parents' role in their children's schooling tended to expand over generations. For example, third-generation parents stressed school more compared to second-generation parents, while fourth-generation parents continued to stress school but also added disciplining for poor performance, rewarding good performance, and holding high academic expectations. Despite that Fuentes parents had regular school experience, with each subsequent generation, they have gotten more involved in their children's schooling.

Why then are Fuentes parents doing more for their children's schooling than they had experienced as children? Here is where the effect of acculturation and American citizenship may be a factor. Now full-fledged working-class Americans and removed from the immigrant experience, some of the increase in parental involvement may have resulted from later-generation parents' exposure to the public campaigns for greater parental involvement. Furthermore, Fuentes parents tended to reassess their childhood in light of these campaigns. In hindsight, many of the

Table 7.1. Fuentes parents role in children's education via parent and child perceptions by generation

Generation	Parent's perceptions	Children's perceptions
Second	Encourage schooling and staying in school Make child a reader Discipline for poor performance	Encourage schooling and staying in school
Third	Encourage schooling and staying in school Stress/prioritize schooling Monitor schooling Be involved in school Discipline for poor performance	Encourage schooling and staying in school
Fourth	Encourage schooling and staying in school Stress/prioritize schooling Be involved in school Discipline for poor performance Reward for good performance Hold high expectation for performance	Encourage schooling and staying in school Be involved in school Hold high expectation for performance
Fifth	—	Encourage schooling and staying in school Discipline for poor performance Reward for good performance Stress/prioritize schooling Hold high expectation for performance

third- and fourth-generation members wished their parents had a greater role in their schooling. Dora commented: "I didn't have the pushing [to do better in school]. I think it might have made a difference. I know that my mother's life, where you work, limited what she should offer in the way of schooling."

Timothy made a finer point on the matter:

Timothy: I don't know. I can't really blame it on my parents. Maybe, the family environment, if like my parents, if dad was a doctor or mom was a professor or something. Where education was #1.

Chávez: It wasn't #1?

Timothy: I don't know if it was #1 because there were so many issues. . . . I mean my parents were just trying to survive, their marriage, keeping the family together, putting food on the table, working. My dad was working in these factories where they refinished furniture. It was hard to stress more education [rather] than just finishing high school.

Timothy understood that parents who had advanced degrees or professional occupations possessed the know-how for children to excel in school, further implying that disposable income and time may provide opportunities to help children. Both Timothy and Dora are not angry or resentful for what their parents were not able to offer them. Instead, as working-class parents themselves, they understand too well the difficulties and hardships associated with raising a working-class family.

Similar sentiments arose in the narratives of fourth-generation parents. Simon, Sr., stated: "I never had any encouragement for grades. Nothing I can remember. Nobody was ever involved in anything. . . . That's why it's important to me to be involved with my kids now." For him, not having his parents help him with school motivated him to fulfill that role with his own children.

Despite their desire to play a greater role in their children's academic lives, third-generation parents had difficulty. First, parents noted that they were unable to help children, because either the subject matter had changed from when parents went to school or parents felt their own schooling was inadequate. Isabel remarked how it was difficult for her and her husband to help with their children's schoolwork: "A lot of the stuff we couldn't help them with. Things like new math, we did not have in our schooling. We didn't have patience to help them with their work. Everyone got frustrated." Parents' unfamiliarity with children's school material also created an atmosphere of frustration that made homework helping sessions stressful for both parents and children.

Ivan agreed with Isabel's point that the change in the school curriculum made it difficult for parents to help. The knowledge and skills they had acquired had become somewhat antiquated, rendering parents a limited resource to their children despite willingness to help:

> We helped the kids until it got too hard. Algebra's changed a lot. Even the way they put their fingers on a typewriter has changed. For example, one kid was beginning high school and I couldn't figure out how to use the calculator. I took Algebra, Geometry, Algebra 1 and 2, but I don't know. I think school has gotten away from the basics.

This same sentiment emerged in fourth-generation parents' accounts, which explained their own parents' limited role in their schooling. Lydia explained why her mother was not as involved with her schooling in the same way Lydia was involved with her own children's:

> I wonder, now, if my mother knew how to do some of these things [parental involvement]. It would have made a difference if my mom could help, in-

stead of me having to wing it. She was not confident [when dealing with school] because she did not graduate from high school. . . . Maybe she didn't know that it was expected of her, because she may not have gotten that from her parents.

Lydia sets in motion here the possible connection between schooling, family socialization, and school experience compounded by the change in school's expectations of parents. Focusing on Yvette's branch, this process can be understood more clearly. In the beginning, Manuela's display of encouragement and insistence on school attendance was the foundation for Yvette's parenting. For both women, their encouragement to do well in school or to stay in school resulted in their children graduating. Like her mother, however, Yvette had not been expected to be involved in her children's schooling and did not model these behaviors for Noemi. This was Noemi's view of a parent's role, as she, and others in her generation, began to experience the pressure to be involved.

Subsequently, now affected by her mother's role in her schooling and her desire to meet the dominant notion that parents need to be active, Lydia arrived at her approach. Although she participated more than her great-grandmother, grandmother, and mother, given her general education, Lydia also had problems helping her daughter once she moved to the middle grades in a private parochial school. Lydia expressed frustration at the difficulty with helping her daughter study world history, "I never had that when I was in school. I could help her with memorizing and stuff like that. But there were things she had to know that I never learned." As a parent, it is difficult to help children advance in school when one has not experienced advanced schooling.

HOW FUENTES PARENTS HELP WITH SCHOOL

From both the parent and child perspective, table 7.2 displays the parent involvement strategies Fuentes parents employed across generations.

At first glance, table 7.2 demonstrates a discrepancy between the strategies parents recall employing and those children recall. In other words, Fuentes parents remembered doing more than Fuentes children remembered. A possible explanation for this is the asymmetrical nature that is at the heart of the parent-child relationship. Specifically, parents undertake many endeavors in the interests of children of which children are often unaware. A case in point is Thomas's admission that he had only recently discovered how his father intervened on his behalf with his high school counselor. As a child, he was not necessarily privy to this information.

Table 7.2. Fuentes parent and children perceptions of parent involvement strategies

Generation	Parent's perceptions	Children's perceptions
Second	Attend school events (carnivals, programs, open houses) Help with homework Take to library Attend teachers conferences	Taught Spanish literacy
Third	Attend school events Help with homework Take to library Attend teacher conferences Pay for extra academic assistance Buy materials for projects Monitor schooling Join PTA	Attend school events Help with homework Buy materials for projects Talk to counselor
Fourth	Attend school events Help with homework Take to library Pay for extra academic assistance Buy materials for and help with school projects Monitor schooling School visitation/volunteering Attend teacher conferences Form study groups	Attend school events Help with homework Monitor schooling
Fifth	—	Help with homework School visitation/volunteering Pay for extra academic assistance

Again, as depicted in table 7.2, parents tended to build on previous generations. Second-generation parents attended teacher conferences, helped with homework, and visited the library; third-generation parents did the same, plus paid for extra academic assistance, bought materials for projects, and monitored schooling status; fourth-generation parents expanded their involvement by volunteering and visiting schools and forming study groups.

Aside from encouragement, one other consistent feature of Fuentes parent involvement has been helping with homework. In the same way that Ivan and Isabel recalled it difficult for them as parents to help their children, other Fuentes members came to the same conclusion about their parents. Tricia claimed that "her mother helped her and her siblings with homework, but could only help so much before [her mother] could do no more . . . [because her parents] only had seventh to eighth grade education." When discussing what people helped him with schoolwork Timothy replied: "There was no one I really could go to for help. I did not really think about doing that. Maybe my mother. As I got older the math got more complicated and I wasn't sure that she even knew about that stuff. She did not finish high school." Parents' school experience had a direct effect on how they were able to help their children and whether children perceived them as sources of help.

In the third and fourth generations, Fuentes parents enacted two-parental involvement strategies generally asked for by schools: monitoring school performance and volunteering. It appeared that third-generation parents, particularly the younger members, were more aware of what was happening to their children in schools, because a few parents intervened to have misplaced children reassigned. Given the increase of Latinos in schools in the nineties, Dora and Timothy had to find appropriate schools or classrooms for their children after the school administrators had misidentified their children as Spanish speakers. When putting her daughter in kindergarten, Dora had discovered she had been put in an all Spanish-speaking class:

> My daughter was placed in a Spanish-speaking classroom. She doesn't speak any Spanish. She couldn't understand anything. The kids did not want anything to do with her. Her last name is Flores. I talked to the principal to change her classroom, but he wanted to wait a few months for things to settle before he did anything. I said, "No. You have to move her now." It took a week to move her. [The other students] shunned her. She didn't like school because of that.

Timothy had a similar issue when he wanted to enroll his son in school:

> I started thinking about schools, when my wife took our kids to school. . . . She wanted to take the kids to the local school across from cousin Dora's house, thinking that it was an open school district. And [the school] told my wife they had to go to the local school, Tujunga Elementary. . . . She took our son there and came home crying. She goes, "I can't leave him there." She says, "Eighty percent of the kids in the class don't speak good English." Because our son only speaks English, my wife was afraid that he was going to get behind. . . . We wanted to put him in a school, not against Latinos or anything, we wanted to put him in a school we felt that wasn't going to hold him back. We didn't know if the teachers were going to have to focus so much on the bilingual, that some of the other kids were gonna suffer.

Timothy and his wife's concern for the quality of their son's schooling resulted in them moving him to a racially mixed school far from their home. In both these cases, race and ethnicity appeared to be a reason for misplacement, necessitating parents to come to school to correct the error.

Unlike previous generations, fourth-generation Fuentes parents began to volunteer and visit schools. Lydia and her husband were required by their daughter's parochial school to volunteer so many hours each month. Perhaps related to her interest in child development, Natalie earlier claimed that being involved with her children's schools as a volunteer was part of her personality, having volunteered at her daughter and her oldest son's school. Simon and his wife also volunteered, chaperoned field trips, and visited their sons' schools at various times. They also attended many teacher conferences when their sons were being considered for retention. Francis, a single parent, did not volunteer, and his sons' school did not require it, but he attended teacher conferences and made a point of having conversations with me about how he could help his sons ("How can I help him with decimals?"). Furthermore, Francis was active in his children's extracurricular activities, having coached both his sons' Little League teams for many years.

Although parental involvement was a new activity for Fuentes parents, it appears members got much from the experience. Simon, Sr., characterized his experience when he explained why he was involved with his children's schooling:

> As a parent you have to be there. You can't just say "okay" and kick your kid over there and expect him to do better. You gotta be there, man. When you see how happy they are to see you come in to read them a story. They're happy just to see you because many parents just don't go.

At the time of the study, Simon, Sr., volunteered and monitored his children's schooling, most of which occurred when he had free time, because he was between jobs. In this response, despite his eagerness and resolve to do more with his children's schooling than his parents had, he implies that there is much more to parental involvement than he knows:

> I don't know much about education. What's a good school and what's a bad school. The only thing I could see here is that the schools appear to be safer. That was it. I had no way to tell if their curriculum was better than the curriculum back home [Los Angeles]. Teachers are more qualified? I don't know how to judge that, you know. Like I said, school was never important to me. So I had no way to gauge it.

Here, not only does Simon attest to the fact that he does not have the depth of knowledge about school to make knowledgeable decisions, but he also shows that this lack of knowledge is directly related to his own past school experience and parent model of involvement.

WHAT IT MEANS TO BE FUENTES PARENTS
IN AMERICAN SCHOOLS

In summary, the shift of the Fuentes family's parental role can be explained in the following way: The Fuentes family is attempting to keep up with new standards of parental involvement despite the constraints of their own school experience (general education), which is shaped by race and a working-class lifestyle (two working parents with a moderate income). In comparison to immigrant parents, like first-generation Fuentes', parents obviously know something about the school system, in that they have made decisions about misplaced children, found private academic resources (Kumon), and helped with homework. They know the importance of stressing school and encouraging children to do well. From this perspective, they are survivors of a social system set against their success as a racial minority and working-class individuals.

Yet, what they do not know has had lasting repercussions. The fact that they do not know how their children feel about their educational experience and their secluded treatment of literacy suggest that there still exists a distinctive separation of home and school characteristic of working-class and Mexican American families (Carrasquillo and London 1993; Lareau 2000). Of no fault of their own, they are unaware of the bridges between school and home that foster strong academic chances for their children, those which are learned through experiencing higher education and congregating with others of that experience base (Brantlinger 2003; Diamond and Gomez 2004). They need more than language interpreters, parenting tips, or life skills. They need access to the cultural, educational, and social capital that has come to advantage middle-class families (Horvat, Wieninger, and Lareau 2003), so that Fuentes parents can make the types of decisions about their children's schooling and upbringing that will break the educational and social ceiling that relegates minority and working-class students to the lower echelons of schools and society.

More importantly, as long as Latinos are viewed only as newly arrived immigrants or their children, the gains in parent involvement that later-generation families like the Fuentes' make are never recognized, and their efforts and success are never validated. Also, without more research on Latino families, their home life and their parental involvement, schools can still impose their singular understanding of parent/family participation, which ignores and underutilizes the unique sociocultural characteristics these families hold and those behaviors they create in adjusting to U.S. society that some scholars are just beginning to acknowledge (Ceballo 2004; Knight et al. 2004; Reese 2002; Villanueva 1996; Walker and Riley 2001; Zentella 2005).

NOTE

1. This chart was based on second-, third-, and fourth-generations Fuentes members' recollections as both parents and children. Fifth-generation children only provided their childhood experience given their ages (seven to twelve).

8

⁄⁀

Conclusion

What the Fuentes Family Teaches Us

Five Generations of a Mexican-American Family in Los Angeles has been a never-before written account of a Mexican immigrant family becoming American. It has put to the test our faith in the American notion of achieving equality, opportunity, and success through solely hard work. Over nearly a century my family has participated in the making of this nation as they picked crops during the Depression, worked in the factories during WWII, fought in major American wars, and contributed in later generations as proud, hardworking Mexican American citizens. They moved from the tenuous lives of immigrants to solid members of the American working class.

Over time, Fuentes' have become American. In their families, they speak predominantly English, and children are strongly socialized to become self-sufficient and independent, to take care of oneself and one's family. Parents aspire to buy homes and cars and find better employment to secure a better life for their children. Children have participated in American popular culture, from bobby socks to Levi's jeans to skateboarding to heavy metal. In regard to schooling, the Fuentes family (like other families) value education and have traditional parent/family involvement: encouraging and stressing children do well in school and monitoring children's academic progress (Christensen and Sheridan 2001).

Yet, by mainstream measures of success (highly educated, entrepreneurial, and upwardly mobile) the Fuentes family would not be considered successful. As Latinos and working class, they are still seen as a problemed people, part of the underclass who refuses to assume the American

151

orientation to living (Moore and Pinderhughes 1993; Portales 2000). Still today, as a nation, we continue to believe in the myths of success for all and ignore the fact that social factors such as race, ethnicity, and class matter in shaping one's life chances to achieve the American dream. *Five Generations of a Mexican-American Family in Los Angeles* clearly demonstrates that the intersection of race, ethnicity, and class in American social institutions has contributed to the Fuentes' maintenance or reproduction of the family's social experience and status across five generations. More importantly, despite the effect of those social factors, the Fuentes family has succeeded in the finest of American traditions.

In isolation, what happens at home, work, and school cannot explain or describe why the Fuentes family has not had more upward mobility. When we consider the intersections of race, ethnicity, and class across these spheres, we illuminate possible reasons for the family's consistent status over generations.

INTERSECTIONS: RACE, ETHNICITY, AND CLASS IN THE FAMILY AND SCHOOL

Chapter 5 clearly showed how race affected the Fuentes family in schools, indirectly linking home and school. On the other hand, ethnicity links the Fuentes family and schools in more direct ways. In the face of the superficial and stereotypical belief that culture (food, holidays, and language) impedes integration into the mainstream, the Fuentes story demonstrates how deeper manifestations of culture persist over time, even though the family has acculturated to the American context. Although Fuentes' still eat some Mexican dishes at family celebrations and some still speak Spanish, ethnicity (including familism) remains as both an identity marker and an economic and social survival strategy. While some may interpret familism as a cause for the family's consistent working-class status, I would argue that it has maintained the family as working class, granting them more options and opportunity than those in the working poor and lower class. The Fuentes family's sense of familism has offset the downward mobility that even the middle class fear (Ehrenreich 1989).

Familism, as a marker of Mexican culture, promotes the establishment and maintenance of personal ties. As Valdés claims, Mexican immigrant families come from a social environment where "relationships and human ties were far more important than options or choices [sic for promotion and advancement]," therefore they emphasize the ligatures or bonds between members, bonds which are "linkages and allegiances 'that give meaning to the place the individual occupies.'"[1] From this perspective,

Mario and Manuela Fuentes encouraged and transmitted the importance of family over all else: "It is how we are; it is how we were raised." Familism and closeness helped the Fuentes' move out of poverty and gave members a financial and psychological safe place in a world that operates on institutional racism and class discrimination.

Next, whether as a part of una buena educación or all on its own, Fuentes' clearly value schooling, having stressed its importance over generations. However, the separation of family and school, associated with an allocation of separate responsibilities, found in Mexican immigrant families also seems to exist in later-generation Chicano families, seemingly setting a standard by which academics are received by children to be outside the meaningful social force of the family (Carrasquillo and London 1993; E. Martinez 1999). Research has shown that families who do not expose their children to the cognitive and language behavior valued in school are more likely to experience academic difficulty (Brantlinger 2003; Lareau 2003; Marjoribanks 2002; Rodgers 2003). The integration of academic life with family life in Mexican American families would likely benefit children's academic success.

But who should assume the responsibility to create or begin this integration? The Fuentes family has shown us that the connection between parents' educational experience and children's academic development are inextricably linked. First, whether as a consequence of race or class, Fuentes parents' relegation to general or vocational tracks affords them little to no experience or skill in helping children move into more advanced tracks. The expectation schools and teachers hold for Latino parents to get involved are unrealistic given how schools have previously and historically schooled parents to assume a lifestyle conducive with a working- or lower-middle class position. Despite later generations' courageous efforts to bridge the gap between their parents' level of participation in their academic development and their level of participation in their children's schooling, fourth-generation parents' traditional parent involvement seems to fall short of making effective and real change as fifth-generation Fuentes still struggle with school. In this case, the blame for students' difficulty does not rest solely on the family's lack of motivation, values and desire; schools' ideology, policy, and practice play a profound role in the replication of the Fuentes family's social status.

Second, irrespective of the persistence of familism, Fuentes' do encourage their children to be self-sufficient, independent, and responsible. Fuentes children are valued for their unique character and personality, and in adolescence, children are expected to choose a career path. The family's value of the individual is salient to members finding happiness and a respectable place in society. Contrarily, white middle-class families delimit and dictate young children's futures through what Lareau calls, concerted cultivation. Here, parents establish, organize, and control activities (i.e., soccer practice, school open house, or conversations with adults) to develop children's talents, resulting in "a robust sense of entitlement . . . [which] plays an important role in institutional settings, where middle-class children learn to question adults and address them as relative equals."[2] This sensibility starkly contrasts with how the Fuentes family cultivates children to be good, respectful, and respectable human beings, deferring to authority, nurturing children's natural talents and inclinations as they emerge.

Parents know their children, make suggestions, or offer learning opportunities and guidance. Even though later-generation families' put children into extracurricular activities, such as music lessons and sports teams, children are never expected to pursue these activities long term. Likewise, children are encouraged to finish high school, and even college, but children still have the option to work if they do not pursue higher education. School is *an* option, not *the* option since "school is not for everyone." Unlike the middle class, which believes that higher education is a "messiah," "capable of . . . improving the welfare of individuals and the social order as a whole,"[3] and whose lives are predicated on a minimum of a baccalaureate degree, Fuentes' working-class lives have shown marginal gain from public education and the possibility to provide one's family with a relatively good and stable quality of life.

At this point, some may rush to blame the family for not having the wherewithal to demand children go to college. The stereotype that Mexican American or Latino families devalue formal education seems to emerge. Nevertheless, this interpretation ignores the links between race or class, schools and families, and the social legacy of policies disadvantaging Mexicans and Mexican Americans and the working class. That is, Fuentes members do not advocate for higher education in that they have found formal schooling to be of moderate value in their lives. Initially, Fuentes members' experience school as a neglectful and isolated environment, which has shaped their lukewarm attitude toward school for generations; school has been seen largely as a hurdle to entering the workforce. Over at least three generations, and in line with other accounts of Latino students, schools have reinforced this attitude by designating Fuentes' to general and vocational classes, offering no mentors, providing unchallenging classes, and poor guidance for academics or careers. Coupled with their working-class status, their experience has sold them on the idea that high school could be a terminal degree. Nevertheless, Fuentes children have over each generation gained more education than the previous, attributed to the family's insistence on finishing school and getting ahead.

INTERSECTIONS: RACE, ETHNICITY, AND CLASS
BETWEEN FAMILY AND WORK

Being working class in America is an experience often nonexistent on the social radar. As stated in chapter 1, working-class individuals struggle to stay ahead of or rebound from economic declines that can have lasting consequences for families and influence the financial and social resources available to future generations (Dohan 2003; Rubin 1987, 1994; Weis 2004). For the Fuentes, being working class has meant being able to attain modest housing, reliable transportation, and sufficient food not available to the first generation. On the other hand, the luxury of the middle and upper classes, college education, has remained unattainable given the financial strain a college education for children would cause the family, because working-class jobs are among the most susceptible to restructuring and elimination (Bernhardt et al. 2001).

Furthermore, A. Gonzalez (2001) suggests that lower or working-class families and have to consider the direct and indirect costs of higher education, such as tuition, room and board, and "the income lost while being a full-time student, [and] the psychological costs of attending, such as being subjected to examinations or long and tedious courses."[4] For working-class families, a large loan burden threatens the family's household income, which is also affected by the hourly wage layoffs and restructuring, and is needed to generate savings for even a modest inheritance for children.

Another connection between the Fuentes' experience and the workplace is how the family values are a greater asset on the job than in the school. The value of buena educación promotes hard work, dependability, punctuality, and responsibility; all values members have claimed helped in their advancement on the job but never mentioned to be of much value at school. In other words, Fuentes' behavior at work, not at school, results in success. Valenzuela (1999) argues that Chicano students' social capital, such as buena educación, is not recognized or validated by schools, which causes feelings of disenfranchisement. The Fuentes story seems to corroborate this point. In this respect, this aspect of ethnicity and the schools lack of respect and validation for it, may lead to the notion that work is a more appealing long-term option than school.

WHAT WE CAN LEARN FROM THE FUENTES FAMILY:
STRATEGIES TO IMPROVE MEXICAN AMERICAN AND
LATINO STUDENT PERFORMANCE

From the Fuentes family, we learn that Latino families are far more complex than has been described. We have for too long blamed them for their failings and ignored the success and triumph they have achieved on a daily basis, for many, over generations. To make a difference in their lives and the lives of future generations we must undertake the task of seeing and knowing them as they see and know themselves. We must acknowledge that the single mainstream definition of success is constraining to individuals who do not possess or do not have access to the social resources and material that make success readily achievable. Families and communities can redefine success to incorporate elements of the mainstream definition with those definitions that are valuable to them.

For example, Caniff (2001) demonstrates how Cambodian American families negotiate a bicultural definition of success through culture, religion, and their emerging social place in American society. Here being academically and financially successful in the American definition coexists with the Cambodian definition of success, being a person that maintains language and culture and that gives back to the family and community—"to be successful Khmer." Likewise, the Fuentes family, having lived through nearly a century of social and political policies and events in and against their favor, view themselves as successful in their ability to stay intact as a social unit and to work toward a better future for their children despite the challenges that race, ethnicity, and class have presented in societal institutions. Families and communities and schools need to work together to arrive at these negotiated definitions.

Scholarship on families and schools advocates for a partnership between families and communities and schools to foster children's academic achievement (Christenson and Sheridan 2001; Wright and Steglin 2003). The result has been an increase in programs and initiatives designed to educate minority parents in the ways Anglo middle-class families interact and behave at home around school matters, neglecting to consider how these programs may be incompatible with other family types. However, as other scholars have noted (Carrasquillo and London 1993; Valdés 1996) any partnership between Latino families and schools must be one that accounts for and contends with the uniqueness of the Latino family, in all its manifestations (Auerbach 2002; Gaitan 2001, 2004; Moreno and Valencia 2002; Quezada, Díaz, and Sánchez 2003; Valverde 2004).

Through parental involvement programs families should be given access to resources and opportunity they do not already possess to reshape family life to maximize children's academic, intellectual, and sociocultural development. The Fuentes family's story makes the point that many families are doing exactly what is being asked of them to get involved, yet, their economic and social position in institutions are not acknowledged as constraints on the effectiveness of that involvement. Instead, I advocate for interventions that focus on the power and strength of Latino families' familism and their right as family members to determine the function and direction of that intervention that will enhance not detract from the health of the social unit. The following are strategies families and schools can implement to improve Latino student academic success.

Strategies for Families and Communities

1. *Become more knowledgeable about schools and how they work.* One of the reasons the Fuentes family and other families like them do not understand how their parental involvement affects their children's academic performance is because they do not understand the ways schools work. How curricula is designed; how subject matter is graded by level; how school's authority is structured; what teachers' roles and power are in schools; how schools are connected to community services; what special programs and assistance are available to families; what procedures exist for how students are promoted, suspended or expelled; what the channels of communication in schools are; what students', parents', and the community's rights in the education process are; what the role and consequences of testing are; what the expectations, procedures, and outcomes of teacher/parent conferences are; what home activities promote intellectual development; what the structure and significance of academic tracks are; are all among the types of knowledge parents and community members do not have in making decisions about their children's education.

    Parents should establish social and information networks in and outside of school whereby they can access this information; community organizations or activists can help families develop these networks by connecting them to culturally and socially sensitive educational professionals, those who understand and will not undermine, but incorporate, the value families place on cooperation and togetherness.

2. *Advocate for your family's well-being.* Most Latino individuals know too well how Latino families are often devalued because of their unique qualities of familism and buena educación, as they have frequently been instructed to be more like Anglo middle-class families who stress school above all else. Yet, many Latino students will acknowledge the crucial role their families have played in making them the productive people they are today (Cabrera and Padilla 2004; Gándara 1995; E. Garcia 2001; Mora 1997; Rodriguez 1982; Vigil 1997; Villaseñor 1991). For this reason, we need to take pride and care in advocating for the well-being of our families.

    Families need to let schools and other social institutions know that they do what they do to help members survive as members of a racial minority and as members of the lower and working class. Without monumental changes to the American social class system, families must prepare their children to persevere and thrive in the face of discrimination and economic struggles. This endeavor does not exclude having children do well in school but doing well in school should not exclude maintaining the well-being of the primary social and psychological resource—the family—which is most likely going to aid them throughout life.

3. *Integrate academics into family life.* Finally, in advocating for Latino children, families need to assume the responsibility of educating children at home, in ways that are going to make a difference in the choices they will have upon high school graduation. This means not only learning about how to develop children's intellect in ways in which they will be successful in school but also in ways which will preserve the practical and precious values of family and together-ness. First, we must realize the tremendous power family has in Latino children's lives and use family relationships and time to show them that school activities and behaviors are part of who they are at home and in public—people with the power of heart and mind.

One of the ways that this can happen is by making school and learning an ordinary and usual part of family activity and conversa-tions. We should ask children to share something specific about what they learned on any given day. We need to be seriously interested in knowing how children feel about school as well as why they feel that way, asking about class work, teachers, classmates, successes, and playground time. If children are going to value all aspects of school, families must model that concern and passion for learning.

Strategies for School and Educators

1. *Acknowledge and change schools' biased and discriminatory policies and practices.* With power comes responsibility. Given the persistent racialized experience of Latino students and their families (Carger 1996; Martinez, DeGarmo, and Eddy 2004; Olmeda 2003; Pizarro 2005; Soto 1995), schools (and other social institutions) have to take the lead to eliminate the bias and discriminatory practices against "other" groups, which are real and historical (Doob 1999; Zinn 1998). Schools need to identify official and unofficial practices, policies, and actions that treat Latino families and students based on racial stereo-types such as: "Latino parents do not care about education." "Latino students are not interested in learning." "Latino students are only in-terested in going to work, not college." Schools need to do a better job of accounting for the various situations and circumstances, which may influence how families and students interact with school personnel, practices, and policies.

2. *Counseling and mentoring of Latino students.* As attested by the Fuentes' account as well as others, counseling and mentorship, or lack thereof, have been key factors in Latino students' school success or failure (Avilés et al. 1999; Cooper 2002; Stanard 2003; Stanton-Salazar and Spina 2003). Schools need to provide frequent and accessible counseling for Latino students, not only about choices in high school but also about the possibilities of college. School must improve the ways in which they identify and encourage Latinos to enter college prep, honors, and advanced placement tracks, and when necessary, provide additional academic support. Schools need to encourage and support mentor relationships between minority students, teachers, counselors, and administrators, noting that more personable and personal rapport is necessary in forging these relationships with Latino students (Canning 1995; Grubb, Lara, and Valdez 2002; Rolón-Dow 2005).

3. *Treatment of Latino students in classrooms and campus.* Given the effect that racial stereotypes can have on behavior, schools should provide teachers, administrators, and staff with quality training in understanding Latino families and students. These programs should get at the root of stereotypical views of Latinos and educate faculty and staff as to the varied and complex ways in which these families exist. Teachers and staff should be supported in reevaluating their perceptions periodically.

4. *Change the institution's perception of Latino families.* Sufficient research on the existence and persistence of biased or insensitive policies and practices toward minority students and their families exists and justifies schools' reevaluation of their ideologies about and perceptions of the Latino students, families, and community (Avilés et al. 1999; Garcia and Guerra 2004). Recent research advocates for a more complex and diverse understanding of the Latino community based on cultural differences from the mainstream as well as in subgroups, language, generation, class, nationality, region, and other factors (Menchaca 2000). Each one of these factors qualitatively shapes family resources and circumstances. Any values or perceptions of Latino families should be viewed as guidelines, not absolutes; differences and exceptions should be expected. Fitting the family to a single model can result in creating inappropriate or ineffective interventions and solutions.

Latino families should be valued and recognized for what families provide for their children, even though they may not identically resemble that of Anglo middle-class families. The importance of buena educación, familism, and the value schooling should be recognized and validated. Parents and other members seriously assume their responsibility to care for their children, including the maintenance of family networks as strength, not liability. Schools need to better understand the connection between the family's resources and the various factors that shape them.

5. *Negotiation, not imposition, should be the basis for family intervention methods and programs.* Schools must first move past the view of Latino families as deficient and instead understand them in their actual sociocultural, political, and economic contexts. School personnel needs to see Latino families as they see themselves—successful. These families are aware of the importance of being a unified, yet adaptive, social unit in an environment in which they are viewed as subordinate. Schools' current understanding of Latino families is a skewed perspective, a biased misinformed one. The belief that these families lack appropriate academic orientation in the home lays the groundwork for blaming the Latino family for their inability to help their children succeed (Valencia and Black 2002). The overemphasis on families as a socializer of school culture ignores the role school and other societal factors play in the lives of these families, as the Fuentes account has demonstrated. Over generations, with the exception of the severely distressed, Latino families increase members' high school graduation rates and their standard of living. If Latino families are going to be criticized for their failure, they must also receive credit for their success—raising socially responsible, respectable, and productive human beings.

In this respect, schools should understand and acknowledge families' success, which is based on a lower- or working-class standard, not a middle-class one. Recognizing the important role family plays in the lives of Latinos can help schools to help families find the appropriate recipe to incorporate academic matters into family life. Ultimately, it is the family's choice to negotiate a new family dynamic and the school's responsibility to see that they receive the necessary help to do so. Families must be consulted about changes, and school interventions must resemble negotiations rather than directives (de Carvalho 2001; Gaitan 2004; Trumbull et al. 2001). Imposed school-determined interventions may develop a breach of respect and trust, two vital qualities that Latinos live by.

In conclusion, policymakers, educators, and others concerned with the Latino community must realize that simply transforming Latino families into their Anglo middle-class counterparts will not work. In fact, this action undermines these families' well-being and the social system they have constructed to survive the harsh realities many of them experience in the United States. Latino families, like the Fuentes family, have come to view themselves as successful, having survived and often, thrived in the face of being lower or working class or being members of a racial minority. They are strong, intelligent, vital, hardworking, and persevering human beings who deserve to be treated with the respect and dignity they afford others.

NOTES

1. Guadalupe Valdés, *Con Respeto: Bridging the Distances between Culturally Diverse Families and Schools* (New York: Teachers College Press, 1996), 170, 171.

2. Annette Lareau, *Unequal Childhood: Class, Race, and Family Life* (Berkeley: University of California Press, 2003), 2.

3. Sandford W. Rietman, *The Educational Messiah Complex* (Sacramento, Calif.: Caddo Press, 1992), 5.

4. Arturo Gonzalez, *Mexican Americans and the U.S. Economy: Quest for Buenos Días* (Tucson: University of Arizona Press, 2001), 72.

Bibliography

Abi-Nader, Jeanette. "'A House for My Mother': Motivating Hispanic High School Students." *Anthropology and Education Quarterly* 21 (March 1990): 41–58.

Acuña, Rudolfo F. *Anything but Mexican: Chicanos in Contemporary Los Angeles.* New York: Verso, 1996.

———. *Occupied America: The Chicano's Struggle toward Liberation.* San Francisco: Canfield Press, 1984.

———. "Truth and Objectivity in Chicano/a History." In *Voices of a New Chicano History*, edited by Refugio I. Rochín and Dennis N. Valdés, 23–50. East Lansing: Michigan State University Press, 2000.

Aguilar, John L. "Insider Research: An Ethnography of a Debate." In *Anthropologists at Home in North America: Methods and Issues in the Study of One's Own Society*, edited by Donald A. Messerschmidt, 15–26. Cambridge: Cambridge University Press, 1981.

Anderson, Margaret L. "The Fiction of 'Diversity without Oppressions': Race, Ethnicity, Identity and Power." In *Critical Ethnicity: Countering the Waves of Identity Politics*, edited by Robert H. Tai and Mary L. Kenyatta, 5–20. Lanham, Md.: Rowman & Littlefield, 1999.

Anyon, Jean. "Social Class and the Hidden Curriculum of Work." *Journal of Education* 161, no. 1 (Winter 1980): 67–92.

Anzaldua, Gloria. *Borderlands/La Frontera: The New Mestiza.* San Francisco: Ante Lute Press, 1987.

Applebaum, Herbert A. *The American Work Ethic and the Changing Work Force.* Westport, Conn.: Greenwood Press, 1998.

Auerbach, Susan. "'Why Do They Give the Good Classes to Some and Not to Others': Latino Parent Narratives of Struggle in a College Access Program." *Teachers College Record* 104, no. 7 (October 2002): 1369–92.

Avilés, Robert, M. Davison, Manuel P. Guerrero, Heidi Barajas Howarth, and Glenn Thomas. "Perceptions of Chicano/Latino Students Who Have Dropped Out of School." *Journal of Counseling and Development* 77, no. 4 (Fall 1999): 465–73.

Baca Zinn, Maxine. "Familism among Chicanos: A Theoretical Overview." *Humbolt Journal of Social Relations* 10 (1983): 224–38.

——. "Insider field research in minority communities." In *Contemporary Field Research*, edited by Robert M. Emerson, 224–38. Prospect Heights, Ill.: Waveland Press, 2001.

Barrera, Mario. *Race and Class in the Southwest: A Theory of Racial Inequality.* Notre Dame, Ind.: University of Notre Dame Press, 1979.

Bearchell, Charles A., and Larry D. Fried. *The San Fernando Valley: Then and Now.* Northridge, Calif.: Windsor Publications, 1988.

Berger, Eugenia Hepworth. "Parent Involvement: Yesterday and Today." *The Elementary School Journal* 91, no. 3 (January 1991): 209–19.

Bernhardt, Annette, Martina Morris, Mark S. Handcock, and Marc A. Scott. *Divergent Paths: Economic Mobility in the New American Labor Market.* New York: Russell Sage Foundation, 2001.

Bettie, Julie. *Women without Class: Girls, Race, and Identity.* Berkeley: University of California Press, 2003.

Blau, Peter Michael, and Otis Dudley Duncan. *The American Occupational Structure.* New York: Wiley, 1967.

Blea, Irene. *Chicano Communities: Social, Historical, Physical, Psychological and Spiritual Space.* Westport, Conn.: Praeger, 1997.

Bobo, Lawrence D., Melvin L. Oliver, James H. Johnson, Jr., and Abel Valenzuela, Jr. "Analyzing Inequality in Los Angeles." In *Prismatic Metropolis: Inequality in Los Angeles*, edited by Lawrence Bobo, Melvin L. Oliver, James H. Johnson, Jr., and Abel Valenzuela, Jr., 3–50. New York: Russell Sage, 2000.

Boggs, James P. "The Culture Concept as Theory in Context." *Current Anthropology* 45, no. 2 (April 2004): 187–209.

Booth, Alan, Ann C. Crouter, and Nancy Landale, eds. *Immigration and the Family: Research and the Policy on U.S. Immigration.* Mahwah, N.J.: Lawrence Erlbaum, 1997.

Borjas, George J., and Marta Tienda, eds. *Hispanics in the U.S. Economy.* Orlando, Fla.: Academic Press, 1985.

Bowles, Samuel, and Herbert Gintis. *Schooling in Capitalist America: Educational Reform and the Contradictions of Economic Life.* New York: Basic Books, 1976.

Brandt, Deborah. *Literacy in American Lives.* Cambridge; New York: Cambridge University Press, 2001.

Brantlinger, Ellen. *Dividing Classes: How the Middle Class Negotiates and Rationalizes School Advantage.* New York: Routledge Falmer, 2003.

Briggs, Vernon M., Jr., Walter Fogel, and Fred H. Schmidt. *The Chicano Worker.* Austin: University of Texas Press, 1977.

Browning, Harley L., and Rudolfo O. De La Garza. *Mexican Immigrants and Mexican Americans: An Evolving Relation.* Austin: CMAS Publications, Center for Mexican American Studies, University of Texas at Austin, 1986.

Buriel, Raymond, and Terri De Ment, "Immigration and Sociocultural Change in Mexican, Chinese and Vietnamese American Families." In *Immigration and the*

Family: Research and the Policy on U.S. Immigration, edited by Alan Booth, Ann C. Crouter, and Nancy Landale, 165–200. Mahwah, N.J.: Lawrence Erlbaum, 1997.

Cabrera, Nolan L., and Amado M. Padilla. "Entering and Succeeding in the 'Culture of College': The Story of Two Mexican Heritage Students." *Hispanic Journal of Behavioral Sciences* 26, no. 2 (May 2004): 152–70.

Camarillo, Albert. *Chicanos in California: A History of Mexican Americans in California.* Sparks, Nev.: Material for Today's Learning, 1990.

Caniff, Julie G. *Cambodian Refugees' Pathways to Success: Developing a Bicultural Identity.* New York: LFB Scholarly, 2001.

Canning, Christine. "Getting from the Outside in: Teaching Mexican Americans When You Are an 'Anglo.'" *High School Journal* 78 (1995): 195–205.

Carger, Chris Liska. *Of Borders and Dreams: A Mexican-American Experience of Urban Education.* New York: Teachers College Press, 1996.

Carrasquillo, Angela, and Clement B. G. London. *Parents and Schools: A Source Book.* New York: Garland, 1993.

Carter, Thomas P. *Mexican Americans in Schools: A History of Educational Neglect.* Princeton, N.J.: College Entrance Examination Board, 1970.

Carter, Thomas P., and Roberto D. Segura. *Mexican Americans in School: A Decade of Change.* New York: College Entrance Examination Board, 1979.

Casso, Henry J. "Higher Education and the Mexican-American." In *Mexican Americans Tomorrow: Educational and Economic Perspectives*, edited by Gus Tyler, 137–63. Albuquerque: University of New Mexico Press, 1975.

Castillo, Ana. *The Massacre of the Dreamers: Essays on Xicanisma.* New York: Plume, 1995.

Caughey, John Walton. *The Shame of Los Angeles: Segregated Schools, 1970–1971.* Los Angeles: Quail Books, 1971.

Ceballo, Rosario. "From Barrios to Yale: The Role of Parenting Strategies in Latino Families." *Hispanic Journal of Behavioral Sciences* 26, no. 2 (May 2004): 171–86.

Chapa, Jorge, and Belinda de la Rosa. "Latino Population Growth, Socioeconomic Status and Demographic Characteristics, and the Implications for Educational Attainment." *Education and Urban Society* 36, no. 2 (February 2004): 130–49.

Christenson, Sandra L., and Susan M. Sheridan. *Schools and Families: Creating Essential Connections for Learning.* New York: Guilford Press, 2001.

Clifford, James, and George E. Marcus, eds. *Writing Culture: The Poetics and Politics of Ethnography.* Berkeley: University California Press, 1986.

Coleman, James. "Families and Schools." *Educational Researcher* 16 (August/September 1987): 32–38.

Cooper, Catherine R. "Five Bridges along Students' Pathways to College: A Developmental Blueprint to Families, Teachers, Counselors, Mentors and Peers in the Puente Project." *Educational Policy* 16, no. 4 (2002): 607–22.

County of Los Angeles Commission on Human Relations. *The Urban Reality: A Comparative Study.* Los Angeles: County of Los Angeles Commission on Human Relations, 1965.

Crawford, James. *At War with Diversity: U.S. Language Policy in an Age of Anxiety.* Clevedon, England: Cromwell, 2000.

Cutler, William W., III. *Parents and Schools: The 150-Year Struggle for Control in American Education.* Chicago: University of Chicago Press, 2000.

Darder, Antonio, and Rodolfo D. Torres, "Shattering the 'Race Lens': Toward a Critical Theory of Racism." In *Critical Ethnicity: Countering the Waves of Identity Politics*, edited by Robert H. Tai and Mary L. Kenyatta, 173–92. Lanham, Md.: Rowman & Littlefield, 1999.

Dauwalder, Donald D. *Education: Training for Technical Occupations, A Study of Industries and Schools in the San Fernando Valley, California*. Los Angeles: Los Angeles City Junior College District, 1961.

de Carvalho, Maria E. P. *Rethinking Family-School Relations: A Critique of Parental Involvement in Schooling*. Mahwah, N.J.: Lawrence Erlbaum Associates, 2001.

Diamond, John B., and Kimberly Gomez. "African American Parents' Educational Orientations: The Importance of Social Class and Parents' Perceptions of Schools," *Education and Urban Society* 36, no. 4 (August 2004): 383–427.

Diaz-Guererro, Rogelio, and Lorand B. Szalay. *Understanding Mexicans and Americans: Cultural Perspective in Conflict*. New York: Plenum Press, 1991.

Dohan, Daniel. *The Price of Poverty: Money, Work, and Culture in the Mexican American Barrio*. Berkeley: University of California Press, 2003.

Donato, Ruben. *The Other Struggle for Equal Schools: Mexican Americans during the Civil Rights Era*. New York: State University of New York Press, 1997.

Donato, Ruben, Martha Menchaca, and Richard R. Valencia. "Segregation, Desegregation and Integration of Chicano Students: Problems and Prospects." In *Chicano School Failure and Success: Research and Policy Agendas for the 1990s*, edited by Richard R. Valencia, 27–63. London: Falmer Press, 1991.

Doob, Christopher Bates. *Racism: An American Cauldron*, 3rd ed. New York: Longman, 1999.

Duarte, Cynthia Michelle. "Between Shame and Authenticity: Negotiating 3rd-Generation Mexican Ethnicity in Los Angeles" Ph.D. diss., Columbia University, 2007.

Durrenberger, Robert, Leonard H. Pitt, and Richard Preston. *The San Fernando Valley: A Bibliography*. Northridge, Calif.: Center for Urban Studies & Bureau of Business Services & Research, San Fernando Valley State College, 1966.

Echevarria-Howe, Lynn. "Reflections from the Participants: The Process and Product of Life History Work." *Oral History Review* 23, no. 1 (1995): 40–46.

Edsforth, Ronald. *The New Deal: America's Response to the Great Depression Problems in American History*. Malden, Mass.: Blackwell Publishers, 2000.

Ehrenreich, Barbara. *The Fear of Falling: The Inner Life of the Middle Class*. New York: Pantheon Books, 1989.

Erdmans, Mary Patrice. *Opposite Poles: Immigrants and Ethnics in Polish Chicago, 1976–1990*. University Park: Pennsylvania State University Press, 1998.

Espinoza-Herrold, Mariella. *Issues in Latino Education: Race, School Culture and the Politics of Academic Success*. Boston: Pearson, 2003.

Fiener, Susan F., ed. *Race and Gender in the American Economy: Views from across the Spectrum*. Englewood Cliffs, N.J.: Prentice Hall, 1994.

Finn, Patrick J. *Literacy with an Attitude: Educating the Working-Class Children in Their Own Self-Interest*. New York: State University of New York, 1999.

Fishman, Joshua. *Language and Ethnicity: In Minority Sociolinguistic Perspective*. Philadelphia: Multilingual Matters, 1989.

Flores-Gonzalez, Nilda. *School Kids/Street Kids: Identity Development in Latino Students*. New York: Teachers College Press, 2002.

Foley, Douglas E. *Learning Capitalist Culture: Deep in the Heart of Tejas*. Philadelphia: University of Philadelphia Press, 1990.

Foley, Neil. *The White Scourge: Mexicans, Blacks and Poor Whites in the Cotton Culture of Central Texas*. Berkeley: University of California Press, 1997.

Fought, Carmen. *Chicano English in Context*. New York: Palgrave Macmillan, 2003.

Fussell, Peter. *Class*. New York: Ballantine Books, 1983.

Gaitan, Concha Delgado. *Involving Latino Families in Schools*. Thousand Oaks, Calif.: Corwin Press, 2004.

———. *The Power of Community: Mobilizing for Family and Schooling*. Lanham, Md.: Rowman & Littlefield, 2001.

Gándara, Patricia C. *Over the Ivy Walls: The Educational Mobility of Low-Income Chicanos*. Albany: State University of New York Press, 1995.

Garcia, Alma. *The Mexican Americans*. Westport, Conn.: Greenwood Press, 2001.

Garcia, Eugene. *Hispanic Education in the United States: Raices y Alas*. Lanham, Md.: Rowman & Littlefield, 2001.

Garcia, Mario. The *Desert Immigrants: The Mexicans of El Paso, 1880–1920*. New Haven, Conn.: Yale University Press, 1983.

Garcia, Richard. *Rise of the Mexican-American Middle Class: San Antonio, 1929–1941*. College Station: Texas A&M Press, 1991.

García, Shernaz B., and Patricia L. Guerra. "Deconstructing Deficit Thinking: Working with Educators to Create More Equitable Learning Environments." *Education and Urban Society* 36, no. 2 (February 2004): 150–68.

Geertz, Clifford. *The Interpretation of Cultures*. New York: Basic Books, 1973.

Gibson, Margaret A., Patricia Gándara, and Jill Peterson Koyama. *School Connections: U.S. Mexican Youth, Peers, and School Achievement*. New York: Teachers College Press, 2004.

Gilbert, Dennis. *The American Class Structure in an Age of Growing Inequality*, 6th ed. Toronto, Ontario: Thomson Wadsworth, 2003.

Gonzalez, Arturo. *Mexican Americans and the U.S. Economy: Quest for Buenos Días*. Tucson: University of Arizona Press, 2001.

Gonzalez, Gilbert G. "Segregation and the Education of Mexican Children, 1900–1940." In *The Elusive Request for Equality*, edited by José F. Moreno, 53–76. Cambridge, Mass.: Harvard Educational Review, 1999.

Gonzalez, Manuel. *Mexicanos: A History of Mexicans in the United States*. Bloomington: Indiana University Press, 1999.

Gordon, John Steele. *An Empire of Wealth: The Epic History of American Economic Power*. New York: HarperCollins, 2004.

Grant, David. "A Demographic Portrait of Los Angeles County, 1970–1990." In *Prismatic Metropolis: Inequality in Los Angeles*, edited by Lawrence Bobo, Melvin L. Oliver, James H. Johnson, Jr., and Abel Valenzuela, Jr., 51–80. New York: Russell Sage, 2000.

Grebler, Leo, Joan W. Moore, and Ralph C. Guzman. *The Mexican American People: The Nation's Second Largest Minority*. New York: Free Press, 1970.

Griswold del Castillo, Richard. *La Familia: Chicano Families in the Urban Southwest 1848 to the Present*. Notre Dame, Ind.: University Notre Dame Press, 1984.

Groger, Jeff, and Stephen J. Trejo. *Falling Behind or Moving Up?: The Intergenerational Progress of Mexican Americans*. San Francisco: Public Policy Institute of California, 2002.

Grubb, W. Norton, Claudia M. Lara, and Susan Valdez. "Counselor, Coordinator, Monitor, Mom: The Roles of Counselors in the Puente Program." *Educational Policy* 16, no. 4 (September 2002): 547–71.

Gutierrez, Kris D., and Barbara Rogoff. "Cultural Ways of Learning: Individual Traits or Repertoires of Practice." *Educational Researcher* 32, no. 5 (June/July 2003): 19–25.

Gutierrez, Ramon. "Chicano History: Paradigm Shifts and Shifting Boundaries." In *Voices of a New Chicano History*, edited by Refugio I. Rochín and Dennis N. Valdés, 91–114. East Lansing: Michigan State University Press, 2000.

Hamilton, Stephen F., and Jane Levine Powers. "Failed Expectations: Working-class Girls' Transition from School to Work." *Youth and Society*, 22 no. 2 (December 1990): 241–62.

Handlin, Oscar. *Boston's Immigrants: A Study of Acculturation*. Cambridge, Mass.: Harvard University Press, 1979.

Hart, John Mason, ed. *Border Crossings: Mexican and Mexican American Workers*. Wilmington, Del.: Scholarly Resources Books, 1998.

Hayes, Katherine G. "Attitudes toward Education: Voluntary and Involuntary Immigrants from the Same Families." *Anthropology and Education Quarterly* 23 (September 1992): 250–67.

Healy, Joseph F. "Diversity and Unity in the United States: Defining Terms." In *Race and Ethnicity*, edited by Alma M. Garcia and Richard A. Garcia, 12–21. San Diego: Greenhaven Press, 2001.

Heath, Shirley Brice. *Ways with Words: Language, Life, and Work in Communities and Schools*. New York: Cambridge University Press, 1983.

Helfand, Duke, Jean Merl, and Joel Rubin. "A New Approach to School Equality: Fifty Years after Brown Ruling." *Los Angeles Times*, May 15, 2004, A1.

Henige, David. *Oral Historiography*. New York: Longman, 1982.

Hernández-Chávez, Eduardo. "Native Language Loss and its Implications for Revitalization of Spanish in Chicano Communities." In *Latino Language and Education*, edited by Antionette Sedillo López, 24–40. New York: Garland, 1995.

Hornberger, Nancy H. "Language Policy, Language Education, Language Rights: Indigenous, Immigrant and International Perspective." *Language and Society* 27 (1998): 439–58.

Horvat, Erin McNamara, Elliot B. Weininger, and Annette Lareau. "From Social Ties to Social Capital: Class Differences in the Relations between Schools and Parent Networks." *American Educational Research Journal* 40, no. 2 (Summer 2003): 319–51.

Hosp, John L., and Daniel J. Reschly. "Referral Rates for Intervention or Assessment: A Meta-Analysis of Racial Difference." *Journal of Special Education* 37, no. 2 (Summer 2003): 67–80.

Jackson, James E. "I am a Fieldnote: Fieldnotes as a Symbol of Professional Identity." In *Fieldnotes: The Making of Anthropology*, edited by Roger Sanjek, 3–33. Ithaca, N.Y.: Cornell University Press, 1990.

Jacobs-Huey, Lanita. "The Natives Are Gazing and Talking Back: Reviewing the Problematics of Positionality, Voice and Accountability among 'Native' Anthropologists." *American Anthropologist* 104, no. 3 (September 2002): 791–804.

Jeffries, Vincent. "Class Stratification in the United States: Method and Empirical Studies." In *Social Stratification: A Multiple Hierarchy Approach*, edited by Vincent Jeffries and Edward H. Ransford, 106–36. Boston: Allyn and Bacon, 1980.

Jones, Delmos J. "Towards a Native Anthropology." *Human Organization* 29, no. 4, (Winter 1970): 251–59.

Keating, Lisa M., Michelle A. Tomishima, and Sharon Foster. "The Effects of a Mentoring Program on At-Risk Youth." *Adolescence* 37, no. 148 (Winter 2002): 717–34.

Keefe, Susan E. "Personal Communities in the City: Support Networks among Mexican-Americans and Anglo-Americans." *Urban Anthropology* 9, no. 1 (Spring 1980): 51–74.

Keefe, Susan E., and Amado Padilla. *Chicano Ethnicity*. Albuquerque: University of New Mexico Press, 1990.

Kerbo, Harold R. *Social Stratification and Inequality: Class Conflict in the United States*. New York: McGraw Hill, 1983.

Kikumura, Akemi. "Family Life Histories: A Collaborative Venture." In *Oral History Reader*, edited by Robert Perks and Alistar Thomson, 140–44. New York: Routledge, 1998.

Knight, Michelle G., Nadjwa E. L. Norton, Courtney C. Bentley, and Iris R. Dixon. "The Power of Black and Latina/o Counterstories: Urban Families and College-Going Processes," *Anthropology and Education Quarterly* 35, no. 1 (March 2004): 99–120.

Knowlton, Clark S. "The Neglected Chapters in Mexican American History." In *Mexican-Americans Tomorrow: Education and Economic Perspectives*, edited by Gus Tyler, 19–59. Albuquerque: University of New Mexico Press, 1975.

Kondo, Dorrine K. "Dissolution and Reconstitution of Self: Implications for Anthropological Epistemology." *Cultural Anthropology* 1, no. 1 (February 1986): 74–88.

Kouritzin, Sandra G. *Face[t]s of First Language Loss*. Mahwah, N.J.: Lawrence Erlbaum, 1999.

Krashen, Stephen. "Bilingual Education: The Acquisition of English and the Retention of Spanish." In *Research on Spanish in the United States: Linguistic Issues and Challenges*, edited by Ana Roca, 432–44. Somerville, Mass.: Cascadilla, 2000.

Kravolec, Etta, and John Buell. *The End of Homework: How Homework Disrupts Families, Overburdens Children, and Limits Learning*. Boston: Beacon Press, 2000.

Kuper, Adam. *Culture: The Anthropologist's Account*. Cambridge, Mass.: Harvard University Press, 1999.

Lareau, Annette. *Home Advantage: Social Class and Parental Intervention in Elementary Education*, Rev. ed. Oxford, England: Rowman & Littlefield, 2000.

———. *Unequal Childhood: Class, Race, and Family Life*. Berkeley: University of California Press, 2003.

Le Blanc, Paul. *A Short History of the Working Class: From the Colonial Times to the Twenty-first Century*. Amherst, Mass.: Humanity Books, 1999.

Levitan, Sar A., ed. *Blue-Collar Workers: A Symposium on Middle America*. New York: McGraw Hill, 1971.

Linkon, Sherry Lee, ed. *Teaching Working Class*. Amherst: University of Massachusetts, 1999.

Los Angeles Board of Education. *Your Children and Their Schools: An Informal Report to the Patrons of the Los Angeles City Schools*. Los Angeles, Calif.: Los Angeles Board of Education, 1937.

Los Angeles Unified School District. "Five Year Review LAUSD Ethnic Survey." Planning, Assessment, and Research Division 2004, available at: www.lausd.k12 .ca.us/lausd/offices/bulletins/5_yr_review.html.

Lyon, Laura Lucile. "Investigation of the Program for the Adjustment of Mexican Girls to High Schools of the San Fernando Valley," Master's thesis, Los Angeles: University Southern California, 1933.

Macgregor-Mendoza, Patricia. *Spanish and Academic Achievement among Midwest Mexican Youth*. New York: Garland, 1999.

Marjoribanks, Kevin. *Family and School Capital: Towards a Context Theory of Students' School Outcomes*. Dordrecht, The Netherlands: Kluwer Academic, 2002.

Marotta, Sylvia A., and Jorge G. Garcia. "Latinos in the United States in 2000." *Hispanic Journal of Behavioral Sciences* 25, no. 1 (February 2003): 13–34.

Martinez, Charles R., Jr., David S. DeGarmo, and J. Mark Eddy. "Promoting Academic Success among Latino Youths." *Hispanic Journal of Behavioral Sciences* 26, no. 2 (May 2004): 128–51.

Martinez, Estela A. "Mexican American/Chicano Families: Parenting as Diverse as the Families Themselves." In *Family Ethnicity: Strength in Diversity*, 2nd ed., edited by P. McAdoo, 121–34. Thousand Oaks, Calif.: Sage, 1999.

Martinez, Fredda Gregg. "Familism in Acculturated Mexican Americans: Patterns, Changes and Perceived Impact on Adjustment to U.S. Society," Master's thesis, Northern Arizona University, Flagstaff, 1993.

Martinez, Oscar J. *Mexican-Origin People in the United States: A Topical History*. Tucson: University of Arizona Press, 2001.

Marx, Sherry. "Regarding Whiteness: Exploring and Intervening in the Effects of White Racism in Teacher Education." *Equity and Excellence in Education* 37, no. 1 (March 2004): 31–43.

Mattingly, Doreen J., Radmila Prislin, and Thomas L. MacKenzie. "Evaluating Evaluations: The Case of Parent Involvement Programs." *Review of Educational Research* 72, no. 4 (Winter 2002): 549–76.

Matute-Bianchi, Maria E. "Situational Ethnicity and Patterns of School Performance among Immigrant and Nonimmigrant Mexican Descent Students." In *Minority Status and Schooling: A Comparative Study of Immigrant and Involuntary Minorities*, edited by Margaret Gibson and John U. Ogbu, 205–47. New York: Garland, 1991.

McNamara, Patrick H. *Mexican-Americans in Los Angeles County: A Study in Acculturation*. San Francisco: R & E Research Associates, 1957.

Menchaca, Martha. "Beyond Internal Colonialism: Class, Gender and Culture as Challenges to Chicano Identity." In *Voices of a New Chicano History,* edited by Refugio I. Rochín and Dennis N. Valdés, 183–95. East Lansing: Michigan State University Press, 2000.

———. *The Mexican Outsiders: A Community History of Marginalization and Discrimination in California*. Austin: University of Texas Press, 1995.

Michie, Gregory. *Holler If You Hear Me: The Education of a Teacher and His Students*. New York: Teachers College Press, 1999.

Mirandé, Alfredo. *The Chicano Experience: An Alternative Perspective*. Notre Dame, Ind.: University of Notre Dame Press, 1985.

Monroy, Douglas. *Rebirth: Mexican Los Angeles from the Great Migration to the Great Depression*. Los Angeles: University California Press, 1999.

Moore, Joan W. "Isolation and Stigmatization in the Development of an Underclass: The Case of Chicano Gangs in East Los Angeles." *Social Problems* 33, no. 1 (February 1985): 1–12.

Moore, Joan W., and Raquel Pinderhughes. *In the Barrios: Latinos and the Underclass Debate*. New York: Russell Sage Foundation, 1993.

Mora, Pat. *House of Houses*. Boston: Beacon Press, 1997.

Moreno, José F., ed. *The Elusive Quest for Equality: 150 Years of Chicano/Chicana Education*. Cambridge, Mass.: Harvard Educational Review, 1999.

Moreno, Robert P., and Richard R. Valencia. "Chicano Families and Schools: Myth, and Knowledge and Future Directions for Understanding." In *Chicano School Success and Failure: Past, Present and Future*, 2nd ed., edited by Richard R. Valencia, 227–50. London, New York: Routledge/Falmer, 2002.

Mufwene, Salikoko S., John Rickford, Guy Bailey, and John Baugh, eds. *African-American English: Structure, History, and Use*. New York: Routledge, 1998.

Mukhopadyay, Carol, and Rosemary C. Henze. "How Real is Race? Using Anthropology to Make Sense of Human Diversity." *Phi Delta Kappan* 84, no. 9 (May 2003): 669–78.

Murguía, Edward. *Chicano Intermarriage: A Theoretical and Empirical Study*. San Antonio, Tex.: Trinity University Press, 1982.

Narayan, Kirin. "How Native is a 'Native' Anthropologist?" *American Anthropologist* 95, no. 3 (September 1993): 671–86.

Norment, Nathaniel, Jr., ed. *Readings in African American Language: Aspects, Features, and Perspectives*. New York: Peter Lang, 2003.

Novak, Michael. *Unmeltable Ethnics: Politics and Culture in American Life*. New Brunswick, N.J.: Transaction, 1971.

Oakes, Jeannie. *Keeping Track: How Schools Structure Inequality*. New Haven, Conn.: Yale University Press, 1985.

Ochoa, Gilda. *Becoming Neighbors in a Mexican American Community: Power, Conflict and Solidarity*. Austin: University Texas Press, 2004.

Ogbu, John U. *Minority Education and Caste: The American System in Cross-Cultural Perspective*. New York: Academic Press, 1978.

———. *The Next Generation: An Ethnography of Education in an Urban Neighborhood*. New York: Academic Press, 1974.

———. "Variability to Minority Responses to School: Nonimmigrants vs. Immigrants." In *Interpretive Ethnography in Education*, edited by George Spindler and Louise Spindler, 225–80. Hillsdale, N.J.: Lawrence Erlbaum, 1987.

Ogbu, John U., and Herbert D. Simmons, "Voluntary and Involuntary Minorities: A Cultural-Ecological Theory of School Performance with Some Implications for Education." *Anthropology and Education Quarterly* 29, no. 2 (June 1998): 155–88.

Olmeda, Irma M. "Accommodation and Resistance: Latinas Struggle for Their Children's Education." *Anthropology and Education Quarterly* 34, no. 4 (December 2003): 373–95.

Ornstein-Galicia, Jacob, ed. *Form and Function in Chicano English.* Malabar, Fla.: R. E. Krieger, 1988.

Ortiz, Vilma. "The Mexican-Origin Population: Permanent Working Class or Emerging Middle Class?" In *Ethnic Los Angeles,* edited by Robert Waldinger and Medhi Bozorgmehr, 247–77. New York: Russell Sage, 1996.

Ortner, Sherry, ed. *The Faces of "Culture": Geertz and Beyond.* Berkeley: University of California Press, 1999.

Osterman, Paul. *Securing Prosperity: The American Labor Market, How It Has Changed and What to Do about It.* Princeton, N.J.: Princeton University Press, 1999.

Padilla, Amado M., and William Perez. "Cultural Orientation across Three Generations of Hispanic Adolescents." *Hispanic Journal of Behavioral Sciences* 22, no. 3 (February 2000): 390–98.

Parker, Richard. *The Myth of the Middle Class.* New York: Harper Colophon Books, 1972.

Parnell, Dale. *The Neglected Majority.* Washington, D.C.: Community College Press, 1985.

Pastor, Manuel, Jr. "Common Ground at Ground Zero? The New Economy and the New Organizing in Los Angeles." *Antipode* 33, no. 2 (March 2001): 260–89.

Pearl, Arthur. "Systemic and Institutional Factors in Chicano School Failure." In *Chicano School Failure and Success: Research and Policy Agendas for the 1990s,* edited by Richard R. Valencia, 27–63. London: Falmer Press, 1991.

Peñalosa, Fernando. "Class Consciousness and Social Mobility in a Mexican-American Community," Ph.D. diss., Los Angeles: University of Southern California, 1963.

Penfield, Joyce, and Jacob L. Ornstein-Galicia, eds. *Chicano English: An Ethnic Contact Dialect.* Amsterdam; Philadelphia: John Benjamins, 1985.

Perruci, Robert, and Earl Wysong. *The New Class Society.* Lanham, Md.: Rowman & Littlefield, 2003.

Pizarro, Marcos. *Chicanas and Chicanos in School: Racial Profiling, Identity Battles, and Empowerment.* Austin: University of Texas Press, 2005.

———. "Searching for Curanderas: A Quest to Revive Chicana/o Studies." *Journal of Latinos and Education* 3, no. 3 (Spring 2004): 145–64.

Portales, Marco. *Crowding out Latinos: Mexican Americans in the Public Consciousness.* Philadelphia: Temple University Press, 2000.

Portes, Alejandro, and Lingxin Hao. "E Pluribus Unum: Bilingualism and Language Loss in the Second Generation." *Sociology of Education* 71 (October 1998): 269–94.

Portes, Alejandro, and Rubén G. Rumbaut. *Immigrant America: A Portrait.* Berkeley: University of California Press, 1996.

———. *Legacies: The Story of the Immigrant Generation.* New York: Russell Sage, 2001.

Preston, Richard E. *The Changing Landscape of the San Fernando Valley between 1930 and 1964.* Northridge, Calif.: Center for Urban Studies, San Fernando Valley State College, 1965.

Quezada, Reyes L., Delia M. Díaz, and Maria Sánchez. "Involving Latino Parents." *Leadership* 33, no. 1 (September/October 2003): 32–34, 38.

Quiroz, Pamela Anne. "The Silencing of Latino Student 'Voice': Puerto Rican and Mexican Narratives in the Eighth Grade and High School." *Anthropology and Education Quarterly* 32, no. 3 (September 2001): 326–49.

Raferty, Judith R. *Land of Fair Promise: Politics and Reform in Los Angeles Schools, 1885–1941.* Stanford, Calif.: Stanford University Press, 1992.

Ramirez, Roberto R., and Patricia G. de la Cruz. "The Hispanic Population in the United States: March 2002." *Current Population Reports* P20–545. Washington, D.C.: United States Census Bureau (June), 2003.

Ransford, Edward. "Social Mobility: Multiple Hierarchy Approach." In *Social Stratification: A Multiple Hierarchy Approach,* edited by Vincent Jeffries and Edward H. Ransford, 522–49. Boston: Allyn and Bacon, 1980.

Reese, Leslie. "Parental Strategies in Contrasting Cultural Settings: Families in México and 'El Norte.'" *Anthropology and Education Quarterly,* 33, no. 1 (March 2002): 99–120.

Reimers, Cordelia W. "Hispanic Earnings and Employment in the 1980s." In *Hispanics in the Workplace,* edited by Stephan B. Knouse, Paul Rosenfeld, and Amy Culbertson, 29–55. Newbury Park, Calif.: Sage, 1992.

Rietman, Sandford W. *The Educational Messiah Complex.* Sacramento, Calif.: Caddo Press, 1992.

Rist, Raymond C. "Student Social Class and Teacher Expectations: The Self-Fulfilling Prophecy in Ghetto Education." *Harvard Educational Review* 70, no. 3 (Fall 2000): 266–301. Reprinted from Harvard Educational Review, 1970.

Roderick, Kevin. *The San Fernando Valley: America's Suburb.* Los Angeles: Los Angeles Times Books, 2001.

Rodgers, Rebecca. *A Critical Discourse Analysis of Family Literacy.* Mahwah, N.J.: Lawrence Erlbaum Associates, 2003.

Rodriguez, Richard. *Hunger of Memory: The Education of Richard Rodriguez.* Boston: D. R. Godine, 1982.

Rolón-Dow, Rosalie. "Critical Care: A Colorful Analysis of Care Narratives in the Schooling Experiences of Puerto Rican Girls." *American Educational Research Journal* 42, no. 1 (Spring 2005): 77–111.

Romo, Harriet D., and Tony Falbo. *Latino High School Graduation.* Austin: University Texas Press, 1996.

Romo, Richard. *History of a Barrio: East Los Angeles.* Austin: University of Texas Press, 1983.

Rosaldo, Renato. *Culture and Truth: The Remaking of Social Analysis.* Boston: Beacon Press, 1993.

Rose, Mike. *The Mind of Work: Valuing the Intelligence of the American Worker.* New York: Viking, 2004.

Rosenfield, Michael J. "Measures of Assimilation in the Marriage Market: Mexican Americans 1970–1990." *Journal of Marriage and the Family* 64, no. 1 (February 2002): 152–62.

Rossides, Daniel W. *Social Stratification: The American Class System in Comparative Perspective.* Englewood Cliffs, N.J.: Prentice Hall, 1990.

———. *Social Stratification: The Interplay of Class, Race, and Gender,* 2nd ed. Upper Saddle River, N.J.: Prentice Hall, 1997.

Rubin, Lillian B. *Families on the Fault Line: America's Working Class Speaks about the Family, Economy, Race, and Ethnicity.* New York: Harper Collins, 1994.

———. *World of Pain: Life in a Working-Class Family.* New York: Basic Books, 1987.

Rueda, Robert. "An Analysis of Special Education as a Response to the Diminished Academic Achievement of Chicano Students." In *Chicano School Failure and Success: Research and Policy Agendas for the 1990s,* ed. Richard R. Valencia, 27–63. London, England: Falmer Press, 1991.

Rueschenberg, Erich, and Raymond Buriel. "Mexican American Family Functioning and Acculturation: A Family Systems Perspective," *Hispanic Journal of Behavioral Sciences* 11, no. 3 (August 1989): 232–44.

Ruiz, Mona. *Two Badges: The Lives of Mona Ruiz.* Houston, Tex.: Arte Público Press, 1997.

Ruiz, Vicki L. "South by Southwest: Mexican Americans and Segregated Schooling, 1900–1950," *Organization of American Historians,* available at: www.oah.org/pubs/magazine/deseg/ruiz.html, 2001.

Rumbaut, Rubén G., and Wayne A. Cornelius. *California's Immigrant Children: Theory, Research and Implications for Educational Policy.* San Diego: Center for U.S.-Mexican Studies, University of California Press, 1995.

Sanchez, George J. *Becoming Mexican American: Ethnicity, Culture and Identity in Chicano Los Angeles, 1990–1945.* New York: Oxford University Press, 1993.

Sanjek, Roger. "The Enduring Inequalities of Race." In *Race,* ed. Steven Gregory and Roger Sanjek, 1–17. New Brunswick, N.J.: Rutgers University Press, 1994.

San Miguel, Guadalupe Jr. *"Let Them All Take Heed": Mexican Americans and the Campaign for Educational Equality in Texas, 1910–1981.* Austin: University of Texas Press, 1987.

San Miguel, Guadalupe Jr., and Richard Valencia. "From the Treaty of Guadalupe de Hidalgo to Hopwood: The Educational Plight and Struggle of Mexican Americans in the Southwest," *Harvard Educational Review* 68, no. 3 (Fall 1998): 353–412.

Santa Ana, Otto A. *Toward a More Adequate Characterization of the Chicano Language Setting.* Albuquerque: University of New Mexico, Southwest Hispanic Research Institute, 1993.

Schecter, Sandra R., and Robert Bayley. "Language Socialization Practices and Cultural Identity: Case Studies of Mexican-Descent Families in California and Texas." *TESOL Quarterly* 31, no. 3 (Autumn 1997): 513–60.

Schimdt, Fred H., and Kenneth Koford, "The Economic Condition of the Mexican–American." In *Mexican-Americans Tomorrow: Education and Economic Perspectives,* edited by Gus Tyler, 81–106. Albuquerque: University of New Mexico Press, 1975.

Security First National Bank. *The Growth and Economic Stature of the San Fernando Valley and the Greater Glendale Area.* Los Angeles: Security First National Bank, Economic Research Department, 1967.

Sewell, Dorita. *Knowing People: A Mexican American Community's Concept of a Person.* New York: AMS Press, 1989.

Shostak, Arthur. *Blue Collar Life.* New York: Random House, 1969.

Shrag, Peter. *The Decline of the WASP*. New York: Simon & Schuster, 1971.

Smelser, Neil J. "Culture: Coherent or Incoherent?" In *Theory of Culture*, edited by Richard Münch and Neil J. Smelser, 3–28. Berkeley: University of California Press, 1992.

Soto, Lourdes Diaz. *Language, Culture, and Power: Bilingual Families and the Struggle for Quality Education*. Albany: State University of New York Press, 1995.

Stanard, Rebecca Powell. "High School Graduation Rates in the United States: Implications for Counseling." *Journal of Counseling and Development* 81, no. 2 (2003): 217–21.

Stanton-Salazar, Ricardo D. *Manufacturing Hope and Despair: The School and Kin Support Networks of U.S.-Mexican Youth*. New York: Teachers College Press, 2001.

Stanton-Salazar, Ricardo D., and Stephanie Urso Spina. "Informal Mentors and Role Models in the Lives of Urban Mexican-Origin Adolescents," *Anthropology and Education Quarterly* 34, no. 3 (Spring 2003): 231–54.

Steinberg, Stephen. *The Ethnic Myth: Race, Ethnicity and Class in America*. Boston: Beacon Press, 1989.

Stephenson, John B., and L. Sue Greer. "Ethnographers in Their Own Cultures: Two Appalachian Cases," *Human Organization* 40, no. 2 (Summer 1981): 123–30.

Suárez-Orozco, Carola, and Marcelo Suárez-Orozco. *Transformations: Migration, Family Life and Achievement Motivation among Latino Adolescents*. Stanford, Calif.: Stanford University Press, 1995.

Suárez-Orozco, Marcelo M., Carola Suárez-Orozco, and Desirée Baolian Qin, eds. *The New Immigration: An Interdisciplinary Reader*. New York: Routledge, 2005.

Suárez-Orozco, Marcelo M., and Mariela M. Páez, "Introduction: The Research Agenda." In *Latinos: Remaking America*, edited by Marcelo M. Suárez-Orozco and Mariel M. Páez, 1–37. Los Angeles: University of California Press, 2002.

Sullivan, Teresa A. "Stratification of the Chicano Labor Market under Conditions of Continuing Mexican Immigration." In *Mexican Immigrants and Mexican Americans: An Evolving Relation*," edited by Harley L. Browning and Rudolfo De la Garza, 55–73. Austin: CMAS Publications, 1986.

Terkel, Studs. *Hard Times: An Oral History of the Great Depression*. New York: Pantheon, 1970.

Trueba, Henry. *Latinos Unidos: From Cultural Diversity to the Politics of Solidarity*. Lanham, Md.: Rowman & Littlefield, 1999.

Trumbull, Elise, Carrie Rothstein-Fisch, Patricia Greenfield, and Blanca Quiroz. *Bridging Cultures between Home and School: A Guide for Teachers*. Mahwah, N.J.: Lawrence Erlbaum Associates, 2001.

Tse, Lucy. "Resisting and Reversing Language Shift: Heritage-Language Resilience among U.S. Native Biliterates." *Harvard Educational Review* 71, no. 4 (2001): 676–708.

Valdés, Guadalupe. *Con Respeto: Bridging the Distances between Culturally Diverse Families and Schools*. New York: Teachers College Press, 1996.

Valencia, Richard R. *Chicano School Failure and Success: Past, Present and Future*. New York: Routledge/Falmer, 2002.

Valencia, Richard R., and Mary S. Black. "Mexican Americans Don't Value Education!: On the Basis of the Myth, Mythmaking and Debunking." *Journal of Latinos and Education* 1, no. 2 (2002): 81–103.

Valenzuela, Abel Jr., and Elizabeth Gonzalez, "Latino Earnings Inequality: Immigrant and Native-born Differences." In *Prismatic Metropolis: Inequality in Los Angeles*, edited by Lawrence Bobo, Melvin L. Oliver, James H. Johnson, Jr., and Abel Valenzuela, Jr., 249–78. New York: Russell Sage, 2000.

Valenzuela, Angela. *Subtractive Schooling*. Albany, N.Y.: State University Press, 1999.

Valverde, Leonard A. "Latino Education: Systemic Change Needed for Serious Improvement." *Education and Urban Society* 36, no. 2 (February 2004): 123–29.

Vega, William A. "Hispanic Families in the 1980s: A Decade of Research." *Journal of Marriage and the Family* 52 (1990): 1015–24.

Vigil, James Diego. *Barrio Gangs: Street Life and Identity in Southern California*. Austin: University of Texas Press, 1988.

——. *Personas Mexicanas: Chicano High Schoolers in a Changing Los Angeles*. Fort Worth, Tex.: Harcourt Brace, 1997.

Villanueva, Irene. "Change in the Education Life of Chicano Families across Three Generations." *Education and Urban Society* 29, no. 1 (November 1996): 12–34.

Villaseñor, Victor. *Rain of Gold*. Houston: Arte Público Press, 1991.

Waite, Linda J., and Mark Nielsen. "The Rise of the Dual–earner Family, 1963–1997." In *Working Families: The Transformation of the American Home*, edited by Rosanna Hertz and Nancy L. Marshall, 23–41. Berkeley and Los Angeles: University of California Press, 2001.

Walker, Susan, and David A. Riley. "Involvement of the Personal Social Network as a Factor in Parent Education Effectiveness." *Family Relations* 50, no. 2 (April 2001): 186–93.

Weaver, Charles N. "Work Attitudes of Mexican Americans." *Hispanic Journal of Behavioral Sciences* 22, no. 3 (August 2000): 275–95.

Weis, Lois. *Class Reunion: The Remaking of the American White Working Class*. New York: Routledge, 2004.

Wells, Miriam J. "Oldtimers and Newcomers: The Role of Context in Mexican American Context." *Aztlan* 11, no. 2 (Fall 1981): 271–95.

Willis, Paul E. *Learning to Labour: How Working Class Kids Get Working Class Jobs*. Westmead, England: Saxon House, 1977.

Wright, Kay, and Dolores A. Steglin. *Building School and Community Partnerships through Parent Involvement*, 2nd ed. Upper Saddle River, N.J.: Merrill Prentice Hall, 2003.

Zavella, Patricia. "Feminists Insider Dilemmas: Constructing Ethnic Identity with Chicana Informants." In *Feminist Dilemmas in Fieldwork*, edited by Diane L. Wolf, 138–59. Boulder, Colo.: Westview Press, 1996.

Zentella Ana Celicia, ed. *Building on Strength: Language, Literacy in Latino Families and Communities*. New York: Teachers College, 2005.

Zinn, Howard. *The Twentieth Century: A People's History*. New York: Harper Perennial, 1998.

Zweig, Michael. *The Working Class Majority*. Ithaca, N.Y.: ILR Press, 2000.

Index

About the Author

A graduate of Stanford's School of Education, Dr. **Christina Chávez** is currently an assistant professor at California State Polytechnic University, Pomona, in the Liberal Studies Department. She teaches undergraduate teacher candidate courses on the history of education, politics of schooling, families and schools, and language, culture, and identity.